T0323002

# ALL THE HOUSES I'VE EVER LIVED IN

# ALL THE HOUSES I'VE EVER LIVED IN

Finding Home in a System that Fails Us

KIERAN YATES

**SIMON &
SCHUSTER**

London · New York · Sydney · Toronto · New Delhi

First published in Great Britain by Simon & Schuster UK Ltd, 2023

Copyright © Kieran Yates, 2023

The right of Kieran Yates to be identified as the author of
this work has been asserted in accordance with the
Copyright, Designs and Patents Act, 1988.

1 3 5 7 9 10 8 6 4 2

Simon & Schuster UK Ltd
1st Floor
222 Gray's Inn Road
London WC1X 8HB

www.simonandschuster.co.uk
www.simonandschuster.com.au
www.simonandschuster.co.in

Simon & Schuster Australia, Sydney
Simon & Schuster India, New Delhi

The author and publishers have made all reasonable efforts to contact
copyright-holders for permission, and apologise for any omissions or errors in the form
of credits given. Corrections may be made to future printings.

A CIP catalogue record for this book
is available from the British Library

Hardback ISBN: 978-1-3985-0983-2
eBook ISBN: 978-1-3985-0984-9

Typeset in Bembo by M Rules

Printed and Bound in the UK using 100% Renewable Electricity
at CPI Group (UK) Ltd

For all those activists who have fought,
and continue to fight, for home

And for my mum, who has always made home for me

# Contents

# Contents

# INTRODUCTION

The desire for home is innate in all of us. For me, home is something that I've learned to make, lose and love thanks to years of moving. By the time I was twenty-five I had lived in more than twenty different houses, and they have taught me everything I know about community, interior design and a failing state.

Each chapter in this book starts with a different house I've lived in. It isn't every *single* house I've lived in – there are more – but I've chosen these because each one reveals something about the housing crisis, its politics and history, and how we live now. They are not even all houses, technically, but the language of home and house feels interchangeable to me. When I lived on an estate, I learned about negligence first hand. When I lived in a car showroom, I learned about what happens when people are housed in places not designed to be lived in. When I went to housemate auditions I learned about optimising yourself online, and when I saw the clinical aesthetics of gentrification close up, I realised just how much taste is weaponised. Researching and reporting for this book has taken me from retracing Asian youth movements in 1970s Britain to sourcing millennial *Monstera deliciosa* plant obsessions and how sounds travelling through a wall impact our ears.

How we manage precarity together is the real focus of this book rather than the architecture of the different houses, though there is some cultural history of interiors, too. If the exteriors of houses tell a story about our history, from the scars of the Blitz on Victorian townhouses to brutalist estates, interiors can reveal our present. We have a history of peering inside people's homes, at the details of a living room, guessing at a house's period and market value, from the first Ideal Home Exhibition in 1908 to Kim Kardashian's *Vogue* videos. In a decade of chaos and political, social and economic instability, many of our homes have adopted a frictionless grey. During the pandemic, people painted arches on walls while they were trapped inside, creating an illusion of escape. When the mainstream adopted a commodified feminism, millennial pink made its way onto our walls. The details that make up our home and interior lives are a treasure trove of housing stories – of large windows, foamy imitation flock wallpaper, buttery magnolia paint, and jewel-tone blue velvet sofas. I have loved all of them.

I wanted to write this book on the meaning and making of home not only because a lot of books about home focus on white working-class experiences of council housing, or overwhelmingly feature middle-class lives. It's also because there aren't enough honest conversations about how it really feels to move around this country, and the precariousness of not having a 'home' that you can always go back to. Moving takes many forms. The movement of the GRT (Gypsy, Roma, Traveller) community with nomadic roots clearly has a different cultural context to moving because of rent or landlord changes. But this is a book that explores how it feels to move and some of the reasons we feel a sense of nostalgia about our old homes. We inhabit the spaces we are in. They give something to us and we give something to them, too.

This book is for anyone who has ever lived in a house and wondered about how long they could stay, who has lusted for Stuff – for pastel-coloured body-positive candles, IKEA lampshades or chintz wallpaper – and felt guilty about it, for anyone who has been refused permission to paint a wall, undergone a housemate audition or simply struggled to pay rent. It is for anyone who has bought a house and has complicated feelings about it. It is both for people who have experienced housing stress – an increasing proportion of the population – and for those who are housing secure. It is for anyone who has ever longed for, lived in, built or loved a home.

This book is also a call to action – to resistance and activism through attending community meetings, emailing MPs, setting up Facebook groups and zines – empowering anyone who has ever felt too small to push back. It is up to all of us to advocate for those at the sharp edge of the housing crisis – trans people who are forced into dangerous housing, Black communities who are targeted en masse by racist landlords, immigrant communities with no option but to disperse. Fair access to housing benefits everyone. It is good for society. It is good for you, it is good for me, because housing is a justice issue.

–

I may have moved more than most people, but my experience is not unique. We all want to find home, and so many of our lives and our housing experiences have been profoundly shaped by the 2008 financial crisis, a decade of Tory rule, and now, a climate crisis and global pandemic. There is no justification for the housing crisis, which is a direct result of the profit motive of capitalism being allowed to run rampant. It hinges on the myth that only certain people can be secure, and that only certain people should have access to housing in a country of finite space and resources. Who is left behind reveals the racism, classism, transphobia and ableism braided into the housing system. These are uncomfortable but necessary truths to reckon with before we can really begin to understand how they impact every element of our lives, including the housing landscape.

In 1919, the introduction of the Addison Act ensured a fair right of abode to some of the most vulnerable residents of this country. I would benefit from Addison's dream, living in a block side by side with others on a council estate in west London. But 100 years later, we are still falling desperately short of equality. According to the National Housing Federation, an estimated 8.4 million people in England are living in unaffordable, insecure or unsuitable homes. We are in a crisis of poor-quality housing, rogue landlords and rampant gentrification.

Years of reporting as a journalist have taken me inside the homes of people across the country, who have shared their stories and their precious tchotchkes with me. People who have taught me the value of a doily, of a curtain, or of a Louis Vuitton decal on a window. I briefly worked for the housing charity Shelter's magazine *Here*, where I first saw the conflicting motivations of people who want to see housing as a human right, and a government who makes this almost impossible for many of our most vulnerable tenants. Housing law is a notoriously complicated part of the legal system – it is not set up to be easily understood, even while it affects every single person in this country.

Home has never felt more precious – and more insecure. Home for everyone – but especially for working-class people of colour – is a political issue. Communities who might never before have believed they had a stake in society are learning how to create space for themselves in a country that doesn't make space for them: learning how to make a place feel like a home. In a housing crisis that continues to chew us up and spit us out, moving is a bigger part of our lives than it has ever been. As the demographic of the UK changes, people are making their home here from disparate global communities, while house prices are simultaneously making long-term stability unmanageable for a generation and, tragically, the safety net of social housing is being slowly frayed to nothing.

–

While I will be using my work as a journalist to report on stories across the UK, I am myself in some ways a case study, never fully removed from the stories I write about. Many of my experiences with housing have been comically bad (in hindsight), but stopped short of being completely bleak thanks to other joys. This book sees homemaking and the pursuit of love as essential, and employs the notion of self-care, where 'self-care' means finding and locating home in any form, as a means of resistance. As we navigate a housing crisis that affects us in increasingly severe and unique ways, finding the joy in home and pushing back together feels like a balm.

Thousands of words have been – and will continue to be – written about home. It is what we search for. Being a child of immigrants renders you nomadic by nature, and so does class disparity, negligence from the state and a fluctuating market. This is a story about what happens when you are faced with all of those things first hand. It is an account of heartbreak and a love story all at once. Moving can be the site of chronic stress but it is also an opportunity to reset. It has taught me, most of all, about finding the beauty in every corner of home – the delicate, fragile curls of chipped paint and the sonic reverbs of thin walls on an estate. We all move from place to place and find stories that make us who we are. Here are some of mine.

# Beresford Road – How a history of activism got us here

I come from a line of dreamers. My nanaji, in the tiny rural village of Bahowal (population: 1,298) in the Hoshiarpur district of Punjab, spent most of his time daydreaming, envisioning what could be. His favourite sound was the primal, full-bodied thud of the dhol, a double-ended barrel drum made from wood, brass, and leather that hangs around your neck like a child. The sound it makes is bassy enough to wake and shake the ancestors from their slumber. Once, he told me why he liked it: 'It sounds like it's building to something,' he smiled.

The house my nanaji grew up in as a skinny, optimistic boy was built from clay bricks dense with the scent of sun-dried earth, mixed with mulchy straw and timber, reaching up and across like a one-room bungalow, around 7 feet high, a sturdy feat of engineering. His father dreamed of building the house up, literally, skyward. He worked in the field and raised eleven children, hoping to see their dreams take them out of the hard labour of the village. His hope was realised when my nanaji, at twenty-two years old, left because he too was building to something.

My nanaji arrived in 'Yookaay' in the early 1960s. He landed in Southall in west London, bang in the middle of a British winter, bones seizing with the cold and motivated to buy a home. This well-worn ambition has many names: 'staking a claim', 'digging in your heels', acquiring a 'better life' for your children, and has its roots in a historical, hopeful – and often unrecognised – pursuit of equality. Though south Asians have been living in Britain for over 400 years, Southall specifically became a place of high-density migration from the 1950s (so much so that it would become locally known as 'Chota Punjab', Little Punjab, and at one time was the largest Punjabi community outside India). This was thanks to its proximity to Heathrow airport and nearby opportunities for work like the R. Woolf rubber factory, where, as the story goes, the general manager had served with Sikh soldiers in the British Indian army and so was happy to recruit them.

My nanaji worked as a baggage handler at Heathrow. He shared a room with a friend in a house on Southall's Lady Margaret Road, the name a reminder of the sovereign exceptionalism built into the ground of the country he'd arrived in. Though Southall attracted people* through its proximity to the airport and being the best place to get lassi in the city (allegedly), the largest contributing factor was affordable housing stock.

---

* It has remained predominantly south Asian: the 2011 census revealed that in Southall, 76.1 per cent were Asian, 9.6 per cent Black and 7.5 per cent white. Southall Broadway ward had the lowest proportion of white British residents of anywhere in the UK – 93.7 per cent of its population were Black, Asian and minority ethnic.

My nanaji benefited from this, and from an existing model for success that had been tried and tested before him: arriving in London with the help of a cousin, finding work, renting a room, sending his wife – my naniji – over, having five children amid the squash, and saving until they could finally buy a house. They did do this, in the late 1960s, helped in part by supplemental income from my naniji's unofficial haberdashery side business where she made and sold intricate sari blouses, and it was there, in 1968, that my mum was born. Home over here made way for more home over there, and any excess money was sent back to Bahowal. Over thirty or so years, my nanaji's family home gained reinforced concrete walls, metal gates with intricate rose-shaped ironwork, and three small bedrooms.

This is how Beresford Road became bigger than a house in my family's imagination. A by-word for magic and marvel, it was a glittering fantasy made real against the grey backdrop of 1970s London. In reality, the house itself was innocuous – just another uniform terraced house with protruding windows and net curtains. If it feels like these houses are everywhere, it's because they are, recognisable by their triangular gables and curved living-room windows that face the street – it was one of the thousands built in Britain in the 1930s after the recession, where new ways of building relatively cheaply, together with mortgages and low deposits, led to a boom in house building which peaked at around 350,000 a year in the mid-1930s (around double the current annual number, for context).*

---

* Many, like the ones on Beresford Road, have been altered from the original design by incorporating white uPVC windows, covering archways or smothering external brickwork in beige plaster, trying but not always succeeding to conceal the holes made by fairy lights put up for weddings and Diwali.

Two of the few white households in the road just happened to be either side of us. On the left of us was Ethel, an elderly lady who lived alone and often asked for help retrieving her cat from various trees on the road. On the other side was a friendly family who eyed us with fascination. The patriarch, Mr Johnson, a carpenter full of warmth and jolly enthusiasm, took it upon himself to rename half the family for ease, which is how my uncle Mukhbir mysteriously came to be known as 'Fred'.

The first room you'd encounter on stepping into the house was the guest-only 'front room', featuring a mahogany Grundig radiogram that played records of Punjabi songs and broadcast the news on Sunrise Radio, with its lilting, elongated theme that reverberated off the walls. Further down the hall was the well-used dining room complete with a black faux leather sofa, glass coffee table and French doors that opened to the garden. To make way for the twin-tub washing machine in the kitchen, a large chest freezer was placed on the landing at the top of the stairs, full of diced onions and garlic pastes. If you made your way upstairs, you'd see the bathroom and breathe in the medicinal scent of Vosene shampoo and Imperial Leather soap. Walk past the master bedroom and you'd come to a box room for my uncle and one bedroom for four girls (Sukhbinder, Jasbinder, Dabinder and Balbinder, a family tongue twister). My mum, Bally for short, all skinny wrists and willowy limbs, shared a double bed in this room with my aunty Jas, while the other two had a bunk bed and all shared a small record player that played the Jackson Five, Blondie, Bananarama, and, from what I can ascertain, shitloads of ABBA. Many years later, this would be the house I took my first steps in.

Under the stairs, my nanaji had constructed a kind of small work studio for my naniji, where she would sit with her Singer and sew, moulding her body to the small angular space guided by the tiny light above her head. If she wasn't under the stairs, my early memories find her in the caramel-tiled kitchen with clumps of pale yellow dough between her fingers, manoeuvring her body around hot oil and pillowy hills of gram flour in a small space that just about allowed her to stretch out her arms and I spent hours watching that choreography. My favourite room in the whole house was the pristine and rarely used front room, because as a very small child I was fascinated with an object given pride of place on the coffee table: a tissue box of gold plastic and black faux velvet, which my nanaji had brought with him from Bahowal.

## LIVING MY LIFE LIKE IT'S GOLDEN

There are specific objects in every home that transport us. In mine, it's a copy of my nanaji's tissue box, a memento of historical decadence. These days, the tissue boxes you see in most south Asian houses are cheaper mass-manufactured plastic copies of the original versions that were made of precious metal. These boxes are adorned with fake velour, usually in black, red or navy, and covered in embossed yellow-orange plastic, to mimic Indian 22-carat gold, fashioned into patterns of intricate vines or leaves or flowers and shipped across oceans so that we might all experience some luxe in our lives.

As a child I would eye my nanaji's tissue box with intrigue and awe, this lump of *real* gold excavated and carved especially for us from God knows where. Once, I acquired a gold pen and got to work seeing what else I could gild, applying a DIY Midas touch to various unassuming objects to make them special: screws, chairs, door frames. For all their ability to fool a child, the sound of these boxes gives them away – if you tap one with an acrylic nail, like I often do now, there is no resonant 'ting' but a hollow, clattering sound. Our soundscapes are formed early and are uniquely attached to our interior environment, and my young eye was tricked so for a while I thought all gold sounded like that.

The story of how these tissue boxes journeyed to Britain is hard to pin down. Their ownership is contested across the global south, but it seems most likely that they are a remnant of the Mughal dynasty, which ruled India from 1526 to 1857. Mughal emperors often embellished metal boxes originally used for holding perfumes, or betel boxes used for storing tobacco leaves, with rich textiles and gem-set jewellery, transforming courts into luxury residences. Some researchers in the quest to find the year zero for these boxes have suggested that they were probably passed down through the opulent courts of maharajas who used them to store cloths for hand cleaning in the beginning of the eighteenth century. As industrialisation ramped up in the nineteenth century, these became replicated en masse as people got a taste for this remnant of ultra-wealth. Other historians suggest that British viceroys found and stole these boxes from Indian residences to adorn their London homes and impress guests, before they fell out of fashion. The details may vary, but what is undeniable is that there are at least 500 years of history being reproduced for a fiver in most high street markets in most cities in the world, cradling cheap tissues. Objects like these tell us something about who we are and where our stories begin. To misquote my favourite sociologist, Ambalavaner Sivanandan, gold tissue boxes are *here* because we were *there*.*

In ancient Egyptian funeral traditions gold was associated with the gods, serving as a conduit between heaven and earth. The Indian relationship is particular, not least because it houses large quantities of the natural resource – recent data suggests that India still has around half a billion tonnes of gold ore reserves. Colloquially known as the land of gold, the element has been a source of significant historical violence in India, namely after the British mined palaces and religious sites, leaving behind the scars of gouged-out chunks, many of which have been preserved today. During India's partition in 1947, when Punjab was split into the arbitrary border lines of India and Pakistan, gold jewellery was buried deep into the ground under homes and surrounding areas by women who planned to return after the conflict but never did. Years later, much of this has never been unearthed – the ground of Punjab is literally filled with gold. The holy Sikh site of Amritsar's golden temple, covered in gold leaf, exists in picture frames in various Punjabi living rooms, almost always shot at the same angle, and looks as it has every time I've seen it in real life – like a figment of the imagination.

One of the ways that many Punjabi houses across the UK – including my first home – built their aesthetic was through migrant sharing networks that helped people get on their

---

* The aphorism 'We are here because you were there' is attributed to Sivanandan, one of Britain's foremost and most influential Marxist thinkers on race.

feet. Aside from gold plastic, rugs and tablecloths were passed around the community to help new arrivals build a home. When I was younger, I would double-take when I saw the same tablecloth over and over again in different homes before I realised it was a kind of uniform – and armour. (Of course, it would be ridiculous to assume that white Britons' homes are completely alien to immigrant ones. After all, my mum's house, on a council estate just outside Birmingham, is filled with the same throws as her white neighbours' homes because they have taken advantage of the same B&M sale; gold carriage clocks passed down from elder members of families who received free gifts from life insurance claims appear to transcend any cultural matrices, and I have visited more than a few aspirational migrants' homes with Middle England's rallying call to 'live, laugh, love' adorning the wall.)

Objects like these are interesting because the process of migration can skew the class politics of taste, where working-class interiors and objects get jumbled and co-opted with middle-class homes in transit, until they create an aesthetic that can feel uniform. A lot of communities tie interior markers with a sense of national identity. In Britain, a pink and blue floral Cath Kidston tea towel *says* something about a person which often signifies a certain kind of British (read: white) middle-class taste, and these items can bring people closer to the margins of acceptability by providing a uniform language. For marginalised communities, there is a different motivation. When the world rarely reflects yourself back at you, it makes sense to use your home to do it instead.

Some of the more functional elements of this south Asian aesthetic, designed to preserve and protect the home, have endured over time. These take the form of lotas in the bathroom (vessels used to wash rather than wipe, dating back to 2300 BCE), thin, intricately patterned plastic tablecloths,* bobbled plastic matting on hallway carpets (for grip), plastic coverings on remote controls and sofas (with their distinctive squeak and crack), plastic multicoloured strip doorway curtains in bright blues, yellows and reds (mosquito repellents in Indian climates) and suitcases on top of wardrobes and under beds (ready to leave in a moment).

Psychologists put nostalgic objects in our homes into two categories: 'personal' objects and 'linking' objects. 'Personal' objects refer to sentimental items that take us back to an individual time and place – a mug from a honeymoon, or a keyring from a childhood trip to Alton Towers, say. When you think of the keyring, you think of the day that you bought it. This is distinguished from 'linking' objects, which tap into a cultural or ancestral memory and take us elsewhere. Think of it like this: a doily, a piece of lace used to protect furniture or humanise technology (and allegedly named after a seventeenth-century London draper and cloth merchant), is widely used across Jamaican homes and can be bought from Brixton market for £3.50 for a pack of five. When the doily is placed on a coffee table it doesn't recall the innocuous rainy day in the market where it was bought but the wider connection to a time and place. Maybe it takes you to a childhood memory of a hot afternoon watching TVJ in

---

* Michelle Obama mentioned 'those relatives who have plastic on their furniture' in a 2008 speech at a predominantly Black South Carolina church as part of Barack Obama's presidential campaign; many commentators claimed that the speech gained favour in sceptical Black communities.

Kingston. These 'linking' objects are tangible ways to make our abstract memories real, to write the poetry of imaginary homelands into our living rooms.

Easily replaced and replicated, 'linking' objects are both precious and plentiful, a secure way of ensuring we can never lose the place they take us back to. This becomes particularly significant to people for whom home is adrift – conflict refugees who left versions of their cities that do not exist anymore, migrants who are scared to visit their home in case they are not allowed back, orphans who have lost their connection to their parents' countries.

My friend Hani has a small white clay (or kaolin) pot called a dabqaad which is used to burn uunsi (frankincense), and which she insists is found in 'basically every Somali household' across the UK and the globe. Traditionally decorated with ornate pattern work and spade-shaped cut-outs, hot coal is applied under the arch with the uunsi on top. As it burns, it fills the air with perfume, as a way of recalling home in a full sensory experience. These too, tell a story about the place of their origin. Somaliland is one of the main global exporters of frankincense. The sap is sold to make perfumes and incense, and dabqaads make their way into western markets, trading via the Horn of Africa (the East African peninsula so named because it is shaped like a rhinoceros horn). Then they travel the way many of these sacred objects do – via packed suitcases ignoring weight limits and gifts sent via FedEx, Mailpac or DHL. The uunsi is burned in homes across the world, with its oud-like, smoke amber notes creeping under the noses of passers-by on British residential streets in Glasgow, Luton, Bedford and beyond. There is something so satisfyingly audacious about sending scent into streets where immigrants are often demonised for taking up space. My friend Hani points out that living in a community of Somalis means that her parents' neighbours seldom complain when the smoke alarms go off.

Another friend, Mahta, once let me photograph their Iranian living room while giving me a running commentary about the importance of having mini pull-out side tables 'to cater for unannounced guests coming to share gossip' and showed me the framed wall rugs and stacks of Persian literature: Hafez poetry books and the gilded, leather-bound *Shahnameh* (Book of Kings). A fellow writer, Vera Chok, told me how her mounted black and silver cow bells from Malaysia took her on a sonic journey back to 'what home sounds like', being woken up by their nearby hollow clanging. One colleague introduced me to candy-apple-coloured ceremonial wedding dolls and scrolls with calligraphic messages of prosperity in his grandparents' house, which take him back to the southern Guangdong province of China, while my Ghanaian friends in our group chat lovingly revere the lace headrests (one of many Venn diagram diaspora crossovers) in their family homes, delighting in plastic garden chairs that feature the omnipresent Akan symbol Gye Nyame, meaning 'only God'.

My reporting on this subject has shown me many more. In 2017, it took me to Seaford in Sussex to speak to Ali Hayder, who showed me his small wooden models of traditional Bangladeshi boats called noka. If he closed his eyes, he could imagine the waves of the seaside town were from Bangladesh, longing for home and fresh fish. In Wembley, Edna Brown told me about the significance of the tropical plants that recalled the breadfruit and mangoes of her home in Sturge Town, one of the first free villages in Jamaica.

Sometimes the object is a memento of something turned to dust. In 2018, I travelled to Handsworth in Birmingham to interview Noor Al Bari, two years after she had fled from Syria as a conflict refugee. She told me about her glassware back home that shook and cracked during bomb activity. That day, she took me on a tour in her living room to the glassware-filled wooden cabinet donated by a local charity, looked into my eyes, and then gestured back at it. 'Look,' she beamed at me. 'It stays still.'

## Don't you think it's tacky?

In April 2021, I speak to Sumit Khanna, who is dressed in a black T-shirt, styled grey hair, with AirPods in his ears – every inch the modern CEO. Khanna is the CEO of Beeta Tissues, a large facial tissue manufacturer based in New Delhi. He started the company in 1992, and in an effort to modernise, has targeted the brand at 'trendy millennials'. It is now a staple in many homes, and the boxes don't require any kind of plastic cover. 'It's a royal thing, so it's subconscious to want gold,' he tells me. 'But India is moving past that now.' He goes on to describe their new Beeta box designs for a cool, changing and design-led market. His team have worked around the obvious challenge of plastic exteriors covering your brand, while also acknowledging the market for decoration. 'We have a box designed with a peacock, which is a traditional Indian look, and we call it the Mirasa line, which is the Sanskrit word for "heritage",' he explains.

If there was ever a good reminder of how earnest lore can cloud our ability to see clearly, it is the observations made by Khanna after I describe my personal affection for the gold versions. 'Yes,' he says. 'But they're quite old-fashioned, aren't they?'

The next day, I join an online event with Bangalore-based artist and curator Chinar Shah, whose work includes long-term research on homes across India.[1] The day I hear her, she is speaking about historical uses of gold and its relation to wealth. At the end, I ask her a question about tissue boxes and gilded interior design and she takes a careful pause. 'Gold continues to be a sign of wealth, even though for a new urban generation, it's known as . . . tacky,' she smiles.

It is a good thing that Indian interiors are not static, and this small sample makes a point about the way a diaspora can imitate culture 'back home', reducing it to redundant mythologies. Owning an item like a gilded tissue box can be a way of trying to grab onto a version of India, the equivalent of flying an Indian flag on Southall High Street, when what you're *really* doing is shouting out the diaspora – and the diaspora likes to dip in and out of homespun aesthetics. I enjoy fake gold for being so audaciously tacky, an ironic look at real opulence that often turns me off. My desire is about something else: a link to my family, who found something precious in what many might see as breakable, mass-produced crap that will likely end up in landfill, not a museum. For me, it's a little dollop of ancestral memory every time a greasy hand reaches over to grab a tissue from a hunk of plastic that I can't bear to throw away.

Mostly, these objects tell us something about the version of 'home' that our parents and grandparents may be longing for, how they have created items of lustre to distract from the negativity outdoors. The India my nanaji left behind in the 1960s, which exists in a time vacuum at a happy standstill, is only one version, when Bollywood stars were modest, when he could navigate the land as a local, and (some) people had gold tissue boxes on their tables.

## COMBAT ZONES IN THE FIGHT FOR HOME

Beresford Road is the last residential road before you get to the Hambrough Tavern pub. If you turn right outside number 27, walk the 50 or so metres to the end of the road, turn left and make the one-minute walk to the bridge, you'll see it, an unassuming locus of resistance still standing to tell the tale.

Throughout the 1970s, far-right white fascists like the National Front regularly drew blood to a soundtrack of a coarse and thrashing subgenre of punk rock called Oi! On Friday 3 July 1981, one of the genre's skinhead bands called the 4-Skins,* with a sizeable neo-Nazi following, were booked to perform at an Oi! gig at the Hambrough Tavern. South Asian locals, worried about being targets of racist violence, implored the pub owners: might they, please, *not* invite droves of people to kick their heads in? At the risk of speeding through history, their request was denied. What followed was an almighty fire at the pub which took place about 200 metres from the house that my mum grew up in and ignited some of

---

* The music was even worse than the name.

the most violent race protests in this country's history, known as the Southall riots.

My mum's recollection of these events is hazy but she remembers her dad, my nanaji, carefully arranging a row of glass milk bottles on the wall outside the house 'just in case' trouble came to their door. Whether he really thought that milk bottles launched by my twelve-year-old mum and her young siblings would do the job of protecting a family from a gaggle of skinheads is unclear, but these rows of terraced houses, like bodies standing side by side, were a defence network of community safety. A *New York Times* article from the next day reported on busloads of skinheads arriving in Southall to fight, describing the aftermath of the streets that included Beresford Road as a 'combat zone', and reporting on 'attacks with petroleum bombs, streets littered with bricks and glass', shattered shopfronts and burnt-out cars.

These events were not unconnected to the soundtrack which was gaining volume thanks to the legacy of MP and one-time Tory minister of health Enoch Powell. His alarmist panic expressed in the now-infamous speech known as the 'Rivers of Blood' was touted as a prediction of what might befall citizens of different ethnic groups forced to live together. Powell made that speech in 1968, the year my mum was born, and just over a decade later, the legacy of it would see her cowering in her home. On the actual weekend of fighting, she stayed in and was tasked with organising the freezer, full of Tupperware at the top of the stairs. While her community elders were out fighting, my mum was stacking frozen onions for future meals – we all have our place in revolutionary struggle.

According to Powell, migrants like my grandparents, who had already settled, posed a danger until they were sent back. The seismic divides between 'us' and 'them' articulated in his speech placed a national debate about immigration, integration and race relations on the frontline, viewing immigrants as unwelcome aliens and creating a language of fascism that braided itself into the fabric of British life.* It is a speech which has become a warning signal of a certain kind of fascism, and while Powell may be discussed as being 'safely in the past', Powellism still informs much of government policy today, from the Home Office and its relentless attack on migrants, to the mistreatment of the Windrush generation, the political legacy of Islamophobia, and referendum campaigns fought on the lines of immigrants taking your jobs, space and resources. All this was explained to me in subsequent years using two characteristically concise words from my nanaji: 'Bad Man'.

None of this made the reality of finding housing easy, even if there were pockets of affordability. The racist approach to renting was seen in landladies' neatly handwritten cards in windows that enforced 'colour bars' or declared that 'no coloureds' were allowed to rent. Homes occupied by immigrants were neglected, and banks refused to lend to many Black and Asian borrowers. Landlords collected money for repairs that never came, and took advantage of tenants who struggled with the English language. This, for many immigrants, was their introduction to housing in Britain.

---

* This all had an impact on the ground, where racist attacks were happening nationwide, targeted at a community viewed as weak, docile and unlikely to fight back. In Southall, men were routinely getting their turbans pulled off, and my nanaji once nonchalantly told my mum that he heard the word 'Paki' at work so often he thought it was the name of a colleague.

When Black and south Asian communities *were* housed, either through private rent or, more often, multi-occupancy social housing provided by housing associations, many were victims of violent racism in majority white estates. In 1976, 34 per cent of West Indian and 41 per cent of Asian households were allocated housing which was 'overcrowded' compared to only 11 per cent of the white population.[2] This gave rise to the myths of overpopulated immigrants spilling out, ready to take over the white heartland of Britain, overbred, fertile and ready to attack.

Communities fought back. One of the reasons that many families across the UK were able to acquire housing was thanks to the work done by grassroots activist organisations like the Asian Youth Movements (AYM) and Black Power campaigns that took place nationwide, across London, Manchester, Sheffield, Burnley, Leicester and beyond. They fought for housing legislation and demanded anti-racist policies that thousands of immigrants benefit from today. (In Southall, teenage members of various AYM organisations would walk schoolchildren to the school gates to protect them from racist attacks.)

Inspired by Black Power thinkers and intellectuals from the US and beyond, activists took it upon themselves to build coalitions across communities and faith groups, many of whom had brought over organising tactics from their own locales, to amplify concerns across employment, education and immigration injustices, and they led to the formation of countless diverse groups: the Pakistani Progressive Group worked alongside the Indian Workers Association, the Bengali Housing Action Group, Manchester's Arawak

Housing Association, the Organisation for Women of African and Asian Descent, and the Bahay Kubo Housing Association Ltd, created to aid renters and still the only Filipino housing association of its kind in Europe.*

One tactic that activists used to fight back was by providing mortgage committees. They helped tenants who were excluded from mainstream banking by enabling them to put down deposits. Activists would pay into a pot (anything from, say, a pound a week) for the primary purpose of raising a mortgage down payment, but the money also funded financial literacy and administrative aid and translation services. A version of this took place in some Jamaican communities in the 1950s and 1960s; they relied on interest-free saving systems like the 'paadna' (a similar system called 'susu' existed in many West African communities),† allowing poorer members to draw ready cash in emergencies, or when their credit status made them ineligible for loans from high street banks. A group of 'partners' agreed to pay a regular sum (or 'hand') to a trusted person (or 'banker', usually an older, respected member of the community) on a weekly basis to be shared and allocated to housing costs,

---

* With special mention to the United Coloured People's Association, the Jamaican Labour Party, the Black Parents Movement, West Indian Independence Party, and the Antigua, Barbados and St Kitts & Nevis labour movements.

† Sam King, an early Windrush pioneer, was one of many West Indians who used paadnas. Interviewed as part of the Windrush Legacy exhibition (produced by Black Cultural Archives and Lambeth Archives) what he is recorded as sharing is truly extraordinary: 'We were the second Black family to buy a house in Camberwell, this was 1950. Over the next twelve years my family played a part in buying about half of all the property owned by Blacks in Camberwell. Because we couldn't get mortgages we pooled all our money together to help others. We called it a "partner", which is the same in Jamaica, and it worked very well.'

building security on money raised by the community for the community.

## THE ROAR OF BHAG

One of the most extraordinary – and locally celebrated – grassroots organisations was the east London-based Bengali Housing Action Group (BHAG). The group was formed in 1975 by Mala Sen and Farrukh Dhondy, alongside tenants, squatters,* unions and the radical campaigning collective Race Today, after demands for decent housing for Bengali workers in the East End were ignored. BHAG put pressure on the state by demanding changes to racist policy that kept many south Asians off council housing lists, and which exposed them to violent neighbours and rogue landlords. Helal Abbas is an activist who was part of BHAG, joining as a teenager in the role of secretary in 1977, and is part of a generation of local activists at the frontline of DIY housing actions back when, he laughs, his knees were strong. Abbas arrived in the UK in the 1970s from Sylhet, a city in north-eastern Bangladesh. He speaks to me from Tower Hamlets where he still lives, after early years squatting on 'Nelson Street, E1'.

'A lot of the people involved have now sadly passed,' he

---

* Squatting has historically been a revolutionary tool and act of resistance, occupying houses that were empty, inviting others to share and negotiate a way of life when there were few alternatives. The famous community activist Olive Morris is featured on the cover of the 1979 edition of the *Squatters' Handbook*, scaling the roof of 121 Railton Road in Brixton. The picture was taken during one of the attempted evictions of the squat. In an interview about it at the time, she said, 'The prices for flats and bedsits are too high for me.' I have a picture of this cover on my wall, forty years later, as prices continue to be too damn high for all of us.

tells me over the phone. 'We used to get cardboard food box pallets from Spitalfields market and use the wood for pickets. We would paint them colours, and make signs out of them.

'Living in poor housing with my parents and my brother sharpened my feelings of injustice,' he recalls. 'The Bengali community were forced to live in unfit housing which were in poor states of repair, plus were full of overcrowding, and we received a lot of racism from the local council,' he says in a friendly but exasperated tone that I've come to recognise in long-term activists. 'The work was voluntary and took place in the evenings or the weekends after work because many people were working long anti-social hours. But you were walking around areas known for racist attacks on the Bengali community so you were at risk.' On his way home one evening, Abbas was attacked by a gang of racists who left him needing five stitches in his skull. 'It was widespread,' he sighs, but it didn't slow him down. Perhaps fittingly, the acronym BHAG in Bengali means 'tiger'.

BHAG continued its work years after Abbas quit his job as secretary there to work on other campaigns in other groups. One significant action took place in 1976.[3] After having sixteen letters demanding better housing conditions ignored by Tower Hamlets Borough Council, BHAG organised a demonstration which saw 300 men and women, who led the charge, bringing children to march to the town hall on 30 June. Once outside they found a spot and sat in the street on the blisteringly hot day until a council rep agreed to speak with them. After twenty minutes, the council agreed to discuss the protestors' demands, which included, among other things, changes to housing policy which made 53 per cent of the Asians applying for council housing ineligible. After they were done, activists drove everyone home.

Abbas tells me that during his time, 'I would organise transport where it was possible so people wouldn't get attacked by racists. Not everyone had cars and public transport wasn't as accessible as it is now because the cost was a barrier to their participation and lobbying.' One universal truth emerges after trawling through the archives: throughout our history of activism, someone with a car is always useful.

## STARTING FROM THE BEGINNING

I think of the actions of 1976 as yesterday, today and tomorrow. This is not history that has been buried, only useful for writers to unearth it. Many contemporary activist groups are still resisting racist landlords and drawing largely on this work, evidence that it is alive.

The history of the struggle is one of the reasons why the beautiful interiors of many immigrant homes continue to be a retreat from a hostile and grey world outside. It is joyful to think about the power in seemingly tacky bits of plastic that adorn our mum's house, that we dismiss when we live there and miss when we leave. Objects like my nanaji's tissue box bring with them a quiet sense of grounding. After all, their existence in our homes reminds us how we got here in the first place. These things can't be shrugged off as fake versions of the real thing, because there's no getting away from the fact that these copies bring something new and real, that they are historically significant, and that they remind us that we are, too.

My mum had an arranged marriage at seventeen and moved into a nearby house in Southall with my dad a year before I was born. An Elvis fan born and raised in the city of Jalandhar in Punjab, he had flown from India a few days prior to the wedding, where he met my mum and acquired a visa and a wife in short succession. It was not a happy marriage, and she spent so much time in my grandparents' house that I have no memory of the one that she shared with my dad. I only remember the Beresford house, dressing as a toddler in home-made foil-shiny dresses in blue and gold with billowing sleeves (a carousel of fashion looks emerging from under the stairs), sidestepping around sharp corners, sitting on the plastic-covered sofa and stroking the embossed ridges of the tissue box. While I was pulling tissues out of gilded boxes, my mum was struggling with the cultural penalty of trying to leave her union. When she finally – and bravely – filed for divorce, she was, at the age of nineteen, with a small child, swiftly disowned. Though I was happily able to continue to visit my maternal grandparents and family throughout my life, she was not and so was quickly left out of any ideas of piggy-backing onto the housing ladder.

Disownment in economic terms is a big deal: in its most acute form, it's not a punishment you bounce back from. It means no generational wealth, no financial support, no offers of a place to stay when you need it. This was the beginning of a housing precarity that would become the constant of our lives, but we both entered it with the knowledge that you can make a home anywhere, with small objects that connect you to a community, time or place.

The house my mum grew up in, where I took my first steps, was a lesson in building comfort and familiarity. It taught me that home is something to fight for. And sometimes, it really does feel like a fight. My mum took me out of this house, imbued with Southall's history, objects of reverence and my grandfather's dreams, into a new one – to build a home for us that did not exist yet. And so, for the first time, we moved.

# Green Man Lane Estate – How we live with social housing negligence

In 1993, after years of short stays with various friends and on the couches of distant family members, my mum and I finally settled into a third-floor flat on the Green Man Lane Estate in West Ealing. The walls of the estate were coated in grey concrete and scratchy pebbledash, with large windows acting as eyes that overlooked the courtyard where I played. If you looked down from the courtyard (and I couldn't, with my short seven-year-old frame), you could see the darkly lit car park below, which looked like a square of the playground had been hollowed out to reveal an underworld populated by grubby vans and rust-covered cars. On rainy days, the smell of soaked concrete sailed into my bedroom and on hot ones, the sun would create blurry heat lines rising from the ground, making the whole estate look like a mirage.

My earliest memories of Green Man involve being mesmerised by the small, jagged shards of the pebbledash glistening in the sun like amethyst and obsidian. I would see magic eye patterns in the flecks and imagine the building as a pulsing vessel for spiritual energy. In reality, pebbledash is just a composite of limestone, sometimes mixed with sand and gravel, that is literally 'dashed' onto external walls.* It has been used on Britain's walls since the 1890s as an insulation cladding but mostly, it is used to hide shoddy brickwork, and it has subsequently become an aesthetic tied to council housing. It's now so unfashionable it can reduce the value of a property by up to 5 per cent (and it's also almost impossible to remove). While I was searching for meaning in gravel and limestone, desperate to excavate diamonds from the walls, I was unaware of the fact that pebbledash conceals negligence.

The walls in our flat were, of course, painted magnolia – a buttery, yellow-based white which is the institutional aesthetic of millions of council properties in the UK.† (With proper immigrant-mum-cum-Hyacinth-Bucket energy, my mum called the colour 'vanilla'.) At night, I would stare up at the ceiling, a pattern of tessellated plaster strokes, and imagine a sky of clustered Japanese paper fans.

From our window, you could see the paint-worn yellow and red metal climbing frames in the courtyard that I would play on under the watchful eye of the neighbours. In the summer, the light shone through the big windows in my bedroom, where I slept beside my neatly arranged rows of 'special stones', which I'd collected from the wall. Above me

---

* YouTube videos show this process in satisfying loops for the pebbledash enthusiasts among us.

† Warmer than pure white, the colour is now a neutral blueprint for many homes. According to colour psychology, the positive attributes of magnolia include hygiene, clarity, purity, cleanliness, simplicity and sophistication, while the negative properties are isolation and sterility.

was a picture of Janet Jackson taken from a *Janet* album CD inlay, unfolded into a long strip and Blu-Tacked on the wall. It would be a few years – and two house moves – before we could afford beds (and many years before I saw the alternative topless *Janet* cover), so I slept on a mattress on the floor. I loved that. I thought it was the height of 'cool mum' fun – I could bounce on my mattress and brag about it to my jealous friends.

Our flat had two bedrooms: one for me, and one for my mum and my two-year-old brother. A brief relationship my mum had after her divorce produced this beautiful and boisterous boy who I adored from the minute I saw his small, jaundiced face in the hospital, and have not stopped. Opposite us were 'Trigger' and Jason, two Jamaican guys in their twenties, who would come over to check in on us if they heard a loud noise, and once after a nameless intruder had kicked our front door in. They played Shabba Ranks and bashment from their windows and told me that if you drank ten cans of Nurishment you would get a six-pack. I don't know where urban myths are born but in estates, like school, they catch on like wildfire, and the Green Man walkways often had the mouth-watering strawberry milkshake scent of Nurishment emanating from cans strewn on the floor and almost zero evidence of the alleged six-packs.

These myths shape our worldview. After the divorce, my dad, learning English and working at Poundstretcher in Southall High Street, moved to the notorious Golf Links estate in south Greenford. It was an infamous place – stories and crime tales from that estate bubbled over into ours and my mum was terrified to send me there. The irony was, of course, that he was equally tentative about approaching Green Man Lane and a few months later, after he had decided to disappear from my life, I learned that they were hearing the same stories about us. (The two things weren't related.)

Around the corner from us was Carisse, a sex worker from St Lucia with cropped, icy blonde hair who had a daughter my age who I played with. I would go to her grandma's house to gorge on ginger cake and learn the dance routine to 'One Cent, Five Cent, Ten Cent, Dollar!', thrusting my bony hips forward with a huge, innocent grin. I later performed this to my mum, who received it with a fair amount of horror. On the bottom floor of our block lived Mark, a white artist with a beard and a single long plait with a coloured bead at the end which changed week to week. He was obsessed with Batman, and had hand-painted murals of Gotham City in his house and a couch fashioned in the shape of a Batmobile.

My favourite neighbour, around the corner two doors down to our left, was Mavis, my Jamaican 'aunty' and Pentecostal Christian. She had seen Jesus and his angels. Whenever I went over she would make me milk and a spiced bun smothered with butter and then describe this divine vision and how it changed her life, and she would explain how if I read every word of the Bible they would come to me, too. (She bought me a children's illustrated version and I now have a forensic knowledge of most stories in the Old Testament, which would serve me well when I would later have an obsession with the music of the GOD channel and Kirk Franklin in my teens.) Mavis's flat, which also had magnolia walls, was adorned with kitschy religious trinkets: a faux-gold Jesus on a cross, printed posters of the rivers of

Ocho Rios, delicate porcelain figurines of doctor birds and rules on how to behave cross-stitched in red onto a blue and white tapestry.

I read about Shadrach, Meshach and Abednego surviving a furnace with the help of angels, and between pauses for hot milk Mavis would tell me about the ones who had visited her. I would beg her for more details, wide-eyed and in awe, and then retell these tales to my mum, who would nod and change the subject. I often dreamed of Mavis and those angels, their gold wings made of light, and thought about how transcendental moments could be happening a few doors down from me. There was otherworldly magic coming from the squashed kitchen and chipped sideboards of Aunty Mavis's house. She taught me early that only an idiot might look at a place like Green Man and think that's all there was to it, that it didn't contain miracles. If I could go back now, I would ask her more about her life and investigate further. A lack of answers means that I'm left with one simple truth: on this estate, angels visited.

I would visit Mavis by walking along narrow concrete walk-throughs, passing green fire doors, used condoms in stairwells or sometimes, thrillingly, a dead pigeon kicked into a corner. The walkways overlooked the school I attended, St John's Primary, where most of the kids on the estate went. Sometimes we'd all rally together for a mass walk-down with various mums who took turns swooping up and collecting children from front doors like a revolving cast of west London von Trapps. It was also slightly sinister – you could terrorise yourself into thinking your mum was always watching you as the balcony walkway outside our front door saw straight into the school playground. The real pleasure of these raised walkways was not only that they were easy to manoeuvre for a kid visiting the neighbours, but that the perspective granted a huge horizon that overlooked the city. I remember standing on tiptoes to hesitantly peer over the edge, fingers curling around the concrete, heaving myself up. On one side, the grey car park stretched out below, and on the other, a sprawling skyline of glittering lights and other blocks like mine, a world for the taking.

If you turned right outside our front door, then right again at the red rubbish chute on the corner, your heart would stop because that was where the heart-throbbiest of heart-throbs I have ever seen lived: Ashvin. He is still unfathomably beautiful in my head because he has the rare luxury of being untouched by the ravages of social media and is instead perfectly preserved in my memories. He was Punjabi too, with floppy jet-black hair like the Aladdin doll my brother had, and a leather jacket. He was about five years older than me and his skin smelled like Lynx Africa and something else . . . fresh laundry mixed faintly with second-hand cigarette smoke. In the narrow corridors of the walkways, the smell of a person often came before they did, and my pupils dilated when I caught his scent in the wind.

I was completely enamoured by Ashvin in the way that young girls who haven't formally reconciled with grown-up desire are, and in the absence of an official fandom to hang onto (my mum wouldn't let me put boybands on my wall) and unknown to him, I made him mine. I would chase him around, heart in my throat, and find excuses to talk to him. He gave me the kind of electricity that would overload great power stations, and send pylons fizzling and melting into static lumps on the ground. My friend once made him, somehow, dance with me at a birthday party held in our living room for my cousin, and so my first dance with a boy was with Ashvin, to Janet Jackson's 'That's the Way Love Goes'. I can still feel my heart physically swell when I think about it.

## PAPER-THIN WALLS

If the pebbledash-coated external walls of Green Man Lane concealed things you didn't want people to see, then the paper-thin internal ones failed to conceal the things you didn't want people to hear. One of my most vivid memories of Green Man was hearing the one-second delay of the *EastEnders*' bassy theme music through the walls as the neighbours watched along with us. (I've spent some time over the last few years trying to find out the average thickness of a wall but I'd put 'paper-thin' as being around 11–12 millimetres.) So this measurement, coupled with the fact that sound can move smoothly through a wall, is part of the reason why music culture thrives in these environments so frequently. All you can do is submit, and we would all hear those iconic 'duff-duffs' through it one second out of time. Our own house was a mixture of bhangra, R&B and pop – Mum loved Mariah Carey, Luther Vandross, and softly sung Bollywood songs from *Disco Dancer* that stuck in her head – which probably shaped the soundtrack of our neighbours' lives, too.

The close proximity to one another that social housing has provided is one of the reasons that music has been able to mutate and evolve so effectively in this country, from make-shift sound systems to eastern European techno. The history of the music from immigrant communities creating new sounds has been long documented – over the last fifty years the residents of British council estates have seen reggae, lovers rock, rap, grime and afrobeats all develop and thrive. They still do, in bedrooms, stairwells, lifts, cars and beyond. It's in these living rooms that thousands of parties and shebeens* have taken place as an act of resistance and refuge from racist club policies.

Hearing sounds through thin walls influences the ears of would-be producers and artists. But there is no known research into how that experience can affect our psychology. In fact, there's no real research about the cultural benefits that come from living on estates at all. After weeks of asking industry experts, including neurologists and psychologists, the most interesting thing I heard on this issue was from London-based artist Yuri Suzuki, a Japanese sound designer who was born in Tokyo and whose work centres on how we live with sound in different environments. On the afternoon I join him in his studio in west London, he neatly explains these relationships. 'Sound moves through materials differently, like brick or plaster, which might seem obvious,' he tells me, dressed in dark denim with a neat haircut and slick, black glasses. 'But these minor details have a great impact on the quality of life people have, and also on how humans behave. When we can hear other humans, we feel safe. Too much silence has been shown not to be good for humans, which is

---

* Famously, blues parties in the terraced streets of Southampton during the 1970s and 1980s.

why these details must be thought about with care. In Japan, we *really* think about sound design in homes.'

This may explain why musical genius courses through estates. When ambient music pioneer Brian Eno once told me during an interview that he made installations of 'sound baths' – a method of therapy by immersion in ambient sound – he could have been talking about the muffled laughs, chatter and TV hums of close neighbours on Green Man. Even when the through-the-wall soundtrack morphs into yells or arguments it can be oddly comforting – my mum says that the sound of something is always less eerie than the sound of nothing and I think I agree. There are some frequencies that affect the human body – sounds at 20 kilohertz can make you feel sick, for instance. There must be others that simply make us feel comforted; the vibrations of many bodies humming together in unison like atoms in a solid mass.

## LEGACIES OF NEGLECT

It's not just the width of the walls that creates communal experience within a council estate – often it's the architecture of the place. But to really understand the current state of social housing, and the history of Green Man, we have to look *beyond* architecture. As much as I am a product of architectural decisions, I am also a product of policy. It is policy that has taken us to where we are now: with many estates undervalued, unloved and neglected.

This history begins with the well-intentioned 1919 Housing, Town Planning, &c. Act or, as it is better known, the Addison Act, named after the then minister of health and housing, Dr Christopher Addison. He was a breed of politician that is, unfortunately, increasingly rare: a doctor, advocate of national insurance, and, later, a Labour Party member who was motivated by social conscience. The Addison Act promised government subsidies for the building of working-class housing, which meant that for the first time, housing became a national responsibility for all local authorities. The Act was partly the result of a campaign to improve the design of working-class homes and a pledge by Prime Minister David Lloyd George in November 1918 to provide habitable homes for the returning soldiers of the First World War, a scheme known as 'Homes fit for Heroes'. These soldiers, it's worth noting, were assumed to be white, neatly erasing the contributions of Black and Brown soldiers from across the colonies, who should also rightfully have had a significant claim to this housing. They were often not granted it.

The Green Man Lane Estate was built in 1977 and was one of many post-war social housing experiments, dense with prefabricated concrete designed to last for up to 100 years and representing a point in history when there was a huge push for increased social housing in Britain. As a collection of different building types within the same estate, it is an example of how for a time, there was a hope that you might stay on an estate for ever, moving from room to room and block to block. The concept of a whole lifespan built into the architecture of an estate is not a new one. Perhaps the best example of it is the Maiden Lane Estate in Camden, built by architects George Benson and Alan Forsyth between 1979 and 1982. The design of Maiden Lane was based on the idea that someone born in one of the three-bed flats for families would later in life move into a studio apartment, then a one-bed flat, then back to the two-, three- and four-bedroom flats on the estate when they had a family of their own. Today there are residents who have lived on and moved around the Maiden Lane Estate their whole lives.

This idea didn't always work in practice. Almost immediately, social housing became a site of derision and neglect. Since the 1980s, the amount of social housing in the UK has steadily declined. One of the reasons for this is the Conservative 'Right to Buy' policy, first introduced in Margaret Thatcher's 1980 Housing Act, which allowed tenants in council housing opportunities to buy their homes, with state subsidies. This essentially privatised the housing stock, which played a big part in the crisis we see ourselves in now by creating a huge deficit of social housing that was sold off and never replaced. The 'good' houses and 'nice' estates were sold, leaving stock that no-one wanted to live in, let alone buy.

In 2017,[1] council homes were sold off almost three times as fast as new ones were built, which should have sounded alarm bells. In 2021, just 6,644 social homes were built across the whole of England, but in the same period we lost 28,796 social homes to sales and demolitions. (This is not enough to cover demand even in the London borough that I currently live in).[2] Activists have been imploring the government to build social housing as long as I've been old enough to remember, but it hasn't happened. Now, the lack of social housing is more urgent than it's ever been.

It doesn't help that the language used for housing stock is notoriously confusing. 'Social rented' is housing owned by the government which is rented at significantly below the market rate. 'Affordable housing' describes housing stock which is privately owned and whose rent is set at up to 80 per cent of the market rate. Housing associations provide both of these.* These terms are used interchangeably, easily being misunderstood to mean that 'affordable' housing is housing that the state provides for anyone to afford. This is not true. 'Affordable housing', which isn't really affordable to the lowest-income sections of society, is increasing, while real, accessible 'social rented' housing is declining.

This affects us all but in 2017, the Race Disparity Audit showed that the households most likely to rent social housing were in the African, Caribbean, Black Other (whatever that stratum refers to), Bangladeshi, Irish, Arab and Mixed groups (with the exception of the Mixed White and Asian group, which puts my family as an anomaly compared to the national average). So social housing in this country is in a bad state, but the penalty is felt even more keenly by immigrant communities.

Access to social housing is also, unsurprisingly, hugely competitive because of its deficit. In 2021, over a million households across the UK were waiting for social housing,[3] and one in ten people wait five years to find a home. On those lists are some of this country's most at risk people – homeless trans people, disabled people, refugees, sex workers. All are waiting for protections that can mean the difference between life and death.

---

* Housing associations also provide shared ownership and commercial lettings, and many have 'nominations agreements' with local authorities, which let the local authority decide who will get the social rented tenancies.

## GRENFELL

On the morning of 14 June 2017 the Lancaster West Estate's Grenfell Tower was set ablaze by a faulty refrigerator. The number of deaths rose over the next few days – 10, then 17, 18, 45, 60, and finally 72. It was a national heart-stop, and reporting on it for months after was the most life-changing thing I'd ever experienced both as a journalist and as a tenant. It put into focus – on a national scale – just how underdeveloped the conversation is around state negligence. On that morning, my mum called me in tears watching the rolling coverage, asking if I was seeing this, too. I was. One news report in the days that followed showed a journalist asking a Grenfell resident if she knew who lived next to her, as it might prove valuable when trying to get a count of people in the building. I remember thinking that the person asking the question must have never lived in a block, never experienced the muscle memory of people squeezing past you on the stairs, the faces who you talked to and the faces that you didn't. Estates are living organisms, a beating heart, a body of voices and sounds and irritants and calm. It's unlikely that you wouldn't know even your worst neighbour, because often, you see each other every day. I could always sense when Aunty Mavis or Trigger and Jason were approaching my house, just from the way they walked: the curve of a spine, a passing silhouette cast on our net curtain by the sink.

Anyone who has lived on an estate knows what it means to be patronised, and what it means for middle-class people to be shocked by living conditions that you regularly complain about to no avail. The archives from the housing associations are surely full of historical complaints made by social housing residents that have gone ignored, about anything from leaky gas pipes to spitting taps. I have been at the mercy of many of these ignored complaints over the years, standing in lines where my young friends acted as translators for their parents in grown-up worlds they didn't fully understand. (The only upshot to this is that I finessed my early writing skills thanks to passive-aggressive letters to housing authorities.)

A group of tenants known as the Grenfell Action Group (GAG) tried to make change in 2016 – and failed. The GAG website details power surges on the estate in 2013 which went ignored, as well as multiple other warnings lodged with the Kensington and Chelsea Tenant Management Organisation. Grenfell was an avoidable disaster, with architectural negligence built in. Let's take the use of the external cladding: highly flammable Reynobond PE, aluminium panels containing a plastic filling, used by a cost-conscious council. While zinc cladding was initially considered when the tower was refurbished in 2015, Reynobond PE was a cheaper option, saving nearly £300,000. This is a process known as 'value engineering', a systematic approach to cost cutting. Tenants were treated with vitriol before and after the fire. During the inquiry in 2020, Simon Lawrence, who was the contracts manager for construction company Rydon during the Grenfell Tower refurbishment, described residents who raised complaints about fire safety and cladding as 'vocal and aggressive'. For working-class people, it often seems that even raising your legitimate concerns must be done in a 'respectable' way – whatever that means.

Nothing sends a clearer message about a systemic failure to

care than the fire at Grenfell Tower. In fact, 'Grenfell' is now a by-word for negligence. It is also a story of unchecked state violence against low-income people, predominantly from immigrant communities, who often bear the brunt of neglect. Of the residents that died in the fire, 85 per cent were from ethnic minorities.[4] In 2017, data showed that the majority of children who lived above the fourth floor of tower blocks in England were Black or Asian.

During the days after the fire, while images of that apocalyptic blaze were striking horror in living rooms, Twitter feeds and group chats around the country, I attended a meeting at the Al Manaar Cultural Heritage Centre in Westbourne Park, where the mosque had been transformed into a community centre to discuss the immediate needs of displaced locals. It was one of the hottest days of the year, during Ramadan, and over 100 people were standing in an airless room, making space for survivors. Inside, there were wails and guttural, high-pitched cries from women expressing their unmanaged, immediate trauma to the room, men demanding justice and mothers holding their hands over their children's ears as people recounted the horror that had taken place four days previously.

At the time, in the absence of local councillors from Kensington and Chelsea Borough Council – and the prime minister – it was members of Muslim aid organisations who were doing hands-on work on the ground alongside citizen volunteers who came from across the country. They called for social housing lawyers and trauma counsellors, and a strategy to begin the search for missing people and long-term housing. Organisations like the Radical Housing Network, a

London-based alliance of thirty housing groups, were simultaneously applying pressure through campaigns like 'Action for Safe Homes' to demand public authorities take urgent action to address home safety.

Local volunteers I met, like Tasnia Aurongozeb and Jehangir Malik, spent weeks organising people and aid in Notting Hill. The Grenfell Action Group continued to publicly expose consistent failings. Mail addressed to the Grenfell Tower tenants was delivered to the Westway Sports Centre car park for collection, so that the people who had lost their homes could still experience a semblance of normality. Local activists set up Oyster top-up stations, where volunteers would put money on cards to ensure residents got to school or were able to move around. Prayer space was cleared on pavements for people observing, and locals bought prayer mats, lining them up side by side. I visited the sports centre, the site and the mosque many times in the weeks that followed, once with my friends who, at a loss what to do, ended up distributing packets of Hobnobs.

Some ex-Grenfell residents were eventually placed in hotels and temporary accommodation where they stayed for months. When I meet 31-year-old Amanda Fernandez she has been staying in a double room in a Holiday Inn Express in west London with her 73-year-old mum for over a year. I meet her on an arid morning in the hotel and we chat downstairs in the restaurant area as cleaners hoover around us after breakfast. She is dressed comfortably in a black T-shirt and leggings, with the demeanour of someone more than familiar with the hotel reception. Amanda, of Spanish and Colombian descent, was a resident of the Lancaster West Estate; she lived on the top floor of one of the blocks directly beneath Grenfell Tower. Falling debris from the fire destroyed her home, and the jets of the fire hoses waterlogged what was left. She tells me that the days following the disaster felt like 'a massive carnival, without the joy.* Everything was just so ... floaty. Nothing felt real. The heat was overwhelming ... and it felt like there were loads of people around, millions.'

There are hundreds of Amandas, whose untold stories piece together a tale of Grenfell that we might never hear in its entirety. She talks about trawling in the heat, asking shopkeepers to charge her neighbours' phones. She describes the glaring oversights by the local authority, who printed instructional pamphlets to distribute to residents in Farsi rather than Arabic so most of the speakers couldn't read them; how the paperwork given to her Spanish-speaking mother without explanation caused her distress. Smoothing her thick dark hair with one hand, she takes a breath and offhandedly mentions how, when her key workers went on holiday, she was asked to retell her story again and again to new people, and the toll that took.

Amanda was eventually moved into a double room in the hotel with her mum. She recalls the claustrophobia of being in a room where the windows didn't open: 'The first thing I wanted to do was just go in and open the windows and feel free.' As we lift our feet for the hotel's cleaner to vacuum under the table, she makes the point that day-to-day life in the hotel brings new stresses. She talks about how strange it is to have a plastic key card rather than a set of metal keys,

---

* A reference to the Notting Hill Carnival, which takes place on many of the roads on which all this was happening.

reminding her that she is suspended from reality every time she absent-mindedly checked for the jangle in her pocket, and it never comes. The hotel has no laundry services so she spends hours in the launderette, watching laundry tumble round and round, and to top it off, the bane of her life: an ugly piece of commissioned hotel art in her room, which is immovably screwed to the wall.

But there are warm stories too: the bond she formed with the doctor who is also still waiting at the Holiday Inn; the Filipino family she had grown up with who she thought had died, but who reappeared at the hotel weeks later, and the tears of relief as they ran to each other. The 'young guys in thobes coming to help during Ramadan'; the building of a new community and the humour she found moments for, throughout the trauma.

Her anger galvanised her, each administrative calamity spurring her on. 'I've been offered [housing in] Harrow,' she tells me, 'which, look, is totally fine for people who want to leave the borough – everyone wants different things. But I was born and raised on that estate. I work locally. Our estate wasn't just a tower.' It's true. Alongside housing, the Lancaster West Estate contained a nursery and a boxing club, and I think about the role of St John's School on my own estate. It's a gross misjudgement to think this kind of community – and home – is easy to replace. Amanda, like many others, was expected to rebuild her life with no-one around her, in the middle of a community where she didn't know anyone. 'I think to myself, "What is the role of a council?"' she tells me, gazing into a plastic tumbler of water. 'These people are there to safeguard you as tenants, and as you've got so many towers in London, it's just worrying. Who do you put your trust in?'

Six years later, the knock-on effects continue and many tenants are still trying to answer this question. Namely, the people across the country who live in properties with potentially unsafe cladding, many of them on estates with no timeline for when it might be removed. Many middle-class leaseholders are currently in spiralling debt and even bankruptcy thanks to rising insurance costs for new-builds with dangerous cladding. All these failures are neatly, and tragically, connected.

## Saying goodbye

We moved out of Green Man after two years because my mum was being threatened with rehousing. This followed plans for a 'regeneration' project which didn't include us, and so I hurriedly made it my business to pack up my tiny shiny rocks into my Coca-Cola pencil case. The estate had been unofficially on the ropes for years. Crime rates were rising and conditions worsening, with bad plumbing and broken latches and thermostats, which all made it easier for the creeping threat of property development to move in with promises of solving these issues. We left when officials told my mum the development was certain. But this impending demolition did not happen immediately – in fact, today, unbelievably, Green Man is still standing, albeit in unrecognisable disrepair.

The Green Man Lane Estate now, according to Ealing Council's website, 'needs a lot of work to address the improvements needed to bring it up to the government's

Decent Homes Standard',[5] just fifty years after being built. The Decent Homes Standard is set by the government, which has historically said that homes should be 'warm, weatherproof' and with 'reasonably modern facilities'. However, this definition is at the time of writing under review. In short, what constitutes a 'decent home', in the eyes of the government, is unclear.

At the time of writing, the website copy reduces the estate to four bullet points, describing it as suffering from:

- anti-social behaviour
- derelict garages
- drug dealing and crime
- too many one-bedroom properties and a lack of four-bedroom properties

It's grimly predictable: the legacy of the estate, of cans of Nurishment and Mariah Carey and hot buns, brutally reduced to four bullet points on a basically defunct website.

It should be clear by now that the dream of Addison will be dismantled, brick by brick, if we don't see a tighter regulation of the rental market and an end to the selling off of social housing to private developers. It's hardly a new position to take – since Thatcher started the decimation of social housing without replacing the shortfall, accessible housing has been in decline. Many activists at the time foresaw the crisis we find ourselves in now and made the same plea. We must, with urgency, build more social housing at social-rent costs, but not before we understand the importance of the communities they can nurture. Part of this is forcing management and decision makers in local government to avoid the cheap replication of tower blocks and to reject 'value engineering'. For many, council estates are not joyful places – they are a last resort and it is clear why. In 1995, the Green Man Lane Estate did have communal spirit, but it was aggressively neglected to the point of abandon. Across the UK, all we can begin to demand is to see social housing not as a collision of fragments but as a connective network of beauty through design, care and thoughtful investment.

I went back to Green Man in 2019 for a Radio 4 documentary on the musical contributions of immigrant communities in Britain. Most of it was boarded up, still waiting to be demolished – by Rydon, the property developers at the heart of the Grenfell Inquiry, which at the time of writing, is still going on. Their website assures me the demolition is happening imminently.[6] My bedroom was still intact, behind boarded-up windows, and rats roamed the burnt-out climbing frame where I used to play. It was worse than gone – it was forgotten, abused by the state and never thought valuable enough to rebuild for its original residents. My old bedroom window stood there, unaware of the bulldozer coming for it.

I share my pain with thousands of people in the country who have said goodbye to a community or home before they were ready. While it's not uncommon to go back to a childhood home and find it destroyed, the message of estates from the state is often that they never really belonged to you in the first place. I think of the amethyst pebbledash being crushed and discarded, ground to dust and swept away in a big skip, with zero reverence of the delight that communities create even amid overwhelming negligence. Sometimes, it is the perceived energy from crystals in a wall or the visitations of angels, and sometimes, if you're very lucky, it is a glorious, heart-fluttering, first dance with a boy.

# Yeading Lane – How we feel 'safe' at home

After we moved away from the Green Man Lane Estate, we did what many people did: relocated to the next social housing that was available on a list. This mythical 'list' – still a source of mystery for thousands waiting on it – took my mum, my brother and me to the noisy main road of Yeading Lane in Hayes in 1995. We lived in short-term accommodation, in a 1930s house with two bedrooms – one for me and my brother, and one for a house sharer in the box room next to us. My mum slept downstairs, in the living room, made into another bedroom.

These houses weren't really designed to accommodate whole families in one room, something I noticed was happening unofficially in lots of houses near us, which gave the whole place a specific kind of chaotic energy, with its busy main road and high turnover of short-term neighbours. This was not a unique situation: it was common for Hillingdon Council to create house-shares with different people on a list before they were issued permanent housing. Yeading Lane was well known at the time because it was a minute's walk from the notorious Willow Tree Lane Estate – allegedly so dangerous that pizza delivery drivers wouldn't go into it. As a result, people would order pizzas to randomly selected houses on Yeading Lane and collect them from there.

At first, we shared the house with 'George' (real name Jafari), a Somali refugee and Jehovah's Witness with an addiction to burnt toast and halal Haribos. He worked so much that my memories of him are hazy, but the copies of *The Watchtower* scattered around the house, with their beautiful illustrations of women lying languidly next to tigers in lush gardens in pastel colours of mauve and pink, remain pin-sharp in my head. When his door was ajar, I would peek into his room to see an inky blue Calor hotplate which created an air smudge from the heat that looked like magic. He used to fry eggs or fish, and the smoky, tangy and – for me – mysterious culinary scent would make itself known throughout the house and in young, curious nostrils. When we crossed paths on the stairs he would smile while I stole a glance into his room, at the religious texts and the bareness that designers might call 'modernist', and others might recognise as 'easy to pack up'.

Every now and again George acted as a scapegoat for my crimes. My mum was very strict about what was appropriate for me to read and I would secretly borrow the illicit books of Francine Pascal's *Sweet Valley High* series from our local library, complete with pictures of thin, smiling, blonde Valley girls on the cover (all my mum needed to impose a ban). When my mum came up the stairs to put clean uniforms on my bed I would quickly throw them into George's room. I can only imagine his mystification when coming back from a night shift to see teen Valley girls adorning his floor by the Bible.

## NUTELLA SPREAD TO FIGHT THE DREAD

My curiosity about the very different life George was leading just next door to my bedroom made me fascinated by people, but also by doors themselves. Most of the front doors that I grew up seeing were ones that were standard issue in council blocks: fire doors with a lacquered sheen that peeled away, often with wire mesh grids built into the glass, which were the brainchild of American inventor Frank Shuman in 1892. In Victorian England, when factory windows were susceptible to shattering from the heat and vibrations produced by machine rattles, this mesh wire was widely used to prevent grisly outcomes. A hundred years later, the mesh would find itself in doors on council estates across the country, the idea being, I guess, that council tenants pose the same threat as 10-tonne Victorian machinery.

Though I loved it when we had guests, it was in this house, at age nine, that I developed a short-lived but acute anxiety around our front door. The door was nondescript, made of heavy, white plastic a hard-wearing inexpensive alternative to wood: uPVC, or unplasticised polyvinyl chloride. Ours had a grid of four skinny slabs of glass covered with a frosted decal sticker that peeled at the edges, and when the doorbell rang I would see the blur of an outline, feel light-headed from adrenaline, get a whoosh in my ears and tremble. My mum would have to sit on our threadbare grey carpeted step and stroke my hair, rubbing my scalp in figures of eight.

Sometimes she'd bring me thickly spread Nutella on white bread and I'd slowly eat it on the step, licking the silky chocolate from the top, waiting for my heart to calm my young body, mystified as to why this was happening to me.

Much later I realised that this was an anxiety I'd unconsciously inherited from my mum. Her unusual skittishness in this house was explained by two things happening in unison in our lives which put peril at our front door. One of them was related to George's visa status, and his fear that at any point someone might be on the other side of the door demanding papers.

George's situation was a new concern for our family, who had dealt with many of the details of housing fuckery, but never of citizenship and the state. In the night, my brother would sometimes climb out of bed and pad up and down the stairs. The sound would jolt George awake, and he would go into the kitchen to make a sandwich, shaken at the idea that someone had come for him. Whether or not this was an imagined or a legitimate fear of an impending raid I'm unsure. I was too young to learn the details. But I was old enough to understand the implication: that somewhere out there was a threat I couldn't see.

Anxiety sends adrenaline speeding through your veins, alerting you to danger through a flight-or-fight response. It quickens your breathing as your lungs try to move more oxygen through your body, in case you need to run and escape. The reason it feels terrible is because our bodies are not designed to be constantly on alert in this way. Over time, chronic anxiety can lead to heart disease, loss of kidney function, circulatory disease and obesity.

Immigration officers create fear by raiding at dawn, and their powers of entry allow them to make welcome places – nail shops, restaurants, even wedding register offices – into sites of terror, all part of the political project of the hostile environment. When someone really pounds on a door, you can feel it in your chest. Our homes are extensions of ourselves, and when the most vulnerable parts are attacked, we respond. After all, most of the worst tragedies in history begin with a door being kicked in.

While these scary low-end frequencies were happening in the background, I did find my own antidotes. The Spice Girls' debut album *Spice* had been released and I was in a state of obsession, playing 'Wannabe' on repeat, making up dance routines to the sexy lesser-known tracks that never made it to singles, and turning the volume up. I would lie for hours on my back, feet planted on the wall, looking up at the 'popcorn' ceiling in my bedroom while meditating on high kicks and girl power. At night, past my bedtime, I played the album low in my room as I mouthed 'LAST TIME LOVER' lasciviously, dreaming of boys with curtains and going to high school. If there was a way of soundproofing a door knock, for brief moments, pop music seemed to work so I missed some of the sounds downstairs that were making the adults sit up. I had learned that music was an effective – and bewitching – world-building distraction.

Reading was another. If I wasn't singing, I was reading. The local library was 50 metres away from our house, a small building with a wild garden outside which was close enough that my mum let me go alone. The only books we had in our house were A–Z manuals, religious texts and my mum's Virginia Andrews novels. I was drawn to the books where you didn't have to leave your bedroom to find magic – C. S. Lewis, who uncovered fantasy lands of ice and snow in a wardrobe, the secret passageways that George and Julian found in old houses during escapades as part of the Famous Five, Borrowers scurrying on bedroom shelves, even the Indian in the cupboard (which I thought referred to me, but definitely did not). Sometimes I tore off the cover to keep a piece of the enchantment with me and I'd make up excuses to the librarian. My imagination, when it wasn't conjuring big bad wolves or fake book accidents, gave me peace then that it still gives to me now – a joyful discovery that took me somewhere else when I needed it.

## THICK NECKS AND SNARLS

If immigration officers were one source of anxiety in this house, another was bailiffs. I came to know them through the bright red notice envelopes strewn on the kitchen counter, issuing threat penalties over missed rent payments. My mum had various jobs at this time, one as a secretary at a beauty parlour in West Ealing, where she wore brown suede mini-skirts and knee-high boots that I thought were the height of glam. She also did bits of babysitting, and sold towels at a call centre which required a telephone voice that was unrecognisable to me. All these jobs were cash in hand (with the same precarity you might attribute to zero-hours contracts now, only with word-of-mouth contracts) and some only lasted as long as the businesses did. When the work dried up she missed rent payments, and had to quickly find another job with no financial cushion in between. As we know, it is expensive to be poor.

So, bailiffs were often part of the conversation in our house growing up, spoken about with such frequency that you might mistake them for an undesirable family member. They were real and scary to me – my friends who also received letters from 'the Bailiffs' told tales of caricatures who were heard about but rarely seen: bully boys with a bone to pick. They were 8 feet high in my imagination, until I heard that my school friend Jack's dad had once beaten one up, which made me feel better. When the time came, maybe his dad could come over and beat ours up, too.

Put simply, the role of a bailiff is to enforce High Court writs and warrants instructed by the court to collect a debt. Say a tenant gets into rent or mortgage arrears – at some point the owner of the property might go to the county court to get the property 'back'. The High Court would then instruct the bailiff to produce that property back to the owner with vacant possession. This can take the form of issuing tenants with a fourteen-day notice of a repossession order, the idea being that this is ample time to find another place to live.

Bailiffs have been recruited to do the dirty work of whatever landowning power needed it from as early as the thirteenth century. Initially, they were legal officers used to settle farm and land disputes, and now they are best known as the people who either take your shit (goods possession), fuck up your shit (house eviction), or both. Their work can move between the sinister and, frankly, the absurd. A bailiff once told me he had to retrieve the contents of a 4-acre fishing lake, which included clearing the lake of thousands of pounds' worth of carp and returning them to the owners. In short, it's unsurprising that the public have long seen them as tyrants. Shakespeare, in *Twelfth Night*, used the disparaging term 'bum-baily', allegedly because they followed very closely behind debtors.*

On earning potential alone, the job of a bailiff can be alluring. In 2022, the *Guardian* reported concerns around the employment model used by most bailiff firms, 'where agents are self-employed workers who earn commission based on their caseload, rather than employees with a salary. One advert for a major bailiff firm – which describes those with a military, police or prison background as desirable candidates – offered "uncapped commission" with "realistic earnings between £35k and £65k"',[1] well above the average national salary. These financial incentives make for scary realities.

More recently, bailiffs have become glorified as moral crusaders through popular bloodlust TV shows such as *Can't Pay? We'll Take It Away!*, *Beat the Bailiff* and *Call the Bailiffs: Time to Pay Up*, making raids and the fear of intruders an entertaining part of our culture. They often appear as caricatures on screen: large, pink, sentient thumbs dizzy on power – a thuggish view of Britain that conjures images of British bulldog tattoos, thick necks and snarls. These shows applaud the idea of people 'getting what they deserve' and are designed to put us on the side of the debt collectors. In 2018, a High Court trial known as *Ali & Aslam* v. *Channel 5 Broadcasting Ltd* saw a family awarded damages of £20,000 after their treatment

---

* In France, the term *pousse-cul* (literally 'push-arse') was similarly used for their equivalent officers.

in *Can't Pay? We'll Take It Away!*. Mr Aslam, who had a foot injury at the time, was awoken in the night. Unedited footage showed the High Court enforcement officer apparently encouraging the landlord's son to try and stir up the situation to make for better television viewing. The incident distressed Mr Aslam, who had a heart condition, and the court heard that Aslam's children were bullied in school as a result of the broadcast. The detachment from, and dramatisation of, trauma has been a big part of reality TV programming. There is no year zero for these shows as a whole but surely the US reality TV series *Cops*, which first aired in 1989, has a lot to answer for. In my teen years I watched many episodes purely out of boredom, part of a generation gawping at the format that follows law enforcement officers on patrol, manhandling sex workers and petty criminals, and delights in the power play and its own skewed version of justice. This kind of 'cop-aganda' is designed to put us on the side of law enforcement, just as bailiff shows want us to side with debt collectors. Over many years this justice has become braided into our everyday – *Cops* is one of the longest-running TV shows in the US.

Paul Bohill is a product of this cycle of media glorification, gaining minor recognisability status as the protagonist bailiff in *Can't Pay? We'll Take It Away!* for four years from 2014 to 2018. He now works as a private contractor. Over five seasons, he and his colleagues made '700 to 1,000' repossessions, sometimes as many as five a day. I speak to him at the height of the first UK lockdown over Zoom from his home. Wearing the same rimless glasses as in the show, and a blue striped shirt, he looks every bit the smart, benevolent grey-haired man–next-door, except this one discusses his minor 'celebrity' status with the same glee as he describes his team's ability to 'drill into the locks on a plastic door within about five minutes'.

'A lot of people who are bailiffs are flawed,' Paul tells me. 'They've got a character defect, a lot of them. They're ex-forces so they still think they're in the frontline. They're the people who wear black combat trousers, big boots, so on.' (77-year-old Paul himself, framed in the show as the 'nice' one, was trained in the police force by veterans returning from the Second World War and Korea.)

It is important to get a sense of the work on the ground of these public aggressors, reduced to myth and TV fame for many. I dig into that throwaway comment about the plastic door and Paul explains that in the case of a home repossession, 'if people were to barricade the door, the writ instructs us to repossess the property. So somebody in my team would be trained as a locksmith and we would carry locks and tools to break into it. We have an absolute right to break into the property and to return it to its rightful owner.'

There is much to hate about this. But perhaps the most egregious aspect of their work is that there is no third-party body in place to adequately police the behaviour of bailiffs. I ask Paul about the extent to which police intervene if called by scared tenants and he explains how he sees this hierarchy with chilling confidence. 'Well, the police are then obliged to assist us,' he replies. 'The authority I hold is the authority of the High Court and there is no higher court in the land.' In fact, there are two higher courts, the Court of Appeal and the Supreme Court.

While there may be caveats to the accuracy of Paul's

comments, it is worrying that a bailiff sees himself this way. And yet, the system empowers this kind of thinking (with details like the fact that if a bailiff breaks your lock, it's up to the landlord to fix it because you can't claim insurance). Paul gets off the call casually mentioning that, after a year of job losses and austerity, business is booming: he has been asked to do 200 possessions over the last few weeks.

The fact is, many of us are closer to a bailiff visit than we think. Before the pandemic, referrals to bailiffs had been rising rapidly, with about 3 million civil enforcement cases in 2019, according to the Centre for Social Justice – an increase of more than 600,000 in five years.[2] In 2022, the *Observer* reported that a debt collector turned up at 53-year-old Faith Gillin's door in Northampton. She had forgotten to update her address with the DVLA, so a fine sent to her old address had gone unpaid. But the council had not contacted her at her new address, despite having the details on record, she says – instead passing the debt to an enforcement firm.[3] There are many stories like this. Charities have warned that the number of cases involving bailiffs is set to surge as rising costs of living push households into debt. New figures suggest they are already beginning to climb, with Citizens Advice receiving 2,704 requests for help with bailiffs in March 2022 compared with 1,884 in December 2021, many of whom will likely be victims of spurious admin and a historic economic crisis.

## THE PRICE OF FEAR

Fear is big business. Private doorbell cameras (which the Met call 'domestic CCTV') have seen a huge increase in sales – the most recent data is in the US, which might tell us something about what we can expect here. It tells that in 2016 the size of the doorbell camera market was $252.1 million – by 2025 it is set to be valued at $2.8 billion.[4] An estimated 400,000 Ring devices were sold in the US in December 2019 alone[5] and one in ten US police departments can now access videos from millions of privately owned home security cameras without a warrant. The sales of doorbell cameras are rising in the UK too (my technophobe Asian aunty has just bought one) and will likely become part of the requirement for future insurance claims. In the US already, companies like Flock Safety that sell outdoor security cameras have sold them to homeowners' associations to equip whole neighbourhoods.[6] Far be it from me to judge the tools which people buy to make themselves feel safe (or to demonise low-income communities of colour who should be able to acquire the same solutions to their fear as affluent white people), but it's endlessly curious to me how this has so quickly become the norm.

This is a booming area of business because, even while these cameras don't necessarily make anybody safer, they reassure people that something is being done in the face of all this danger. Sales increase in line with how people perceive crime rates, regardless of whether they are actually rising or not.[*] In fact, in 2021, the Centre for Research and Evidence on Security Threats shared research that showed that fitting these doorbells could even make your home more unsafe, giving an 'affluence cue' to potential burglars.[7] These cameras

---

[*] According to the Pew Research Center in 2019, opinion surveys regularly show Americans believe crime is up nationally, despite the general downward trend in both violent crime and property crime.

have the potential to limit the privacy of neighbours (where there are UK precedents of neighbours being awarded damages on these grounds), can expose users to hackers, and, at worse, can create a civilian surveillance network vulnerable to abuses. The 'something is better than nothing' line is often used to justify these surveillance systems, which only serves to intensify a climate of anxiety for everyone, making it almost impossible for people to trust each other.

In an essay entitled 'Luxury Surveillance',[8] professors Chris Gilliard and David Golumbia illustrate how people of colour are disproportionately surveilled in their day-to-day lives. 'One of the most troubling features of the digital revolution', they wrote, 'is that some people pay to subject themselves to surveillance that others are forced to endure and would, if anything, pay to be free of.' Facial recognition technology, in its current state, is simply not as effective at distinguishing between black and brown faces as it is at identifying white faces. This leaves Black and Brown people open to racial profiling, with reports of neighbours, and even estate agents, being reported for trespassing. Even if you are immune to these particular issues you may have other ones. In 2020 UK consumer group Which? tested a slew of top-selling doorbell cameras on the market and found problems with each one: all raised privacy issues for the owner, with many devices vulnerable to hacking.

What this all boils down to is that safety is sold as our personal responsibility. In an increasingly individualistic world it is not surprising that we feel like we only have ourselves to rely on, believing we can purchase a safer life. But who is a doorbell camera protecting if it's open to racial bias and hacking? This is not as simple as 'We don't need alarms, we need to look after each other more' (which I think is true); it's also about understanding that alarms and surveillance systems alone can be harmful, and that better neighbour relationships lead to a better sense of safety for everyone. One of the most used techniques to enhance relations between warring neighbours is mediation, which is usually advised before legal costs spiral out of control in the courts. Teaching these techniques in mutual aid groups or Zoom workshops for communities, funded by government or local organisations as standard, could bring enormous benefit. We live in a moment where people are increasingly asking the same question – how do we look after each other?

Mutual aid groups provide various tips. (My neighbourhood one tells me: don't oil your hinges, so you can hear it if the gate opens! Have a cricket bat under the bed! Get a pitbull!) These may be well-intentioned suggestions, but what might be more useful are solutions on how to think beyond the individual alone.

My mutual aid group also urges me to enhance my home's 'kerbside appeal', though it doesn't use that exact language. The term refers to the fact that an attractive exterior can add up to 10 per cent to your home's value because it makes the neighbourhood feel safer. It's easy to see how the construction of kerbside appeal – a sort of reverse broken windows theory – which includes hedge tidiness, pillars in front of your house and bin placement – gives rise to local antagonisms. What happens when people suddenly cotton onto the idea that the way that other people's houses look is tied to the value of their own? The answer, in my experience, is that they start descending into micro-managed chaos. It's why my mutual aid group on WhatsApp, born out of the local need of three streets during the first Covid-19 lockdown, can't be the only one which quickly morphed into a nauseating request line for kale and a passive-aggressive surveillance tool – shaming people for the bins and overgrown hawthorn on nearby roads. What feels to me like arbitrary policing of respectability has real-world consequences. An unsightly neighbouring property can reduce the value of a home by up to £29,000, and in 2017, more than 2.5 million Brits confessed they hadn't bought a property because of the décor of neighbouring houses.[9]

The quality of your front door can also add to your kerbside appeal and Victorian and Tudor doors are some of the most coveted. They often have patterned mottled glass to limit visibility, and composite door designs with names like 'Elizabeth Red' or 'Clarence' with angular lines and stained-glass middles. There is also, apparently, a thriving market for companies trading on aesthetics that offer the symmetry of Georgian panelling, or the graphic coloured glass patterns of the 1930s art deco period. Even the sound a door makes can be aspirational. In a brochure from the London Door Company a perplexing line about sonics reads, 'You can hear the quality when it closes behind you.'

In an attempt to override my childhood anxieties, I pretend to be the owner of the house I rent and invite a salesperson from a popular London door company to inspect my front door. A week after booking, a small blonde woman dressed in a black pencil skirt and form-fitting shirt arrives at my house. With a manner that is somehow both sunny saleswoman and sober doomsdayer, she illustrates just how lucrative a commodity fear is. Like a survivalist preparing for nuclear fallout, she points and baulks at the weak spots in the front door. She tells me the panels are feeble from years of warp and because of the material – cheap pine and non-reinforced (modified Accoya wood is apparently the hardiest), and flicking her eyes up and down them, she lets me know she could probably 'kick them in'. The clear glass could, apparently, be easily punched through (she recommends double-glazed toughened glass). Her agenda is to make my home strong and stable, and really, when has that phrase ever failed?

In what might come as a shock for anyone whose childhood – and adult life – featured an instruction to 'put the chain on' for safety, she tells me that it is, in fact, obsolete. The much better choice is something called a Banham lock, costing around £500. It is apparently the gold standard lock because the keys are difficult to replicate, it's ultra-strong, some versions are even saw-proof and crucially, you can design your own finish. She recommends something called a 'rigid hood' to prevent hands coming through the letterbox, and finally, goes through a range of colours for me to pick from. At the end of the door consultation, she quotes me a figure: £8,877 for some (stylish) peace of mind.

## PUSH BACK

Looking back, what would have helped me, my mum and everyone in that house, really, to dissipate those fears into smoke was simply, more information. It would have helped to know what bailiffs are allowed to do, to know what to say to the officers who might come to the door, which local activist organisation you could call to buy more time, or even the places that could provide sites of refuge – flyers with directions to local libraries, skate parks or gardens.

Abolitionist work urges us to abolish our reliance on the systems that oppress us, so that we can look after ourselves. It does a good job of answering some of these fears with solutions that do not require us to purchase our safety or call a police force who might be particularly heavy-handed with communities of colour (and who, incidentally, can't help you ward off bailiffs or immigration officers). One of the founders of the Black Lives Matter movement in the US, Patrisse Cullors, in her book *An Abolitionist's Handbook: 12 Steps to Changing Yourself and the World* tells us that in order to have an abolitionist approach to community problem solving we must start small in our communities and work from there. She advises small but significant things to practise: have courageous conversations, value interpersonal relationships, think imaginatively.[10] The conceit is that if some of us are at risk from the state, then we are all vulnerable. To see these connections in our community is to begin to think about alternative – and potentially more effective – ways of keeping us safe. Abolitionist arguments centre on the idea that you help yourself by helping each other, to begin conversations that provide solutions that go beyond dogs.

Think of the common pushback against bailiffs, for example, where activists recruit people to link their bodies to create a wall in front of a door to ward off bailiffs or eviction officers from tenants. This activist strategy is one of stalling, rather than solving, to give tenants more time to find other housing or come up with the funds. Across the country, people are using their bodies to save doors getting kicked in by agents of the Home Office and creditors, to protect women, young trans kids, victims of violence and many more. Activist organisations like Taking Control advocate for bailiff reform by offering sample complaint letters, videos on your rights and a national debt line.

The Anti Raids Network was set up by Latin American precarious workers based in London to resist the presence of immigration enforcement in migrant communities. For them, and organisations like them, the key tactic to stop this abuse is knowledge – the more that people know their rights, the more power they have to resist collectively. They encourage people to print leaflets, to film and challenge officers, attend work-shops, and to tweet @AntiRaids and @CopwatchNetwork. In May 2021 in Glasgow, crowds gathered on Kenmure Street to stop a deportation van forcibly evicting their neighbours. Hundreds of activists, organised by the local No Evictions Network, and local citizens surrounded the van and eventu-ally, the migrants' release was negotiated. One campaigner told immigration officers: 'You've come to the wrong city.' So, how do we make every city the wrong one? The answer lies in repeating these actions – in the months that have fol-lowed, groups have resisted charter flights to Rwanda and eviction officers in London, Coventry and beyond.

It might be – increasingly – up to us as neighbours to learn what to do when bailiffs and immigration officers turn up on our street as we ward off the most aggressive government policies. Had I felt assured that my neighbours would have known what to do when bailiffs came around (other than

Jack's dad) I might have missed out on months of anxiously nibbling Nutella toast on that scratchy carpeted step.

It took time for me to feel relaxed at home at Yeading Lane. After a few months, the shadows that walked by the door no longer disturbed me so much. The bailiff's letters continued to pile up but luckily, no-one ever did bang our door down. It became less and less frequent that I sat on the stairs, trying to quiet the tinnitus in my head. But living in a state of suspension, waiting for something to happen, kept me held in a state of tension that was its own kind of agony. Eventually, I grew out of the door anxiety, trembled less and less day by day, felt more able to stop the adrenaline coursing through my veins, until the only sounds in my head came from the Spice Girls telling me to high-kick my enemies away.

We shared the space for a few more months with Jafari before he left without explanation, leaving only remnants behind – the bottle-green African net sponge in the bathroom and countless *Watchtower* booklets for my collection. My mum told me he'd gone back to Somalia, and that it looked like the pictures on the cover of all those copies, a verdant place where tigers and people lay beatifically next to one another. I loved the idea of this, that he was settled and happy and somewhere too far for officers to find him, luxuriating in that pastel green grass.

After a year, our family were asked to leave to make way for another family due to replace Jafari, which would have made living a literal, and emotional, squeeze too far. My mum took this as a sign to take us to our own green space full of pastels and friendly wildlife and off we went, leaving the skinny slabs of glass which terrorised me for so many months behind. This move allowed me to commit my last book-related crime: taking with me handfuls of paperbacks, lovingly stacked in my backpack, each of which had the front page stamped with the inky print of Yeading library's crest.

# Meifod Cottage – How we breathe in green space

At the end of 1996, my family moved to a stone cottage that was colossal compared to Yeading Lane. It was in a small village called Meifod, in the deep countryside of Mid Wales. The exterior was made up of large, hand-to-elbow-sized blocks of stone in elephant-skin grey, sourced from a local quarry, and cream cement which looked like it had been thickly smoothed on with a finger. It stood alone, a remnant of preindustrial mass building, miles from any other houses, and was surrounded by bluebells and vast squiggles of dirt-trodden paths: places to get lost and find your way home.

The story of how we ended up in a cold cottage in the heart of Mid Wales can only be told through family folklore. My mum attended Featherstone Secondary School in Southall in the late 1970s where she made friends with a classmate, Bali. The small alleyways of Southall created a network for teenagers like my mum to socialise without being too far from the house. 'Little Bali' lived close by and they bonded there, connected by their shared love of skipping, sweets and conversations about boys that could only happen outside the house. Where my mum was a goody two-shoes, desperate to please her parents, Bali had a rebellious streak, which my mum was morbidly fascinated with.

Then, there was a scandal. At sixteen, Little Bali was due to have an arranged marriage. She revealed this to my mum, who was too young to understand the gravity of the situation because she lived in a house where having an arranged marriage was inevitable, not just for her older sisters (one of whom had already done it) but for her, too. She thought nothing of it, but noticed Bali wasn't in school the next day. A week later, the community was bristling, teeming with gossip, the Tabloid Aunty Network in overdrive – Bali had run away. No-one knew where she'd gone, and she was promptly disowned. The shame was palpable. It cast a thick, bruise-coloured cloud over Bali's house, and for many years, she was exiled to the island of disowned children, even more mythical pre-internet, not seen or heard of again. She became a morality tale and for all I know, the legend of Bali is still being told now to young cousins in the UB1 postcode.

Years later, after my mum had left her own arranged marriage, of which I was a product, and been disowned, Little Bali started to creep back into her thoughts. My mum's logic was that she was already an outlier, so she might as well make it worse and reconnect with another one. She tracked Bali down through a convoluted system of investigations which included friend-of-a-family calls, the Yellow Pages, sightings and rumours, and eventually found out that Bali was living in a mysterious place – to us anyway – called Wales.

My mum called Bali and they met up in the Hayes McDonald's (where else?) for a reconciliation. Despite my mum's shock and bemusement at the fact her friend had turned into a real-life 'hippie' (like a Bollywood folk-devil story she had committed the ultimate crime: chopped all her hair off, dyed what remained red and purple, and was 'shacked up' with a *gora* in the countryside), by the end of the meal, Mum saw Bali with new eyes. In the months that followed, they became closer than ever. Though Mum wasn't entirely impressed with Bali's lifestyle, I think she was inspired by it. Bali had run away, left the community, and lived to tell the tale. Wales began to represent a world away from bailiffs and being shamed for being a single parent, a place where maybe she could escape, too.

It was looking like we'd have to couch-surf again, and my mum had had enough, so when Aunty Bali offered to let us stay with her, she agreed before she'd seen the place. A few weeks later we were on a train, hard navy plastic suitcases banging against our shins under the train tables, the cityscape whizzing by us. She wanted something for herself, something different – and it didn't get more alien than what came next – upping sticks to a place where I'd find myself looking up at the sky, wondering why it had suddenly expanded.

Leading up to the cottage was a mile-long track-marked pathway with fart-scented pools of brown swampy rainwater. The first time I walked down that lane the fetid water seeped into the Kwik Save carrier bags wrapped around my feet and I screamed like my life was ending. Instead of wellies, I had a pair of Reebok trainers, crisp white, mint green and turquoise. My cycle of new trainers moved at a grinding pace, so I was used to avoiding mud and grass in the city to keep my Reebok Classics fresh. Eventually, I had no choice but to submit to the mud, letting my feet sink into the gloopy quicksand, which later dried into a thick crust, squelching and sliding down the lane to the front door. Most of the houses I've lived in haven't had gardens; the outside space was marked by the distance between the front door and the front gate, usually a metre and a half of paved concrete. Here, overgrown bushes scratched my arms and sticky cleavers like long pieces of hair clung onto my body, following me home.

I didn't immediately realise that we had permanently left Yeading Lane and when I found out, I was inconsolable. Not because I missed the house, but because I was addicted to *Newsround*, watching Lizo Mzimba religiously every day after school, and was wild about the idea of being a reporter, a person who got to have their say. Every year they had a Young Reporter of the Year competition, and in 1996 I applied, painstakingly writing a personal statement and a long essay about myself and my chosen subject: 'WHY LIBRARIES ARE IMPORTANT!!!' I asked my mum to send it off, with accompanying pictures, a satisfyingly thick wad of card in an envelope, and I waited to hear. Sometimes, I would imagine that letter arriving and missing it, and cry. (It's ok, I became a journalist.)

But there was something exciting, too, about the adventure of living in a cottage in the country. I spent my time walking Aunty Bali's sheepdog, Billy (I can't believe I did this; I really do not have an affinity for dogs). I adored learning about the power of dock leaves to cure nettle stings and I would glee-fully rub the nettles on my leg before realising that purposely stinging myself to administer this antidote was a game with limited longevity (but I had my next *Newsround* topic in the bag). It was with surprise and jubilation that I was allowed to explore nearby woods on my own, where I first encountered bluebells, and pulled their long tails out of the ground with a satisfying tug of resistance. In the winter, ice formed on top of the ground and made a satisfying crunch, the sound of devouring crisp iceberg lettuce, and I would walk aimlessly, padded up to my eyeballs. Often, I would take my mum's CD Walkman and I got obsessed with Motown, singing badly to no audience about stopping a postman in his tracks before realising that I hadn't seen a real one in ages thanks to the fact that our postbox was located at the end of the lane, beyond our line of vision from the house.

While I was skipping through sour puddles and having profound interactions with bluebell roots, my mum was incredulous at how anyone could live this way, asking the same questions you might ask if you were stranded on a desert island or in a conflict region – how long would it take an ambulance to make its way up this country road, exactly? Where are your neighbours? How frequent are the bus routes? Who do you call on when you need help? I ignored all of them, letting her anxiety bounce off the stone while I tried to find the fun in this mad old house.

Welsh cottages have historically been built through the know-how of local builders and local communities who shared blueprints, hoisted timber and helped source local materials like thatch and rubble stone. I might have been able to appreciate this act of community building with more tenderness had this particular community not appeared to completely disregard the small matter of being warm. I was used to London council blocks, living beside neighbours who danced well into the night, their heat radiating through the walls. At Meifod Cottage there were no neighbours for miles, and the heat came only – meagrely – from the radiator. Many nights I curled up in bed, freezing, feeling the warmth escape like it had somewhere better to be.

Sometimes I would stare from my bed out of the window at the sky, so dark that all you could see was stars. I would listen to the quiet and wonder what I was doing in a house where none of my friends would know to knock for me. It was as if I had been left out in the – literal – cold, with no community of people like me to speak of. I got so used to the sound of my mum tossing and turning next door it became a sort of lullaby, syncopated shuffles which sent me off to sleep, too young to recognise that I was falling asleep to the sounds of my mum's discontent. We are moulded by the sonic textures of our surroundings and it took time to acclimatise to the noise reduction. Our ears are impacted by urban planning – pedestrian crossing beeps, traffic, the chatter of neighbours – and Meifod concealed a world of noise from me. Many of us in cities have learned how to filter the noise out. Meifod was a lesson in tuning out of urban noise and tuning into my body. Thinking back now, it reminds me of the experience of silent anechoic chambers which are used for testing speakers, which are so quiet that you are able to hear your own heartbeat. The quietest place on earth is Minnesota's Orfield Laboratories, which measures at negative decibels, −9.4 dBA, and the average human can only withstand 45 minutes inside it at any one time. Sound, and a lack of it, is a crucial component to how we live.

Throughout the house were grey stone floor tiles which sent icy jolts up my legs like stepping into an Arctic fishing lake, as I made late-night trips to the bathroom. Rugs made of thick woven cotton bought from Southall market were intermittently laid out on the floor as an attempt to remedy this, with limited success. In the end, I just scattered my jumpers on the floor to the bathroom, hopping over them like a cold little frog needing a wee. At times, all this felt like Victorian cosplay (down to the Indian textiles), only exacerbated by the fact that at one point, my mum had to hand-wash our clothes in the bath because of months of frozen pipes and problems with something called a 'well'. I had to help her, wringing out brown water from towels and sheets, puffed out over the side of the porcelain tub, and eventually finding joy in squishing the clothes with my bare feet as if I was making some kind of revolting wine.

During this time I very briefly attended a local school (I have missed a lot of education through the cracks of moving), which felt like such a bizarre fever dream that all I can remember was that the class sizes were so small that there was more than one year in each classroom. Years 5 and 6 were put together and the students just listened to the part of the curriculum that applied to them while getting on with their work the rest of the time. (I think I benefited from this, absorbing a lot of the work from the year above me, and so by the time we came back to London I was ahead, by pure luck of circumstance.) Once we went on a school trip to Ironbridge, to a heritage museum where people dress up as Victorians, complete with butter churners and child chimney sweeps. We shuffled around, and as I watched these young children washing their own clothes, making fires and living cold, hard lives of limited luxury, I couldn't help but think of that laundry squishing at home. It's safe to say when I got back I had much to articulate about how unimpressed I was at how we had gone back in time 150 years. After that my mum bought me a diary to write 'all my thoughts in'.

## WHO OWNS OUR GREEN SPACE?

People have been escaping to the countryside for hundreds of years. The reasons are obvious: the air is fresh, the people friendly and Wordsworth seemed to really like the daffodils. But all green space is not created equal. Guy Shrubsole, author of *Who Owns England?*, reports that half of England is owned by less than 1 per cent of its population, and less than 10 per cent of England's land is accessible to the public. The findings suggest that about 25,000 landowners are made up of 'newly moneyed industrialists, oligarchs and City bankers', a picture, he argues, that has not changed for centuries. (He also, interestingly, calculates that the land under the ownership of the royal family amounts to 1.4 per cent of England.)[1]

Ownership of homes is also increasingly divisive in areas that have more readily accessible nature than cities. Before the pandemic, government figures showed that 495,000 households in England had second homes.[2] Part of this boom is thanks to the fact that amid the worst housing crisis in our generation, the government has lavished subsidies and tax breaks on second-home owners. This has had real-world impact. In Cornwall in April 2021 for instance, there were more than

10,000 properties listed on Airbnb for holidaymakers, but just 62 offered on Rightmove for rent to permanent residents.[3]

The homelessness charity Crisis reports that as of 2021, around 227,000 people were experiencing the worst forms of homelessness – rough sleeping, sleeping in vans and sheds, and stuck in B&Bs – across England, Scotland and Wales.[4] By this measure, there are roughly twice as many second homes as there are homeless households. This has a number of consequences. It makes both rural and urban living unaffordable, and it breaks down communities as rural gentrification runs rampant. All this might make us think more carefully about what we mean when we talk about space in housing.

Once, Aunty Bali took me outside the cottage and asked me how far I could see. I'd always thought the Green Man Lane Estate showed me a whole horizon but here, looking out at the woodlands, it occurred to me for the first time just how much *world* there was. That thought has stayed with me for my whole life.

## 'TAKING' THE AIR

There is historical precedent for the fight for green space and clean air. Victorians would often 'take the air' from seaside and country as respite from the asphyxiating plumes of industrial factory smoke that circled the city and found itself in poems by Thomas Hardy and, less poetically, in the lungs of residents whose cilia were ravaged by innovation. Unregulated coal burning darkened the skies in Britain's industrial cities, but air quality was not measured and monitored until very recently. According to Defra, it is only since

1961 that we've been properly measuring air, after the UK established the world's first co-ordinated national air pollution monitoring network, called the National Survey, which monitored black smoke and sulphur dioxide across the UK.

We are all born naturalists. Humans are particularly adept at differentiating between shades of green, for example (there are six types of chlorophyll, though most plants contain teal-green chlorophyll A or soft yellow-green chlorophyll B[5]), which helps us to distinguish different kinds of vegetation. But modern life and geography often separate us from the natural world and our instincts. In 1986, American biologist Edward O. Wilson coined the term 'biophilia' to describe the necessity for modern humans to be in contact with nature. Some countries take this more seriously than others. In Japan, research into the health benefits of *shinrin-yoku*, or forest bathing, has shown that being in nature calms the stress response in our central nervous system, and can contribute to blood pressure reduction and improvement in autonomic and immune functions, as well as alleviating depression. In the US, some physicians have begun giving 'park prescriptions' to encourage people outdoors. In China, which has some of the most heavily polluted cities in the world, 'fresh air' tours to the country are provided for stressed urbanites, with Yangshuo being a particularly popular destination.

So clean air has always been hotly pursued, if not always accessible. During the height of an airborne pandemic which attacked respiratory systems, a certain kind of countryside exceptionalism narrative played out. Those who worked from home and could afford an idyllic second home in the country were able to escape the lockdown with fresh air and perhaps a seafront. For many, the idea of living in the countryside is billed as a utopian option, a reaction to the circling boa constrictors that squeeze you into urban submission. During a national lockdown, people in cities who either chose to stay or were unable to leave often created makeshift gardens in the street by dragging chairs onto kerbs and roads, bulk-buying houseplants, and, like one of my friends, having wildlife pictures as Zoom and laptop backgrounds.

To breathe easy is the most basic of human needs, but inequality is at the core of access to clean air. The poorer you are, the more likely you are to live in a polluted area – which might include old sites of industry that discharge various types of air pollution, to go to work in a polluted area, for your children to go to school in a polluted area. All of that is affected by your ethnicity, sex, disability and age.

In 2013, Rosamund Kissi-Debrah, a grassroots campaigner, shone a light on the link between pollution and racial inequality following the death of her nine-year-old daughter, Ella. An inquest ruling in December 2020 showed that pollution from the South Circular Road in London was a contributing factor to Ella's death. This might be the first admission of pollution leading to someone's death recorded in the UK. 2023 will see the Clean Air (Human Rights) Bill, also known as 'Ella's law', move through UK Parliament with the aim to establish the statutory right to clean air across England and Wales. The case drew to light how Black Londoners are more likely to be exposed to toxic air,[6] with Black children more likely to be hospitalised due to exposure to high levels of nitrogen dioxide pollution in London than anywhere else in the country. Black and other minority ethnic people are at least twice as likely to be deprived of green space compared to a white person in the UK.[7] In Southall, where I grew up, there has been a long-running campaign by CASH (Clean Air for Southall and Hayes) resisting toxic air from nearby gasworks. There is, incidentally, a disconnect between who causes air pollution and who breathes it, globally. In 2019, NPR reported that after accounting for population size differences, white people experience about 17 per cent less air pollution than they produce, through consumption, while Black and Hispanic communities bear 56–63 per cent more air pollution by consumption than they cause.[8]

This is not a new area of study, but it is as urgent as it has ever been. Hilda Palmer is a biologist who focuses on chemicals and air quality and currently works alongside the Greater Manchester Hazards Centre and Trade Union Clean Air Network. Over Zoom, she speaks with the authority of someone who knows, to the decimal point, how dangerous letting our air pollution go unchecked can be. 'There is no safe level of PM2.5s,' she explains, referring to the tiny particle pollutants in the air that measure up to 2.5 millionths of a metre in diameter, which are released by car exhaust fumes, industrial smog and wood burners, and everything from pesticides to cleaning materials. We know it can get into the body, get into the lungs, can get into the bloodstream, and can get across the blood–brain barrier, get into the placenta, and can get to every part of the body.[*]

---

[*] The effect of atmospheric pollution can also be measured by disparities in men's heights. For men born in the 1890s, the average height (when they enlisted for the First World War) was 5 feet 6 inches (168cm). Those who grew up in the most polluted districts were almost an inch (2.5cm) shorter than those who experienced the cleanest air, leading researchers to argue that height can be a clear indicator of pollution.

Statistically, I have not been well served by the air in London. If there was a dot on a map to denote dense areas of air pollution, Yeading Lane would have one of the biggest in the country, a swollen pustule compared to the tiny pinprick of Meifod's bluebell forest. It's hard not to think of Meifod as a moment of respite for my chest, singing loudly on muddy lanes to Motown and TLC (two of my mum's albums) on my Walkman, while fresh air made friends with my red blood cells.

Now, as I write, I think about all the asthma in my life. My naniji's wheezing in the night would keep me up when I stayed with her, terrified by the sound of it, a ghostly rattle and whistle. My sister as a baby was given a huge plastic inhaler the size of her face that looked like a gas mask, which, after I had to administer it a few times, sparked a short-term fear of gas masks, snorkels, anything that covered a mouth and nose. Though other organs function in utero, life starts the moment that our fluid-filled lungs inflate, for the first time, with our own breath and from that moment we take almost 22,000 breaths a day. For so many of us, pollution affects our lungs from the moment we are born.

## ALL I HAVE IS MY HOUSEPLANTS

There was very little language around flora and fauna in my world before I moved to the cottage. After I left, I would recall the new names that I'd learned, my obsession with bluebells, and wonder why flowers were expensive when you could pick them for free. This botanical interest didn't return until later in life, and it wasn't until I felt settled in one of my rental properties, thanks to a two-year tenancy contract in my late twenties, that I started to find new ways to make nature come alive for me and began amassing houseplants.

I think I had my first meaningful emotional connection to a plant other than a bluebell in 2015. My mum gave me a peace lily, which I held in my arms on the train all the way from Birmingham to my flat in Peckham. It survived three moves (a prerequisite of modern living is that plants must survive moving houses) and I took all precautions, staying up late watching YouTube videos on care, downloading apps that diagnosed brown spots, buying gnat repellent. When I had my heart broken by a long-term boyfriend I couldn't make my limbs move and I used a water spray bottle to wake me up, out of my depression. I would spray the leaves, then my face, feel the droplets cool on my nose, wipe them away and have an excuse to leave my bed and dry it.

While I found it hard to look after myself, I became obsessed with looking after something else. Latin words have now accrued strange muscle memory in my mouth: *Monstera deliciosa* (Swiss cheese plant), *Dracaena trifasciata* (snake plant), *Epipremnum aureum* (devil's ivy). These names were most likely given in the 1700s by Carl Linnaeus, a Swedish – and notoriously racist – botanist tasked with taxonomy, which included naming plants in texts such as *Systema Naturae*. The communities who tended to these plants long before Linnaeus took ownership would not recognise these strange new names. Despite this, learning the names appealed to me, and personifying them helped them become more real.* (I felt this

---

* Saying that, I draw the line at endorsing the current trend of calling myself a 'plant parent'.

too when my houseplants took on different personalities – my high-maintenance fiddle-leaf fig, the dramatic peace lily and my notoriously difficult Boston fern.)

I delighted in watching my indoor plants grow, delighting in how they took up space. This term, 'taking up space', has been politicised to describe the way in which we occupy any place which has not always been shared with us; marginalised people are often told not to take up any at all. Speakers delivering TED talks use the technique of 'power posing', spreading their body out in an expansive stance, illustrating how taking up physical space makes you feel powerful. Yoga teaches us to spread into a goddess pose, to stretch our limbs further and further, taking every unaccounted-for inch for ourselves. Watching a sprawling pothos dominate my room, doing what I can't always do in life, is a specific kind of satisfying. There is something to be said for how many people like me, who have not had green fingers built in from childhood, find this kind of greenery a lifeline. For so many of us, it can become a necessity, satisfying a yearning for control and growth in periods of social, economic and even political inertia.

Houseplants are fashionable again, firmly a part of modern interiors. In 2017, a now widely shared *Washington Post* headline declared: 'Millennials are filling their homes – and the void in their hearts – with houseplants'. This was backed up by data collected in the 2016 National Gardening Survey, which found that out of the 6 million or so Americans who started getting into gardening that year, 5 million fell into the 18-to-34 age bracket.[9] In 2021, seven out of ten US millennials called themselves 'plant parents', and houseplant sales increased by 50 per cent to $1.7 billion between 2017 and 2019.[10]

Rooms might often be tiny but aspirations of greenery are not. In 2022 in the UK, the high-priced plant *du jour* is *Monstera deliciosa*, whose image is reproduced on everything from towels to lamps, and which can cost hundreds of pounds. The Victorian equivalent of *Monstera deliciosa* was the indestructible aspidistra, (*Aspidistra elatior,* nicknamed the 'cast-iron plant'), which was first introduced from China in 1823. It was hardy enough for the most low-lit and fume-polluted Victorian homes. The plant became so popular that George Orwell, in his novel *Keep the Aspidistra Flying* (1936), made it the emblem of middle-class conformity, 'There will be no revolution in England while there are aspidistras in the windows,' says his protagonist, Gordon Comstock. Meanwhile, from the 1850s, fern fever gripped Victorian Britain. These plants were notoriously temperamental and required glasshouses, known as ferneries. But the start of the twentieth century saw a shift in attitudes towards house-plants. After the First World War, when modernity entered the home, plant-heavy interiors dropped out of fashion and lower-maintenance choices like cacti and succulents became the houseplants of choice as their more architectural shapes fitted the design styles of the day.

While houseplants may be for some a damning indictment of our increasingly depressing and squeezed living, for others they are an attempt to resolve poor air quality and decreasing mental health. For the green evangelists, houseplants can be a personal pursuit of better air, acting as a small-scale counter to pollution. This holds up according to NASA, who named, following their 1989 Clean Air Study on indoor air pollution in closed environments, the Boston fern (*Nephrolepis exaltata*) as the top houseplant for removing formaldehyde, while snake plants did a good job of filtering the air of formaldehyde, xylene, benzene, toluene and trichloroethylene.

Much of the history of exotic plants in this country is linked to colonial conquest. The showcasing of houseplants was a useful tool for an empire that boasted of its spoils and agricultural pillaging from colonised lands. And while the British Museum is often criticised for its exhibitions of colonial excess, places like Kew Gardens get off relatively lightly. *Monstera deliciosa* comes from the tropics of South America,[11] and you don't have to stretch a metaphor too far to acknowledge a plant taken from its home in the sun to the cold climate of British living rooms, growth stunted and unable to bear fruit, so that we might enjoy some of its aesthetic. Like most pleasures in the modern world, personal guilt is attached to even this pleasure. These plants are shipped halfway across the world to the UK so I can revel in the joy of a green interior. These are all thoughts I have as I patiently and diligently clean each individual leaf of dust, imagining them exhaling a direct line of oxygen straight into my lungs.

Monsteras might be the plant of the moment but I have an affinity for spider plants (*Chlorophytum comosum*), which arrived in Europe in the nineteenth century from South Africa. My mum had these growing up and I love being around them now – the lithe leaves looking like deceptively strong arms that might haul themselves out of the pot and walk around at any minute. It's hard not to acknowledge that there's something unnatural about confining nature to the small spaces of rented rooms and I like the idea that one day, my spider plants might just break free.

## GREEN FOR EVERYONE!

Living in the countryside to escape the high rents of the city is often touted as an alternative to the misery of market capitalism. But there are penalties to these decisions, and living in a utopian clean-air area of the UK can hinge on having a community where you can belong. Climate activism must, of course, make air safer for everyone through policy. But in the present, we must make the outside accessible – economically, socially, culturally – for everyone.

Designing green space into urban planning is important not only for aesthetics. In the US, neighbourhoods that were previously redlined (where lines were drawn around Black and Latino neighbourhoods which were then denied crucial services) in the 1900s are today 5 to 12 degrees Fahrenheit hotter in the summertime than their non-redlined counterparts. This is because redlined neighbourhoods have fewer trees and cannot benefit from shade and transpiration cooling (the process by which plants release water vapour that cools the air around them). This has social consequences too. A 2001 study of a public housing development in Chicago was the first to link vegetation with actual counts of crime from police reports, suggesting that an abundance of trees can help deter crime.[12] Researchers found that for every 10 per cent increase in tree canopy cover, there was a 15 per cent decrease in violent crime, and a 14 per cent fall in the property crime rate. It is clear, then, that all housing should be built with green space in mind for reasons other than what might seem obvious. Green space is a right, and a public health issue.

Though countryside living is good for us, it isn't always where we feel at home. There are of course many people of colour who live in the countryside, presumably frustrated that much of the discourse of lived experiences in the UK is dominated by urban communities. But there are also invisible border lines in operation – according to recent figures, about 17 per cent of the population – some 9.7 million people – lived in rural England in 2020. BAME communities made up less than 2 per cent of that number.[13]* Part of this is thanks to the racism tax of living in predominantly white areas (difficult to measure, but felt by anything from lingering eyes to comments mumbled in a pub), and a racial wealth gap that has given white people more than a headstart in land and property acquisition.

It is doubly frustrating to consider that many immigrants in this country come from rural landscapes. Many of our ancestral beginnings are rooted in nature, from my Punjabi farming family who taught me about the five (punj) rivers (ab) before I could walk and who grow spinach and maize, to my Chinese friends who come from fishing families, to my Jamaican family who grow mango trees; from poems in Pakistan about the River Jhelum, to stories about the Corn Mother spirit in First Nation communities who have always cultivated land.

---

* The term 'BAME', which lumps many diverse experiences of immigrant communities into one, has been used widely in government and census data. Though limited, this is why it appears, where relevant, in this book. While it can be useful as a data metric, I believe the term is not fit for purpose as a signifier of identity.

We need to find ways of building greenery into housing so that those in urban centres, who are entitled to the cooling, mental health and air-purifying benefits of nature, can enjoy it. This might start with making public health advice a reality. For instance, the World Health Organization recommends that every city provide a minimum of 9 square metres of urban green space for each person.[14]

The public park as we know it today was invented by the Victorians and it was a breakthrough. These parks aimed to democratise green space, boost the local economy and give people of all social classes pride in their communities. Printed on a sign in the gardens of the William Morris Gallery in Walthamstow is the well-known local story of the Lloyd family, who owned Water House. In 1898 the family gifted the land and house to the borough of Walthamstow on the condition that the council bought more land, extending the green space for local access. Today it is a well-used public park.

The ambition of an accessible park for everyone has not evolved in the right direction. Across Britain, 2.78 million people live further than a ten-minute walk from their nearest park or green space, and the poorest areas of England have less than a third of the private garden space enjoyed by the richest. This might be part of the reason why society at large doesn't necessarily associate immigrant communities with green space. In lockdown, when British people were told not to sit on park benches, TV personality Alesha Dixon was heavily criticised on Twitter after uploading a picture of her and her family sunbathing in a large green space which was assumed by Twitter users to be a park. She later clarified that she was, in fact, in her own garden. The same year, a white journalist went viral after declaring, upon seeing a Black stylist on Instagram having a picnic outside a country manor, that she was 'leaving Instagram' because of the offending image, citing 'wealth fatigue'. It's a puzzling response in a country where depictions of Black and Brown country homes are so few and far between thanks to a history of structural inequality.

There are communities invested in making these connections between climate justice, land reform and Black resistance. They span from online groups like the UK-based Flock Together, a birdwatching collective for people of colour, to the popular Hike Clerb in Los Angeles, who arrange hiking meet-ups in an effort to reclaim denied green space and centre marginalised voices. The Facebook group POC in Nature is a large UK network which acts as a message board for climbers, running groups, plant swappers, climate researchers and climate activists.

'My grandfather was a cocoa farmer in Ghana,' says Karen Larbi, founder of POC in Nature. She grew up in Beckton in east London with Ghanaian parents, and speaks to me over Zoom from her bedroom in New Cross while the UK is still in lockdown. 'So there was very much an ancestral connection to the land through subsistence farming. I pray to Asase Ya, who is the earth goddess of my people, the Akan people of Ghana. She reminds me that I am always home wherever I find myself, which gives me confidence to be able to go and venture out to green spaces where I stick out like a sore thumb. When the spaces are majority white I don't feel like I can be my full self. I know that if I'm the only Black person in that space and I'm experiencing a micro aggression or overt racism, I am the only one who can speak up and advocate for myself,' she explains.

I ask her if it's worth it, about what happens to her body in the space, and she breathes deeply before answering.

'Yes. I feel a sense of . . . letting go.'

## PERMISSION TO PAINT POLLEN

My aunty Bali would spend her time outside Meifod Cottage in the garden, dusting the pollen from flower to flower with a paintbrush, encouraging pollination. From afar, it looked like she was painting the colour on the petals with agonising concentration. I learned a lot from this patient disposition, from somebody who – unwittingly – gave me an opportunity to act on the connection to nature that we are all born with.

My mum, conversely, truly hated living in Meifod, but the experience taught her how to be on her own terms. It was, in some respects, a non-traumatic period of self-realisation, and while I was running around making friends with dogs and picking flowers with a gusto bordering on mania we both had a shift in space. You can make space for yourself, the world is bigger than the streets you grew up on, and for women of colour, routinely taught to shrink themselves, maybe, just maybe, you could start to expand.

There is very little to connect me to the literal earth I was born from. Though my ancestral history is farming, I never grew up on a farm, didn't have land or grounds to wander through, and my mum often didn't have the time or know-ledge required to explain each flower in the high street pub garden on the way to the bus stop. Instead, I carry over the things that have made me feel something – plants from places I've never visited and flowers from places I have. As second homes and rural gentrification hike up rents, it is disturbing to consider that we are a society that prices people out of the countryside. As I write, I have a clutch of bluebells that take me back to a time of my life where I had to learn how to adapt, where I was offered something different. I am still in anticipation for a time when I will live securely in a place long enough for my vines to really take root, to swirl their bodies around curtain hooks and shelves and walls. I am waiting for the next opportunity to take up space; one day I will forget to wait and act on my own permission to do so.

My mum would only last six months in Meifod Cottage before needing to move back to London for her sanity. (The last straw was when a couple of locals asked to stroke her arms.) We packed ourselves up and my brother and I were bundled up in the back of a white van, covered in blue padded lumberjack shirts, quilts and blankets. As we drove over speed bumps, with rattling boxes of utensils, I held a bunch of bluebells wrapped in string that Aunty Bali had given me, cradling it all the way like a newborn baby.

When we moved to our next house, the bluebells didn't last long but I kept my muddy Reeboks in a plastic carrier bag as a reminder of this reckless abandon. They had to stay in the bag – our new rental property was not as forgiving when it came to clumps of dried mud on the carpet. I loved knowing they were there, though, and I dreamed of clapping them together to disperse a confetti of maroon flakes through the air like the final scene of *Edward Scissorhands*. In one dream, they turned into butterflies that I caught with a net, in another, the dock leaves grew up to my window and I slid down their stems right into my trainers. The next house we lived in woke me up from these fantasies and the outside world shrank again, the green space limited to the distance from the front door to the front gate, but I'd banked enough Welsh air to get me through the smog.

# A note on finding home in community

My family moved to Swanage Waye in 1997, a stone's throw over the bridge separating Southall and Hayes in west London, which marked an invisible but *significant* divide.*
This divide was on racial lines (Asians in Southall, whites in Hayes, which is similar today, where Hayes has around 25 per cent Asian British population compared to Southall's 76 per cent).

It was a semi-detached privately rented house, also in 1930s style, on a street that linked to the main road, and was safe enough that I was able to knock for my mates, Nagina and Sylvana, to go rollerblading near the house. I would run in when the blades were still on, bounding up the stairs, and mum would slap me upside my head before I ran out again. The house was wrapped in embossed foamy wallpaper with a pattern of tiny flowers which I would press

---

* By 'significant', I mean only to the people who live within a few metres of this imaginary line, as is so often the case.

97

my nails into to make dents, letting the next tenants know that I'd been there.*

The kitchen was very small, catering for only two people at a time, which was often a large aunty and me, a small skinny teen. I'd come in to throw things into oil and back away, or to pour out and guzzle Sunny Delight – that fluorescent thick juice that most of the country believed was vitamin enriched but was later taken off the shelves for being mostly corn syrup and E numbers. One summer, I drank so much Sunny D (after the cash and carry started stocking it) that my skin smelled of it and I'd rollerblade at high speed, wired, up and down nearby streets, getting to know everyone, which is how I found out that I'm apparently, distantly related to half the borough.

The decision to live here was based solely on wanting to be near this community; it was one that we had some agency in, thanks to the fact that we were able to afford to privately rent. This house was rented below market price from a family connection – an (unrelated) 'uncle' recommended by an aunty that lived two streets away. Part of the reason why this community has endured is because anecdotally, south Asian locals have been careful not to sell houses and retail property to white developers owing to historical racism. But their scepticism is also linked to the BCCI (Bank of Credit and Commerce International) scandal of the 1990s. BCCI,

---

* These floral motifs have existed on wallpaper since its inception in the sixteenth century. Originally made from powdered offcuts of the wool industry, it gave houses a luxe texture, smoothing over uneven walls underneath. The one in my house was a cheap – but still satisfying – replica of this opulent flocking, and instead of wool it left a sort of congealed white paste under my fingernails.

not a huge high street name but infamous in UK south Asian circles, was owned by Pakistani financier Agha Hasan Abedi and was known as the 'listening bank' throughout the 1980s because it would offer mortgages to the local community when racist lenders would not. To cut a long story short, internal corruption in BCCI meant that in 1991 the bank folded, leaving thousands of south Asian people in huge debt, savings and houses lost, and some business owners reporting that they lost millions. BCCI is now a by-word for scandal, still a painful warning to keep your money close. Many locals decided to create a sharing economy to keep money within family, or among people they knew directly. We were one of those families that somehow made it onto the 'good-will' network.

My mum was working two jobs at this time – as a receptionist at a beauty parlour during the day and at night housekeeping at the Marriott hotel – and it meant we could afford to rent; it was a rare moment of feeling extremely wealthy and settled. She also met a partner who worked as a cash-in-hand builder, and though he wouldn't always be a firm presence, this was our family's first taste of a joint income. It was here that my stepdad, my dad, came into my life. Born in Manchester, he was a wanderer by nature, drifting in and out of my life throughout my childhood and formative years. He is a tender, strong presence, with the kind of Northern coolness that makes those rare 'I love you's when you get them so particularly delicious. Aside from his young life spent in the army, as a builder he has had a hand in much of London's infrastructure. In his late twenties he helped construct the foundations for the financial centre of the city on the docklands in Canary Wharf. Later in life, in Hayes, he built patios for local uncles and brick walls of temples where he learned the basics of Punjabi to get by: a characteristically low-key but exceptionally talented craftsman who has given me reverence for the process. He has built houses across this country without ever owning his own, but his presence has always felt like comfort. He was on opposite hours to my mum's night shifts, so for a while I didn't see much of either of them, but in the early morning, as I was getting ready for school, gelling my baby hairs, my mum would come back with little treats. Tiny, perfectly decorated cakes with light icing and designs smudged from the train ride home; big punnets of strawberries with the fragrance that filled your nostrils making you salivate, and juice that dripped down your mouth and onto the grey carpet, worn thin by my rollerblades. It was here, as a result of this union, that my mum got pregnant with my baby sister, the great love of my life, who I was immediately infatuated with. She was the product of a Caesarean and I was maybe inappropriately maternal. At times, I had to hold her up to my mum's breast to feed, her heavy 9-pound solid mass in my spindly arms, and I understood that a community like this was important for her, too.

I attended Hayes Manor School, where two thirds of the children were from immigrant communities, predominantly Punjabis, and rated by Ofsted at the time as 'below average'. It was what most underresourced inner city comprehensive schools are made of, fighting to survive, being called a boffin because I was obsessive about perfect marks, and scrambling around for the green free-school-meal tickets (which 43 per cent of the student body were in receipt of, at that time, well above the national average). It was frenetic and overpopulated, with a soundtrack of people swearing in various languages, and jostling to be part of the rich Older Cousin Black Market who would gather at the school gates, where I bought a very treasured tape of Dr Dre's *2001* for £2. In a look, the school was slicked-back hair and high ponytails for the girls, eyebrow slits for the boys, and there was cacophonous noise, all the time. (To give you a shorthand of the ethnic breakdown, my classmate Manjeet Tamani used to call me a coconut relentlessly and made fun of my initials – then K.K., for Kieran Kashab – saying they should be KKK because I had 'so many' white friends. I had three.) After school, I would ride the five stops on the 607 to Southall to get 40p samosas and sour sweets, terrorising the general public with noise and drawing graffiti on the top deck. Hayes Manor, like many London state schools, came with a particular brand of bedlam; a result of teenagers metabolising all the energy of new people and complicated difference.

## MTV, Missy Elliott and Simran's wedding

The most desirable feature of living on Swanage Waye was its proximity to the circular economy of recorded music videos that made the rounds courtesy of Sylvana's older sister, Crystal. This sharing network stretched for three streets. The one I had was a VHS that had been taped over an anonymous person's wedding video, a memory embedded between the music, where somebody was surely missing it, but it was for ever lost to teenage living rooms. It was taped from MTV, which we didn't have, and featured J.Lo's 'If You Had My

Love', Left Eye (RIP) and Missy Elliott in inflated black leather. Now and again a moment of blank space between Missy Elliott and Jennifer Lopez's choreography revealed the faces of 'Simran and Monu', whose names would flash up on the screen in cursive letters with a red border graphic, as is typical of Indian wedding videos. This rupture happened enough times that you caught the sangeet, a second of the gurdwara and a brief glimpse of an aunty eating a piece of cake as the dancing happened (sometimes when I see one of these videos on YouTube I still expect to see the interruptions of that aunty in the orange sari pop up). All in all, it looked like they had a nice day.

Living in a place like Hayes is to be part of a 'type', a shorthand for a specific – and local – kind of British Asian identity. This made it impossible not to think of yourself as a global majority and I'm lucky that I never wanted to be white, because people that looked like me dominated the streets, schools and social environments I spent time in.

The ongoing debate in this country about integration, belonging and multiculturalism largely hinges on immigrant communities, where they choose to live and the language they choose to speak (cue the common complaint about streets where English is no longer spoken). Marginalised communities congregate not only for historical and economic reasons, but for safety, culture and self-preservation. For many immigrant communities, these are places to grab rest from zero-hour contracts, from hard office space, from working conditions that break our backs, from homophobia that sours kisses in the street, from air pollution that introduces smog into your lungs, or whiteness that bears down on you like an industrial crusher flattening a Coke can. It's a place to loudly be yourself inside, bellowing a mother tongue. If you're really lucky, you might sample somewhere like Swanage Waye, where being loudly yourself is OK because the street reflects you, too.

The evolutionary advantages to being in a group come down to safety and security – finding food, defence from outside attack, migration across landscapes and changes in habitat (climatic or seasonal). Primitive man may have sought the group to increase their chances of evolutionary survival, but now we tend to gravitate towards communities for different reasons. 'There's a search towards shared identity, shared experience and commonality,' counselling psychologist Dr Jaspreet Tehara tells me. '"Push factors" are internal factors or personal choices that push someone towards seeking groups. There are also "pull factors", which are external factors (like social conformity, internal group rules and logics). Often, psychological well-being is mediated by those who can strongly hold their sense of individuality while remaining within the bounds of what the group finds acceptable. If this isn't possible people either move into different and more accommodating groups, create their own groups, modulate their behaviours to conform more, or live with a sense of distress if none of those things seem possible to change.'

Communities come together through shared ideologies and values, but more often than not, they are created in real time, by geography. This can make it easier to find like-minded individuals, or to find solutions for how to live together with different worldviews. It is why Stokes Croft in Bristol has a reputation for socialist politics and psy trance, and why Chipping Norton in the Cotswolds is seen as a hot-spot for Tory politicians who all live in close quarters.[*] The so-called 'culture wars' would have us dismiss the concerns of minorities because they are too small in number to really think about. In fact, how we treat small communities and their concerns tells us something important about who we are.

Of course, these communities aren't always truly safe – they may not be as socially liberal as we might like, they may need to unlearn and dismantle anti-Blackness, racism or homophobia, say. But these failures give us something to work from – we see them, raise them, find what we love, and challenge, improve or outright reject what we don't. They give us the confidence to believe that we can create a new world, if not there, then elsewhere.

The problem with moving to and from a place with such a strong sense of identity is that you can feel like you lose your own when you leave it. Living on Swanage Waye felt like being held, all the time, and it wasn't until years later that I realised that I would have always needed to work out my own identity for myself rather than just relying on the locality to provide it for me. I had uncritically absorbed a lot of what was around me, but leaving taught me about the things you take with you and, happily, it gave me permission to leave things behind.

My time at Swanage Waye was blissful in many ways, but I was unaware of the fact that my mum was buckling,

---

[*] If there really is a minority group in Britain, it's the rich, white, Cotswolds Tories. It is curious then that the framing of anyone but rich white people as simultaneously a threatening monolith and a small minority obviously doesn't represent reality and is a wild ploy to both create a threat and delegitimise a high percentage of the population.

and when the rent on our house shot up, it became simply unmanageable. We were given one month's notice to leave after the landlord sold the house (with us still living in it) to his brother. When my dad went to the estate agent that handled the property to retrieve our £2,000 deposit, the agent's office was empty. They had, it appeared, done a runner with (according to local gossip) over 150 deposits.

The high rents and a promise of building work for my dad elsewhere led us to pile inside his tiny, blocky, white Yugo (a by-word for terrible car design produced in the former Yugoslavia, and we had one in yellow, and then later, this one in white) and drive somewhere else. Though I felt guilty for creating a tear in the network, as a balm for my devastation at leaving this chaotic utopia, I took that MTV VHS with me, hugging it all the way down the motorway.

# W. R. Davies – How to live in places not meant to be lived in

The constant moving affected me in ways I am still discovering. Moving as a child is a very different experience to moving in your twenties to another house-share, or in your thirties to a bigger house, or in your forties to a quieter neighbourhood, say. Moving as a child is to lose control over the small world you've built for yourself, and while I enjoyed the variety of people and places, it took its toll. The lack of agency made a negotiator of me. I began bargaining with my mum – if I do *this*, if I do well in class, if I tidy my room, can we stay? If I sell some of my trainers to get more money, can we stay? If my friend's mum agrees to look after me for a while, can I stay with them? When the bargaining didn't work I developed little anxious routines – I was careful not to step on the cracks in the pavement, became obsessed with even numbers (only going up stairs in twos, and feeling itchy and irritable when the volume on the TV was an odd number) and bit my nails for 10 minutes at a time. These all helped to make me feel a bit more like the master of my universe. When retreating to my room to read wasn't an option, I concentrated on these routines to allay the trauma of all those little losses.

For most of the moves up until W. R. Davies I had generally been at ease, receiving the news at having to pack up with a sigh but mostly excited for the adventure. By the time I was settled as a teenager at Hayes Manor this had changed. When we were priced out of Swanage Waye we bounced around rooms and family in London for a few months, but finally settled back in Wales, relatively close to Meifod, where a friend had told us the housing was cheap. I did not want to go. I held on with every fibre of my being and I was furious, refusing to leave, heartbroken at losing my community. I cried all the way down the M4, in the front of the van with my dad, listening to a *Now That's What I Call Music* CD on my Walkman playing 'Toca's Miracle', praying for one myself. When we drove into the place we were staying in, down the winding roads of a small town in Mid Wales called Welshpool, where no-one looked like me, I stared out of the window at boys in baggy trousers with chains swinging from them, girls with matted dreadlocks smoking roll-ups outside phone boxes, and the culture shock was almost too much.

We rented a flat on top of a car showroom named after an invisible owner: W. R. Davies, the name of the family business that owned the dealership and, I guess, provided housing stock on the side. The flat was framed by huge, wall-sized windows that let oceans of light in and made us – a Brown family in the smallest town I'd ever spent time in (population: 5,948) – even more exposed.

We lived on one floor, with the active showroom in use

downstairs, and our flat had a large living room, a small bathroom and a concrete stairwell leading up to the kitchen. The layout of the place was not really intended for family living – it felt like an extension built for use by workers that the landlord had hastily made into a flat, illustrated by the fact that we shared it with unkempt wires, and disembodied copper pipes that got hot and gave me a burn in the shape of Pikachu on my leg. Now and again, the distinctive smell of Turtle Wax and CarPlan Triplewax Car Shampoo would fill the living room, a smell I can still distinguish from a mile away. In the corner of Mum's room was a concave weak spot on the floor that had to be avoided in case we ever fell through it onto a new Ford Fiesta. Sometimes, I put my finger in a little hole in the corner of the living room, amused at the idea of a salesman showing someone around a fancy car being distracted by my finger poking out of the ceiling. Downstairs, people were selling cars for thousands of pounds (you could occasionally overhear hearty laughs interrupting the TV when a sale was agreed) while we hopped over wires to avoid electrocution. But I loved the open-plan nature of the space so much none of this bothered me. I liked the idea of inhabiting a glass palace above those expensive cars. It felt like I was moving up in the world.

Because of the nature of the space, we had to be pro-active about making it look like a home. My mum did this by buying fabrics, pinning picture frames on the vast white clinical walls and adding macramé plant pot holders in the kitchen. She filled the small concrete balcony with terracotta pots of flowers with a vigour bordering on mania, decorating them with seashells caked in hot pink and blue glitter glue by my younger sister. The result was garish and extravagant, a sort of Mardi Gras kitsch made up of an array of brightly coloured pots with sparkly squiggles and blobs which stood out a mile and confused passers-by with their sheer brazen confidence.

I watched a lot of Laurence Llewelyn-Bowen on *Changing Rooms* and was fairly certain that I, too, had a certain interior flair. I brought my room to life with a garage mix from Nagina that I played on repeat. I put a poster of Craig David on the wall, listened to 'A Little Bit of Luck' and the catchy, sexy R&B production of the Spice Girls' new direction as a foursome on 'Holler' which marked their growing up, and at fifteen, mine too. Later, I shared a room with my baby sister, playing music low as she slept, her dreams permeated with the low-frequency hum of Sweet Female Attitude. As I listened to *Born to Do It* on loop I thought of Sylvana's older sister and my friends in Swanage Waye who told me tales of Garage Nation and champagne dances. This white town might be looking at me but I couldn't feel alone because I came with a collective of people who were like me, who shouted 'Re-re-wind' and grabbed a mic when they wanted to be heard. Suddenly, this flat was full of my dancing, making fuzzy silhouettes in the window to UK garage mixes and rushing to find purple bedsheets that I'd seen on *Moesha*.

My room had its own sink, which I thought was the height of glamour and mature sophistication. It was made of white porcelain, and in delicate grey cursive writing had the intriguing name of who I thought was the previous owner, 'Armitage Shanks'. I emulated what I thought was a cool detail by scratching my name into the bottom corner of my bedroom window. After all, if there's one thing the serial renter has a gift for, it's making the best out of badly designed flats. I'd learned early on how you can feel special in a space that wasn't designed for you – to luxuriate in details like huge windows and a personal sink.

At W. R. Davies, light was not in short supply. The windows that surrounded the flat might even be likened to Le Corbusier's idea of the ribbon window – a series of windows set side by side to form a continuous horizontal band. In his five-point plan for optimum architecture, *Les Cinq points de l'architecture moderne*, published in 1927, he posited that windows should run the entire length of the house, so all rooms can get equal light. (While I like this thought, he also set ceiling heights according to his 'ideal man', so safe to say that we can take or leave much of his design.) Though he wasn't exactly advocating car showrooms for all, it's worth mentioning that natural light is not guaranteed in homes across the country, thanks to planning loopholes which have allowed developers to build properties without windows. Only as recently as 2020, the government proposed to ban the building of windowless flats (though the many already built may remain as they are).

Light has always been revered for its healing properties. My favourite example of this is 'sun therapy', which really took off in 1920s Japan. It was connected to the widespread use of windows during the Meiji era which allowed great swathes of restorative light in buildings and made a connection between new technologies and public health. This therapy was used in sanatoriums across the country as a way of healing its inhabitants. (At the famous Omi Sanatorium, built at the base of Mount Hachiman in 1918, a feat of window-centric design, it was even used as a cure for tuberculosis.) As a happy teenager, basking in the rays (my name, after all, means 'rays from the sun' in Hindi), my displacement was healed in part by this light, receiving the warm sun therapy amid the exposed wires.

## NET CURTAINS

The month we moved in, my mum painstakingly sewed and hung up cheap, white net curtains with exquisite panels of patterned flowers and swirls to combat some of our visibility. She sewed and darned for what felt like weeks, making them out of reams of polyester fabric – a hangover in her DNA from her haberdasher mother – and I remember feeling absolutely sure that my mum could do anything. The curtains, gossamer-like, covered the 8-foot-high sealed windows, dropping down to the floor, and one of my jobs was to wash them once a fortnight. She worked nights at the local nursing home and I think this task would have sent her over the edge, as my dad spent weekends away working, a domestic entrapment too far which became my burden.

A burden is no exaggeration. Putting up those net curtains was comically arduous – the kind of finicky task that is proper hell when you're 5 foot 3. The process required delicately lifting and gathering layers of heavy faux lace, letting the open-weave patterns fall between my fingers onto the floor, stuffing them into a washing machine, heaving them out with added water weight, drying them on the balcony on a makeshift washing line that was too short, before carefully hooking them back onto the curtain wires. Sometimes, during this process, my mum's bangles (which I was prohibited from wearing, but wore while she was at the nursing home anyway) would get caught and tear the fabric. I would try to conceal these misshapen holes by ripping new holes in to match, creating a pattern: two irregular blobs in a row. (When I finally made a friend, his mum said she thought I was a cleaning lady after seeing me as she walked by, from the other side of the glass.)

Britain has a particular affinity with lace because of its ability to catch dirt, while allowing for privacy and light in darkly lit middle-class Victorian homes. Though our version was cheap, lace was a covetable fabric across Europe during the nineteenth century. The introduction of industrial power looms, like the Nottingham lace curtain machine of 1846, meant that fabrics could be mass-produced cheaply, and by the mid-1880s in Britain, many of these intricate designs of flora and fauna* – like ours with dancing tulip stems – had made their way into working-class homes. This way, working-class people could, in the form of net curtains, afford something close to luxury. Of course, I didn't know any of this as I painstakingly huffed and sweated over the heavy folds and maintain that they are hell.

If you're into it, there's a whole community of lace aficionados and fanatics, from Facebook group meet-ups to PhD

---

* I am – unsurprisingly – more enamoured of the luxurious Madras style, so named for the origin of the Indian method, which is made by weaving a 100 per cent cotton muslin layer of cloth through a lace loom, which then passes over a second time, creating an overlay of pattern. The weaving process for Madras lace is slower and the cotton is woven onto a net that is so sheer it resembles silk.

theses. Artist and academic Carol Ann Quarini, the founder of both the LaceThread blog and the Lace Research Network on Facebook, is one of the leading thinkers around net curtains, calling for us to pay attention to the art of making home. In her thesis, 'The Domestic Veil',[1] she observes that net curtains can be underestimated as 'a flimsy inadequate boundary ... but it is also dangerous because it is a silent witness in the home retaining a memory of what it has encountered; its folds and creases conceal hidden depths'.

Quarini is writing about the domestic pressures of women in the nineteenth century, not an Asian family in the early 2000s living above a car showroom. But the words resonate. They make me want to rub the fabric between my fingers like a rosary, each ridge like a delicate story in Braille that connects me to women throughout history. I feel closer to understanding how important those translucent boundaries between us and the outside were, something sheer and soft to encase us in.

Textiles invite the traces of human labour and life into our homes, and there is something to be said about how female-centric the responsibility of homemaking is. It has been historically devalued as 'women's work', which patriarchal capitalism sees as nothing more than unpaid, unprofitable labour. We need to fight this assumption. It is radical to be able to look beyond the shell of a house and see not just what is there, but what *could be*. While I was lounging around like Audrey Hepburn, polishing my personal sink and feeling like the 1 per cent, my mum was teasing thread through a needle to make those fucking curtains, hell-bent on just making at least one thing that worked.

The home as a domestic sphere has historically been linked to morality. Victorian etiquette literature, aimed mostly at women, propelled the idea of cleanliness being close to godliness. In reality, when it comes to 'making' home, there is a huge possibility for ungendered collaboration and community which has always existed. In 1919, unrealised inventor Jennie Spangler* designed a prototype vacuum cleaner that was meant for three women to use at once. A purple and pink contraption with three handles snaking from the middle, the intention was that labour would be shared, that it would encourage visits to neighbourhood houses, and this could become collective work. As corporate interests banked on individualising labour for profit, Spangler's invention sadly never took off, but it is useful to think of the idea of 'collective house pride' being a community endeavour. The most encouraging point of this is to recognise the fact that learning how to build home for ourselves enables us to build it for other people too, in the workplace, in community activism and beyond.

## Your home as a headline

We don't have enough housing. The UK requires 220,000 new homes each year to keep up with demand – not to mention making up for the undersupply from previous years. In the year to September 2014, only 141,000 new homes were built.[2] Things have improved a bit – in the 2019/20 financial

---

* The daughter of James Murray Spangler, who invented the first personal suction cleaning device as an antidote to his struggle with asthma, when he worked as a janitor.

year, 211,000 new dwellings were completed. The building solutions to this crisis have taken many forms over the years, one of the most egregious being the creation of quick-build, low-quality homes that often do not work in practice.

People are forced to live in a grim variety of properties in this country. 'Bed in a shed'-type living, where landlords let out cramped garages and garden sheds often with no running water or toilets, is on the rise. Every day, Twitter threads share the most outlandish stories of rogue landlords,* an epidemic of low-quality housing solutions. You might read a story from 2017 about a former RAF engineer in Bristol who spent eight years in a lock-up garage to escape the terrible conditions of hostels he was placed in by the council, or the listing on Rightmove by a landlady renting the basement of her flat for £1,000 a month and requiring two hours of housework from the tenant every day. Maybe you've seen the mezzanines to let, or the former office blocks that people rent at huge cost. These stories have become so widespread that there are whole columns dedicated to exposing how desperate the situation is. To pick just one, Joel Golby's column in *Vice*, named 'Rental Opportunity of the Week', is a guide to the 'hell that is renting in the UK' and spins dark comedy from chaos. A brief glance at this and you'll find a windowless basement tunnel for £2,000 a month, or a dilapidated conservatory in Catford for £1,000 a month. These are all examples of housing developments being unfit from the point of design, even before years of neglect, and can be found all across the country.

---

* I started screenshotting tweets, news stories and viral images about these for my own reference, and after I had amassed over 100 in a few weeks I stopped for my own sanity.

With regard to 'inventive' low-cost and low-quality solutions to the lack of housing stock, there should be a clear distinction made between the unfit housing provided by private landlords, such as sheds and conservatories, and the unfit accommodation provided by the government. In 2021, news broke about the untenable conditions experienced by asylum seekers in Napier Barracks. Photographs of the camps showed dirty, cramped, jail-like rooms reminiscent of the makeshift mobile wards from Second World War films. Further reports revealed that asylum seekers were being housed in the cells of former courthouses, complete with cell windows, cell doors and prison-style bunk beds. The Home Office's inspiration for housing seems to be drawn from prisons, consciously inviting connections between being an asylum seeker and punishment through these conditions of restriction and hostility.

The reality of unfit housing is that people are tasked with trying to 'make the best' out of impossible conditions. In 2021, a damning audit by the Bartlett School of Planning confirmed officially what, by this point in the housing crisis, is obvious: that the vast majority of new housing developments should not have been built due to their shoddy design.[3] It found that of its sample of 140 developments across England built since 2007, 20 per cent should have been rejected outright by planning authorities. A further 54 per cent should have been rejected at planning stage, and only built if the developer came back with 'significant improvements' in the design – which of course, many didn't. It is clear why desperate people are forced into accepting poor housing. It is even worse that the state legitimises this dangerous housing by giving it a new, sinister name: temporary accommodation.

## SASHA

During one of the community meetings I attended after the Grenfell fire, someone flippantly suggested housing residents in shipping containers as a temporary solution. At the time, I thought I'd misheard, that this was some kind of throwaway comment born of grief, or a comment on the quality of the government's response. Weeks later, after revisiting the audio transcript, I paused the tape to research further. The suggestion, which was new to me, was, it turns out, a serious one.

Approach West Ealing's Meath Court (incidentally, just a 15-minute drive from the Green Man Lane Estate) and you will see a large eagle two storeys high, painted in tones of burnt orange, black and grey. It flies above a painted wild garden of crimson, lilac and sunshine-yellow flowers which have been worn away by rust. Corrugated steel lines form the backdrop of this scene, as part of a stack of four shipping containers on top of one another, which are marred by smudges and graffiti marks. The name of this area, and the mural, smacks of a grim sort of irony: Hope Gardens.

Meath Court's 120 shipping containers make up two estates separated by a small triangle of concrete, some benches and patches of green. They are divided into colour blocks – painted in green, blue, orange, red, to denote different areas, with access to each requiring a unique key code at the gate – or would do if the gate wasn't broken. On the day I visit I don't realise that and so a girl carrying shopping lets me in and we climb the rickety steel staircase to her flat.

As we walk through the labyrinth of neon green steel sheets, I notice that the panels that make up the staircase are

perforated with holes, some of which are stuffed with cigarette butts and bits of foil from chewing gum packets. The
green paint is peeling as if it has been here for centuries, but
when I visit the site it is only four years old. As we ascend,
the acrid smell of pennies held too long in your hand becomes
stronger in each stairwell.

Over two levels, we pass disused prams, dishevelled blankets made mouldy with rain, used nappies, rusted iron railings
and boarded-up doors with numbers scrawled on them in
Magic Marker. One door we pass has a Louis Vuitton decal
cut into a thin rectangle. Each step sounds like a hollow 'ting',
followed by a rattle, uncomfortably connecting you to a network of steel structures, precarious in every sense.

The girl who invites me in is nineteen-year-old Sasha.
She pulls up a plastic chair outside her front door and with a
big smile, revealing pink braces, she describes her own first
impressions of the containers. Sasha and her daughter have
been here for nine months (despite being told it would be no
longer than six weeks) so her reaction is fresh. She was made
homeless after she had a baby and had to move out of her
mum's one-bedroom flat. 'The first place [Ealing Council]
offered me was a one-bedroom but it had mould which isn't
good for babies,' she explains. 'So after they said, "OK, we'll
offer you one more place and if you don't take it that's it, we're
not helping you."

'When they gave me the address I went on Google and
was like, "Nah, this can't be the place." I saw the houses and
was like, "No, this isn't right." Then when I came here I was
like, "Oh my God, they've put me in like . . . metal things?"'

'Nah' is a fitting response to what Ealing Council describes as the 'short-term' temporary housing which many of Sasha's neighbours have spent years in. Her container features two bedrooms, a kitchen, a living room and a bathroom. She pays £60 a month (including bills) but any justification about this being under market price is doing a lot of heavy lifting. It is riddled with problems – the electrics in her room are in danger of blowing from the condensation, the bunk beds that came with one bedroom can't be moved to make space for a cot, the sockets hang off the walls, mould forms over the panels (Sasha rejected the former place because of mould and now she has it anyway), there is no lift for her pram, the fridge light is gone. 'If "they" think you can deal with it yourself you have to deal with it, basically,' she says. 'I've tried to call the woman that placed me here and she doesn't answer the phone or email.' She opens her door and I see panels of white, shiny plastic like a whiteboard over all the walls and ceilings, which means she can only use Blu-Tack to put up pictures. As I look closer, I notice that a panel is coming off the ceiling because heat has melted the glue that secures it.

'Everyone who lives here knows that when you're bidding you're not going to find a house for years,' she tells me, a soundtrack of the low metal clang echoing under our conversation as neighbours descend the stairs. 'A neighbour moved out yesterday and she lived here one and a half years and I thought they were going to another permanent but they weren't, they were going to another temporary. So, this is classed as "short-temporary" but apparently there's "long-term temporary". You could be here for two years, but they won't tell you that, the neighbours will tell you that.' Unofficial neighbour networks have proved more reliable than official state communications time and time again. If history has taught us anything, it is this, and at nineteen Sasha is wise enough to recognise it too.

She takes a minute to pause because articulating these issues is taking its toll. She breaks the tension by showing me the curious placement of a wardrobe in the kitchen, as it was when she moved in, and bursts into fits of giggles. 'I have beans in here!' she laughs. 'I couldn't move it out!'

We talk about the small culinary pleasure of chicken and rice, which is Sasha's, who is of Spanish and Jamaican descent, go-to. She shares recipes and bemoans the death of her tomato plants which couldn't endure the heat of the kitchen. She longs for a windowsill. It's just as well she can cook, she sighs, because Deliveroo drivers have trouble finding the place. One of the many anachronistic elements of this block is that no-one has Wi-Fi. 'I have unlimited [data] on my hotspot so I hotspot my Netflix for my TV because you're not allowed to install it,' she sighs. 'You can buy an aerial like I have but it's so bad.'

In the summer on Meath Court, it gets so blisteringly hot (because, well, they're big vats of metal) that tenants open their front doors wide and keep them open until as late as 10 p.m. – precarious when people can walk in and out of the broken security gates. I notice there is no chain and no peephole on Sasha's door and I focus on this, unable to take my eyes off it, guilty at the thought of leaving her alone here.

I speak to various tenants in this block over the following weeks: single men with disabilities, conflict refugees, women escaping abusive partnerships. One of the women I speak to lives in the container just across the stairs from Sasha, a refugee from Afghanistan. She tells me in broken English, with the help of her husband on loudspeaker, that she previously moved from a migrant camp to Southall. She was moved here with her small daughter and partner three years ago and while she talks I notice the peeling floor as the heat rises to a bristling sweat in the early afternoon sun. I wonder how women who complain rarely, who might have few advocates, who may not speak English as fluently as Sasha, might be exploited by this system. After a few minutes, I ask her if she likes living here and she pauses, possibly unconvinced that I am not really an undercover housing officer looking for reasons to evict. 'I am very happy,' she tells me slowly, holding my gaze. 'It is . . . great.'

Many residents at Meath Court have made makeshift curtains from wrapping paper or crisp, white, fitted bedsheets expertly tied to conceal light, some puckering at the sewn-in elastic designed for a mattress. Others have net curtains, jumpers on a line, material that looks like sari fabric, crimson chiffon and ornate cottons folded to look like thick velvet drapes. One has a wooden pallet slab leant up against the window with blue graffiti of a smiley face on it. On the drive home I pull over, think about the hours spent putting up those net curtains in W. R. Davies, close my eyes and think about my mum.

## Dream big, live tiny

The US company Backcountry Containers sells its products using other names: 'tiny houses', 'modular' or 'container homes' which it describes as 'unique, modern [and] durable' on its website. In the UK, Container City offers 'social and cultural hubs made from shipping containers' which are sold as 'eco-friendly alternatives to more traditional architectural forms'. (Steel might be recyclable but calling it eco-friendly is a stretch.) Another UK company, Discover Containers, provides e-books and floor plans for shipping containers so that you might be inspired to do it yourself. In the US and Canada, some luxury homes are made by a company called Honomobo, which provides steel units factory-built to create light-filled, airy homes straight out of the style pages of *Elle Decoration* for around £40,000. These boxes are sold as aspirational for those who are priced out of traditional home ownership options.

If temporary housing by the state illustrates the plight of the poorest and the most vulnerable in society, aspirational tiny homes demonstrate, potentially, a different problem: the squeezed middle class in this country. These companies (and countless TV shows like *Tiny House Nation* on Netflix which refer to the 'tiny house movement' which has 'swept across America') tap into that need for affordable housing and flip it, repackaging cramped living as stylish and modern. This marks a strange turn, as size and space for all has long been a housing battle.* In the UK, these tiny houses often feature on holiday home rental sites and Airbnb. Not all metal boxes, it seems, are created equal. The fact the middle classes are looking for these kinds of solutions exposes the failures of affordable housing stock. If the business of non-traditional living solutions is to continue, we need to ensure the dwellings are of a good enough standard to keep people safe. But

---

* In 2020 the World Health Organization claimed that living spaces must be able to guarantee adequate privacy, be accessible and usable for extended users and be large enough to accommodate people at different stages of the life cycle. Following that claim, housing for many in this country falls quite substantially short.

how can we trust the promise of adequate conditions in non-traditional homes given how badly the housing system is regulated now?

The existence of Meath Court reinforces how damaging the intervention of local councils can be, how negligence runs deep in our housing system and how temporary, quick-fix solutions can create long-term problems for vulnerable tenants who have been forgotten. Despite being a campaign promise of every party for as long as I can remember, public investment in high-quality council homes has not been delivered by any government. It is impossible to fathom how we can reduce the use of 'temporary' accommodation without it.

Those in power have been slow to recognise the link – if they do at all – between crumbling economic policy and the specific repercussions felt by already marginalised communities. There are lots of reasons why people are driven to homes not meant to be lived in: ex-prisoners looking for a home after incarceration, LGBTQIA+ teenagers kicked out of their homes, victims of domestic abuse – the list is long. Vulnerable people, often from marginalised communities, are more reliant on state provision and are chronically underserved, frequently granted low-quality housing and told to be grateful for it. Consider for a minute the fact that one in six ethnic minority families in the UK have a home with a category 1 hazard, which describes housing where the 'most serious harm outcome' is likely.[4] This can be anything from permanent paralysis or loss of a limb to death.

All landlords should be required to demonstrate that their homes meet good standards. Community union ACORN, founded in 2014 in Bristol, boasts over 5,000 members, mostly low-income tenants, in twenty-two cities across the country. In their Renters Manifesto, they share some surprisingly simple and practical proposals to hold landlords accountable, including the idea that homes should be subject to an annual 'housing MOT' where rent can only be collected once they meet the standards set out by local authorities. They recommend putting pressure on the government to provide a clear definition of what constitutes a 'decent home'. ACORN also advocates for local authorities to ensure that temporary and emergency housing is safe, secure and part of a quick, clear path to a permanent home, with standards monitored and data on the extent and public cost of temporary accommodation made publicly available. There are conversations to be had about who might enforce these processes, about penalties for rogue landlords, about the distinction between state and private housing, and which doors to bang down.

Being taught about architecture in school might give us a vocabulary to pinpoint what exactly works and what doesn't, and a way of seeing that would enable us to push back – to laugh in the face of a developer touting broken properties as liveable. Raising the standard of living for everyone is paramount. That has to begin with a much sharper awareness of the conditions that so many people in this country are forced to endure. Only then can we fight for the prioritising of tenants' needs.

## New-builds, old problems

Privately owned new-builds are often touted as solutions to the housing crisis, but they are not immune to unscrupulous negligence either. In fact, low-cost finishes on new-builds have become so widespread that Instagram accounts like @new_home_quality_control (114,000 followers) which give repair tips have become enormously popular.

Flat-pack new-builds populate this country. Travel along most motorways in the UK and you will see adverts for new identikit villages that pop up quickly and are rarely built to last. Anecdotally, I know many people who have moved into homes that no-one has ever lived in before, who complain of cracks, loose sockets, faulty plaster and more, thanks to rushed contracts that are required to be completed at high speed, or jobs allocated to unqualified builders and not protected by a third-party regulator. 'New' does not automatically mean high quality.

New-builds are also often not future-proof. Retrofitting a house to better accommodate people with disabilities, for instance, is extremely expensive and rarely done. In 2018, the Equalities and Human Rights Commission found that an enormous 93 per cent of 8.5 million rental homes in the UK were not fit for disabled access.[5] The London Renters Union's disability caucus often flags these issues up – of able-bodied developers and landlords not designing with disabled people in mind (or as if our population was immune to ageing). If it was standard, say, for all houses to be built with ramps, it would improve the lives of millions in this country. (If we are forced to make an economic argument about this, just think of the reduced impact on the NHS alone if we designed new-builds to limit the likelihood of a fall.) In fact, in 2021, the Building Research Establishment Trust estimated that that poor housing could be costing the NHS as much as £1.4 billion a year.[6]

'Home' is an active word. There are ingenious and beautiful ways that people make home from places that were not built to be lived in. But that can't take away from the fact that many of these houses should be criminalised. We need policy change, but we also need to see a renewed cultural reverence for homemaking, and recognise when it can be radical work, especially by people making the best of what little safety or support they have. Often, people create warmth in spite of their circumstances, which takes me back to the knowledge I learned from this flat: that home is made from the inside out, one curtain at a time.

W. R. Davies was my home for only a year before we were kicked out to make way for a more profitable enterprise. The building where I watched countless reruns of *Moesha* and basked in the sunshine that flooded in felt short-lived; just as I started to make friends and have a place to invite them back to, we were told to leave. I lamented the lost fantasy of palatial glass, and left the curtains behind, wondering what was going to be built on this place filled with my teen memories. Today it is a petrol station.

# A note on kindness

After we were kicked out of the showroom, my family all piled into Penny's house. Penny was the mother of one of my school friends, Tom, and she acted as an unofficial fosterer for our family. There were two spare rooms in her house – one for my mum, dad and baby sister, one for my brother and me – and it was truly the most incredible house I'd ever seen close up. It was three storeys high, with five bedrooms, a basement and an attic. It looked, I have now come to learn, distinctly middle class – what you might call 'shabby chic', complete with a dusty piano in one of the rooms, exposed wooden stairs and a green Aga in the kitchen. It was a house built to last, sturdy and not in fear of a bulldozer. I always thought it was a wonderland for a teenager. Before I moved in, I'd knock and ask if Tom was in, and Penny would shout up the stairs in an operatic bellow to see if there was a response. It was worlds away from the tight ship I'd come from – small rooms, tight vigilance.

This was when I really woke up and looked around at the

place that we had moved to. Welshpool is a market town that has a population of less than 6,000 people, and looks like most towns seemingly forgotten by the rest of the country: populated by countless residential homes, charity shops and at that time, supermarkets – Kwik Save, Morrisons, Somerfield, and of course, the holy beacon of many small towns, Spar. (These have not all lasted after Tesco ostensibly put them all out of business in 2011, and in a tale as old as time about corporate might, they not only set up shop here but also rerouted the whole town around it. Now the Tesco 'Superstore' is the monolith that the town happens around.) Outside Spar was a wooden bench and grassy clearing where teenagers congregated, where I later shuffled through to buy Rizlas and dangerous amounts of sour Skittles. The town is maybe best known for Powys Castle, though, surrounded by deer and a short walk south of the high street, a site of stolen goods amassed during the British colonisation of India by Robert Clive, or 'Clive of India', who collected deities made of silver and gold, weapons, armour and textiles, things of pillaged beauty.

My mum found the town oppressive but I – eventually – enjoyed the fact that I could complete it in 15 minutes, and the limitations of the town's offerings worked for me eventually because they forced me and my friends out, to explore new parts and challenge any intolerance I came across. At W. R. Davies, I sort of stayed indoors, stubborn and angry and depressed, making very little effort to really make friends. When I finally did, Stefan, Kasha, Jed and Tom delighted in taking me into fields and watching me squeal as I spun my legs over gates, agonised huffily up hills and gave a guiding hand when I had no choice but to squat and pee in a field.

## It's not only P**is that get bashed

Welshpool is 4 miles from the Wales–England border and has some of the jingoistic furore that comes with border towns. One year, the National Front marched down the high street and I was surprised to find that while I was hesitantly side-stepping getting bashed, it was some of my Welsh friends that felt really uneasy – having been beaten up in school by Welsh-hating English yobs. That completely blew my mind. (Later, I realised, it made sense – they couldn't have all been there just for me.) It was in this house that I heard about 9/11, watching the towers fall on a TV in my mum's bedroom. It turned out that Welshpool was an unfortunate place to live when Brown terrorists had just bombed an American landmark and 2001 was a year that would mark a fracturing of Brown identity and what some call a generational trauma.*

On my first day of attending the local secondary school I walked through a corridor where the walls were covered with historical school pictures, rows and rows of white faces, and I remember thinking that I might not survive this. Later, I suffered a brief humiliation when I realised that it was the father of a gel-slicked, blond-tipped, football-playing boys in

---

* The artist Kazim Rashid reflects on this in a short film titled *2001: Pressure Makes Diamonds*. He says that in 2001, Brown identity was shaped and ruptured by three key events: three months of race riots in his home town of Oldham, the events of 9/11, and the crushing defeat of boxer Prince Naseem as he lost his first ever fight. I didn't make this connection at the time, but this analysis gives a sense of what it was like to feel a change in the air.

the class who was my family's landlord at W. R. Davies and it was a weird connection to have – a 'your dad is making me homeless, see you in class' kind of thing. Generally, at first my arrival seemed disappointing to some of the bohemian hippie children, who wanted me to be wearing a bindi and gold-threaded paisley skirts. I would often find myself being asked about Asian Dub Foundation and Nitin Sawhney, only to underwhelm them when I had no opinion. They weren't banking on a garage fan, and most of my music references to Dr Fox's chart show recorded on my tape player, or the thrill of the club music that had trickled its way down from older sisters into my imagination, did not seem to be rated. I wasn't quite the right sort of Brown person, arriving in a denim jacket, thickly lined lips with a purple Maybelline gloss, full of local slang from a London school. But I made unlikely friendships with the other alternative kids, anti-establishment thinkers, and relaxed into being with people free from the rigid social factions and tribalism of Hayes Manor.

## METAL IS THE ONLY THERAPY

It didn't take long for me to gorge on metal bands like Disturbed, Korn and Linkin Park for the next few years (and understand why these are so popular in rural or suburban places where you feel like screaming – teenage angst aside, the sound of Jonathan Davis roaring wakes up sleepy towns). I was also sitting on rage and frustration propelled by endless instability that sometimes had no other way to escape my body than by my inhaling deeply and yelling 'OH WA A A A' as a primal scream. I became part of another sharing network: this time CDs, mostly with my small circle of friends and my first boyfriend, who introduced me to the emotional pull of someone called Kurt Cobain – I was pretty much hooked from then. It led me to a full obsession with Brian Molko, which has endured, to Deftones and Radiohead and beyond, all enjoyed on a slight delay from the rest of the country. My mum agonised over these greebo teen years when I would wear baggy torn black jeans that had wine-bottle-sized pockets (which clinked when I snuck out of various houses) and soaked up rainwater. She hated this so much that many of my memories of that house are of me standing, shivering after the rain, in my knickers after she made me take my jeans off at the front door. Nu metal captured a kind of directionless angst for a whole generation. My rage was not aimless – it was at the lack of control, and collided with my first experience of feeling political, like I could maybe actually, really change things if I shouted loud enough.

Years later, I attended Download Festival for a documentary and saw a sea of black hoodies – a uniform as comfortable as a weighted blanket. I felt a pull to this awkward solidarity – other white boys and Asian girls shuffling around crookedly murmuring pleasantries out of the side of their mouth before screaming their lungs out to Korn as release, smashing bodies into one another as therapy.

The merging of our families was a squash that worked. Mum would send me out to buy gallons of milk and she'd make huge vats of rice pudding for everyone, and Tom and I spent hours talking in the sanctuary of his room, pushing our names into the soft polystyrene ceiling tiles, listening to Rage Against the Machine, and laughing until we were breathless. The overload of family happily drove us out of the house, which – luckily for me – gave Penny an opportunity to try to convince my mum to be slightly more liberal in her parenting, and I was inspired by the warmth of their unlikely friendship, too.

It was also at Penny's house that my sister went through a phase of collecting shiny objects like a magpie, which included bits of KitKat foil, sweet wrappers, thimbles, 5 pence pieces and sequins. She would empty her pink purse of these treasures and line them up by her bed. I forgot about this until years later in 2015 when I was reporting on the Syrian migration crisis and came across a piece in *Time* which showed photos of the items that Syrian refugees had taken with them, clutching little moments of home in an unstable world. I wondered if my baby sister had felt that all along.

## Lake Vyrnwy is a humbling experience

Penny's house was about 20 miles away from the valley of Lake Vyrnwy, famous for its chilling history. The valley once held the village of Llanwddyn, consisting of thirty-seven houses, a church and two chapels, three pubs and a population of around 500 people. In 1877 the valley was identified as a potential reservoir which could service the city of Liverpool. An act of Parliament was signed to push through plans to construct a reservoir and dam – a process which did not consult the locals, who resisted the proposals. In 1889, Llanwddyn was completely flooded and the residents relocated. When we visited my brother swore that he could see the roof of a church under the water and I thought about it for weeks after. I thought of how overlooked these small places were, that you could have the audacity to just flood them. Looking back now, I understand the deep divides between country and city more clearly, of how small populations can be discarded so easily. In those initial months, I reduced Welshpool to just a weird, provincial place, but seeing the scale of the water made me think of the value of those displaced lives, of how 500 people is a lot and how a community is important and special, even if it is tiny.

We were able to move out after my mum got a job at a local residential home and we rented on the other side of the town, but I still came back to help Penny wax the piano when I was having difficult times with my family and was full of frustration and hurt. Despite having a more stable home, our family was breaking down – my dad had left, and my mum had a cancer diagnosis and a breakdown in quick succession. I came to Penny, who received my tears with warmth, handing me a yellow cloth and guiding my hand into the circular swirl. It was just us, a forty-year-old white woman and me, finding common ground. When I think of that smell now, I'm back there with her, rubbing the piano in a gentle circle. I would hug her and breathe her in too, Imperial Leather and buttery flapjacks, and chat to her about some of the things she loved that I discovered for the first time: the *Guardian* and the theatre, squash soup, stuff which I ended up enjoying, too.

The kindness of people like Penny makes me well up when I think about it. Taking in a family, building a relationship, thinking nothing of providing a stopgap, responding to a need. There are 45,370 fostering households in the UK,[1] and countless, unreported houses which are opened up by friends just to help out. There is very little data to measure just how many people are offering their homes out of kindness, picking up the slack from the state because they see what they have as a gift to share. Of course, when it comes to rolling this kind of support out at scale there should be a process built in: training, due diligence, background checks, especially when thinking about, say, supporting refugees or vulnerable young people. But this raises an important question: what if we always thought first of the sharing potential of what we have?

After a few months, I gained respect for the history and the language of the place where I lived. I became familiar with names that previously looked like a smash of letters, words that made me think of my dentist telling me I had too many teeth in my mouth. Llanfyllin, Llanymynech, Rhayader. I fell in love with the Welsh coastline of Barmouth and Shell Island and Tal-y-Bont. Once, I camped on the island with my friends, delightfully cut off from the world when the tide went in, and it felt like an island full of teenagers.

I owe my friends everything for breathing life back into me; they picked me up when treading water in the pursuit of a stable home started to get too tiring. Stef taught me the history of Welsh subjugation. Jed taught me about the spirit of left-wing anarchy that existed in pockets of the countryside. Kasha taught me how to put friendship and love (and climate consciousness) first, how to be your own person and to reject the parts of life that don't serve you. Tom taught me how to laugh from my chest, and the restorative power of independence; he, together with his family, reminded me that there is beauty, and kindness, everywhere.

# Mill Lane – How we make a case for welfare

After another move (a house at the top of a hill called Bron-y-Buckley, walking up which gave me bulky calf muscles that did not go with the rest of my body), my mum had to quit her job thanks to her declining health, but her housing benefit allowed her to rent a three-bedroom house on a council estate across the border in England. Relations between us were fraught from the coming and going of my stepdad and what I now understand to be a genuine panic about my rebellion, which she tried to clamp down on with an iron fist. I was made of material unable to concede, a bouncy ball springing back into shape after being squashed. In reality, this was about our struggle to deal with my mum's breast cancer diagnosis, which threw us into a suspended state of terror and hysteria. Any grievances we had only added to the monumental stress of the situation and she made a decision to prioritise her own mental and physical health and move away.

So she went with my siblings to a new house, figuring that

I wanted to be independent and she wasn't in a fit state to manage me. I was eighteen, and it was agreed that I would leave, with my mum at limited capacity to do much else. The news of this sent me into a spiral, but I understood the logic and was at the same time excited at the prospect of living alone, as most precocious teenagers might be. Plus, at least my siblings would have their own rooms. And so, I made my way to the familiar space of the benefits office, on the grounds of being estranged, though I visited weekly (which I didn't tell the Department of Social Security about) and looked after my siblings when my mum stayed with family either in London or Canada for recuperation.

I stayed with Penny for some time, waiting for a flat to reveal itself from The List, and one eventually did. So much of the organising of this in 2005 was done in analogue, using paper and stamps, and having no digital record of this makes it feel like a crack in the atmosphere, where time bent out of shape. Mill Lane was a new-build council property with a neat red brickwork exterior and the distinct smell of institutional living, bleached concrete steps painted a deep burnt orange, the colour of roasted peppers, with weighty fire doors that required me to push with the entire force of my slight, teenage body. The interior was a small hallway with three doors coming off it, one for my bedroom, one for the bathroom and one for the living room, which the kitchen was connected to. All in all, I could walk the whole flat in about three seconds.

The first night I spent there I had no furniture, apart from a bed. I sat on the MDF floor with a care package Penny had brought, and we ate bread and chicken Cup-a-Soup together. When she left, I drew an outline of myself on the floor in a blue biro, like a crime scene, a way to document that I was here.

I eventually got a coffee table and sofa donated from a local charitable organisation, while friends provided CD players and a TV which fed an addiction to *Big Brother*. A few months after the move I saw a picture of Zack de la Rocha in a black and red room in the pages of *Kerrang!* Unaware that I wasn't allowed to decorate, I spent my benefit at a hardware shop and painted all four walls crimson.

## WELFARE FOR EVERYONE

Government rhetoric has for many years encouraged middle-class voters to see themselves as a separate interest group to the working class. The modern welfare state, which many of us have benefited from since the second we were born, is indebted to the policies that followed the Second World War, which exposed the social needs of a nation decimated by conflict. There was a raft of new policies at this time, namely: the National Insurance Act in 1945, creating compulsory contributions from employees and relief for unemployment, death, sickness and retirement; the Family Allowances Act, providing payments for large families; the Industrial Injuries Act of 1946, aiding people harmed at work; and Aneurin Bevan's mighty 1946 National Health Act, which created a universal, free-for-all social healthcare system. The modern welfare state is less than eighty years old, and perhaps its newness makes it appear fragile and easy to dismantle by the political right. After all, we didn't always have a welfare state, and unless we fight for it, we won't necessarily always have one, either.

As long as I've been aware of political discourse, there has been pressure from both major parties to reduce the amount that the 'average person' (whoever that is) should spend on supporting other people. Since its introduction in 1988, Income Support has been the main benefit available to those who are out of work but not seeking employment. When I received mine, I signed on at the post office every week in exchange for a stamp and £44.05 in cash. I lined up alongside pensioners and harassed single mums imploring their kids not to grab handfuls of cola bottles from the Perspex pick 'n' mix boxes, sugary mouths smiling back at them in happy disobedience. I was given the money in cash, and would make it stretch across shopping and bills until the following Tuesday, a practised weekly choreography from the post office to Morrisons.

Universal Credit has replaced the system I relied on. It provides monthly payments for low-income Britons or those out of work. The average monthly amount for a single claimant is £265.31, or £61.22 a week, and it is no small operation – as of July 2021, there were 5.9 million Universal Credit claimants.[1] And yet 'benefits' has become a dirty word. Bizarrely, though the word suggests an advantage, a happy addition to living in the UK, it often just means the bare minimum for a western country with a GDP of £1.9 trillion. These benefits typically serve a range of different purposes. They provide protection for those who are homeless; they offer paid maternity and paternity leave and allowances for children; they support low-income groups, whether out of work or, increasingly, in work and on low pay; they provide financial support for additional costs arising from disability; and they provide state pensions.

There is a disconnect between the substantial right-wing media messaging that state reliance on benefits is sending us into poverty and the reality. The UK offers some of the least generous benefits in Europe.[2] In 2021, the five most generous welfare states were France, Finland, Belgium, Denmark and Italy. Research from 2021 showed that unemployment support in the UK was on average 12.5 per cent of the claimant's previous salary. For context, in Germany claimants are given 66 per cent, and in Italy 75 per cent.[3] Surely the pandemic should have proved that anyone can find themselves in circumstances that require state support but alas, some ministers still think this is too much. The benefit cap was introduced in 2013 as an attempt to limit government spending. When ministers talk about 'cutting tax'[*] they are taking money away not only from crucial public services like schools and hospitals, but also from people who rely on the welfare state to exist, to make toast, to browse Twitter, to feel warm in their beds.

In 2022, the Tory government, then led by Boris Johnson and under the fiscal guidance of current prime minister Rishi Sunak, enacted the biggest overnight benefits cut in modern history by cutting Universal Credit by £20 a week, the response was immediate – people would simply not be able to feed their children with ease, and decisions would have to be made about whether to 'eat or heat' during the punishing winter. Under the current system, claimants have

---

[*] This is most aggressively seen on the political right but has long since crept into those centrist and right-leaning MPs within the Labour Party, too.

three months to find work, but a 2022 government proposal would reduce this to four weeks. Also in 2022, during a period of historic instability, inequality and decline, a tape of former prime minister Liz Truss was leaked in which she commented that British workers needed 'more graft' in order for the economy to get back on track. This callous attitude ignores the Department for Work and Pensions' own data, which shows that 40 per cent of people who receive Universal Credit are already in work. The power of this cognitive dissonance about why people are struggling, and the kinds of people who might have somehow brought it on themselves, infects everything. Individual policies aside, this is part of a culture of demonisation where the governance, details and individuals in power may change but the central idea does not. The caricatures of people like eighteen-year-old me are potent, and chillingly enduring.

Conservative political rhetoric has named vulnerable people as 'scroungers', gluttonously gorging on the state to live out luxurious lives of sloth. In the context of housing, the cultural and political depiction of people who live in council housing has the knock-on effect of making it hard for managers and landlords to take tenants on benefits seriously. These negligent depictions go hand in hand with an aggressive and often gleeful demonisation of working-class people on our TV screens. 'Poverty porn' TV shows are their own genre: *Benefits Street*, *Benefits Britain: Life on the Dole*, *Immigration Street* and *Skint*, to name but a few, enjoy sizeable ratings as they rampantly peddle the 'shirker' narrative. These shows on Channel 4 and Channel 5 teach us that these tenants are obese, lazy subjects of ridicule, and pits the white working class against communities of colour in a fabricated fight for resources. These representations have real-life consequences; they make it more difficult to advocate for change.

At Mill Lane I routinely behaved in ways that make my face hot with shame now, stuff which would surely encourage a Channel 5 TV crew to gleefully stick a camera in my face: forgetting what day the bins were emptied and just putting rubbish outside whenever I remembered, not bothering to heave bags into a wheelie bin, leaving my front door unlocked, smoking inside, and not once mopping the stairs. It might not come as much of a surprise that I was not popular in that building, which was mostly populated by older, white locals who had never left the town and routinely made offhand racist remarks on the stairs. There was a lot of anger about my 'intolerable' behaviour, like the time I sang Skunk Anansie on the staircase, bellowing about how I had no tears for an imaginary lover, only for a neighbour to come out of her flat wielding a broom and telling me to shut up. Once, owing to the various male friends who came to visit, I got reported for being a sex worker by one of my downstairs neighbours and had to take Penny's partner, a legal representative, to the housing association as a character witness to save me from potential eviction. Another time, the same neighbour, a balding septuagenarian, accosted me outside my door, accusing me and my friends of urinating in the stairwells. Luckily, the complaints didn't stick but there is probably a file on me somewhere detailing all these grievances, ready to be unearthed. I'd like to read them.

## THE COMFORTING RHYTHM OF TOPPING UP A GAS KEY

I spent most of my time in this flat on my stomach in the kitchen, igniting the pilot light of the boiler: holding the button down, listening for the click, watching the blue flame through a tiny circular window, releasing the button, then seeing the flame go out. I had to do this around thirty or forty times until the flame held. It was such a dizzying moment of air-punching delight when it finally caught that I would feel my heart beat in my ears like I was coming up.

It was a short-lived joy, really. When the boiler finally turned on I had to keep it on, along with the lights, by topping up gas and electricity cards. My gas and electricity meters in this flat lived outside the building, which required me to trundle downstairs, wrapped in blankets on cold nights, to activate the emergency credit. I had two separate blue cards that I topped up with £5 a week each, and I watched the digital display happily light up when the meter ate my money.

This wasn't new to me – as a child I remember the fun of the navy-blue plastic pre-payment keys that we had to top up and stick in the meter like an expensive game. Growing up, one of the rumours abounding (physics-related rumours were rarely the subject of salacious gossip so I was fascinated by this one) was that you could get free electricity by attaching to the meter a strong magnet (sourced from classrooms around the city) which, allegedly, moved the metal disc inside backwards. If true, this is an act of genius that saved people thousands of pounds across the country (but is no longer effective now that the technology has changed).

My sister visited often, and we danced to her excruciating

music choices: Pink, the *Hairspray* soundtrack, *High School Musical*, until all the fun of musicals became a by-word for her own joyful, exuberant presence, which has stuck. I stroked her dark curls in bed next to me, sang her Hindi lullabies, and she always managed to fall asleep *just* before the leccy went. (There are people across the country who know the very specific kind of rupture you get when the electricity cuts out in the middle of a film. It is uniquely disruptive – sometimes the whole room goes dark, but without the frantic search for a candle that takes place in every home when the whole street has a power outage. It's instead a very personal, individual kind of darkness.)

The dark times are only set to continue. In the UK in 2022, inflation increased to the highest rate in thirty years, up to 9.9 per cent at the time of writing. Utility bills in the UK are at an astronomical increase of 74 per cent over the last year, and rising. For my mum, that's an extra £100 pounds a month to watch the same episodes of *Columbo*, which seems hefty at best. The impact of this hike in inflation and energy prices is hard to overestimate. The value of a pound, how far it can stretch, becomes much more important when it means being able to boil the kettle for a cup of tea or watch the end of a film before the power cuts out.

I learned a lot about the reality of living on your own through the gas and electricity meters. When I went to university and didn't have to think about those costs at all, it felt like a bizarre step backwards in the responsibility of independent living. I got used to it quickly and by the end of the first term I was luxuriating in my self-made sauna, whacking the heating up full blast through the winter months with reckless abandon.

I lived at Mill Lane for a year while I went to college and organised my university submissions. As soon as I received an offer for a place at university, I started the process of packing up my stuff. I had no idea about what to do when you leave a house and no-one told me. I simply walked to the benefits desk one day, told them I was leaving and signed a piece of paper. When the day came, I packed up my stuff, gave the rest away to friends in need, or to the centre where it'd come from, to make its way to another house. That day, I left without so much as running a hoover over the carpet – I discarded what I couldn't carry or didn't want (burned CDs, a shisha pipe, odd socks and coat hangers) and I'm fairly certain I left the bin bags full of trash in the kitchen.*

Mill Lane was a sanctuary provided by the state. I've never had to sign on for such a long period since, or lived on my own for as long. It became a solitary glitch in real life, made up of glorious set pieces – Kasha coming over and making chai and eating Dairy Milk, Tom buying me a CD player, Chris helping me with that fucking pilot light, revising with my friends, and the mums who all quietly, knowingly, helped me out with dinners and sleepovers. My day-to-day survival was thanks to a community of friends who gave me the kind of unspoken support that exists in the form of jokes and KitKat deliveries.

Over time my relationship with my mum healed, as she did. I visited her in hospital while she recovered from radiation therapy and the time apart brought some perspective. Within a year she was in remission. The first thing my mum

---

* I really thought someone would come to pick them up.

did was to arrange for carpets to be installed in my flat, through the good timing of a Carpetright closing-down sale. They covered my weird murder scrawl, and she didn't even comment on the fact that I chose the colour black (finally, greebo acceptance). By the time the year was over, we were close again, and when I moved out, the summer before I started university, it was to her house, to share a double bed with her for summer. We spent nights chatting. I'd put my legs on hers and as she got more uncomfortable she'd huffily kick them off. As the eldest daughter in a single-parent family, our relationship can at times feel like a partnership, but that summer we regressed into old roles – small child, angsty teen, friend. I started noticing her age and the fact that she'd started to snore. Staring through a gap in the curtain at the moon, I lay awake beside her in bed and thought about how at my age she had a child. I thought how squeezed you can feel by family, how lonely it is without them. I kissed her forehead and spooned her as she muttered private prayers to herself in her sleep.

After I started university I decided it was probably best not to mention this year to the new friends in halls, so I just nodded along to complaints about making solo dinners and washing up for the first time. My suspended moment in time during that year in Mill Lane became a memory very quickly. There was nobody else to witness me dancing to D'Angelo and doing pretend cooking shows while I made toast, all those times I moshed on my own. I could almost forget completely, but now I write for a living and can go whole days without saying a thing if I want. Those are the moments when I remember my little flat.

# A note on all the shops I've ever lived above

## SNAPPY SNAPS

For about six months in 2011, I lived above a Snappy Snaps in Clapham. The shop front was sunshine yellow, so bright you could see it from a mile away, and I lived with four people in a three-bedroom flat. I was having a hellish time working in my first full-time office job for a voucher discount company, and had made firm friends with an Australian colleague called Diana, in the way that you do when a colleague can save you from the anguish of office labour. We spent every day together, eating lunch, Skyping constantly, walking out of work for 'errands' for hours at a time. I fell completely in love with her. It was the kind of friendship that existed so richly at work that at first, we had little idea about each other's home lives – to visit after work might feel like overkill. But when she saw me bawling in the office toilets after a break-up, she offered me a room at her house and introduced me to the nomadic lifestyle of a certain kind of foreign tenant in London. Bouncing around was not new to her – she had gone on a Europe-wide coach tour a few years earlier, sleeping in hostels and on friends' sofas for a whole year. She lived with two other Australian girls, aspiring graphic designers, and a French boy she'd met on her travels. As luck would have it, Diana and said man started a relationship – lucky for me, I mean, because they shared a room, which meant there was a single bed going in a room with one of the designers. No-one in the house, used to hostels and dorms, found the room share weird.

I *did* find it weird but was in too much of a fog to think anything of it. I got to know my roommate in a clinical, matter-of-fact way, all bathroom routines and alarm clock timings. The flat itself was icy cold – there was a smashed window in the living room hastily fixed with masking tape and cardboard, and during the winter we slept with two fan heaters blasting over our jumper-clad bodies. The whirr of the heaters concealed the noise of drunk people on the high street loudly singing Australian songs on Australia Day, except when my housemates joined in.

The flat was devoid of homely furnishing. The living room was stacked with suitcases and each morning Diana and I would run to it, shuddering and shivering as we put clothes on to go to the jobs we hated. I was going through the motions, living on packaged tortellini and Ristorante oven pizzas, so when my ex suggested getting back together, I optimistically agreed, making way for the next person to take my place.

There was a running joke that I was going to print our faces on cushions and mugs at the Snappy Snaps downstairs, and populate the house with them, but in the end, I decided against what would, for me, have been an eye-wateringly expensive joke. I used to be snobby about the gaucheness of Snappy Snaps, making fun of my mum who does actually have a pillow with my face on it, but after years of watching delighted parents, aunties and newlyweds leave the shop with choreographed pictures of toddlers in sleighs and anniversary kisses on a beach, even I became sentimental. They would stop, take them out of their carrier bags and admire them, their squeals of delight making their way into our living room – hard to be snobby about that.

## THE BUTCHER/FLORIST HYBRID

Anyone who has ever lived above a shop knows how you become in tune with the rhythms of the work day – when bins are emptied, the clatter and screech of the shutters as they go up. My family lived above both a butcher and a florist, which were next door to each other, the flowers not quite potent enough to mask the smell of meat. Our flat was extremely small and densely packed, with one bedroom for me, my mum and my brother. I was about ten or eleven and had just discovered boy bands (E17, 5ive) so Mum had to endure me singing along to lyrics about girls 'wanting it', whatever 'it' meant.

Both the florist and the butcher were up early. By the time I passed them to walk to school in the morning the fluorescent lights were on, chalk written on the sandwich board. There were times I had to walk past a pig's head in the alleyway to reach the iron stairs to our flat, and I would scream, close my eyes and break into a run. The smell of day-old meat would stay with me until the school gates, my queasy intestines gurgling all the way to assembly. The florist gave me a wicked case of hay fever (it was here I discovered I was allergic to lilies) and in the summer when the flowers were outside on the pavement, the pollen invited itself in through our window. My mum bought three boxes of Cien tissues a week as I spluttered and wheezed before she finally decided to keep the windows closed and we stayed cool via a cheap small, blue electric fan. I nearly boiled that summer.

## AN EX-POST OFFICE

This wasn't strictly a working post office, but in 2014 I lived in a top floor two-bedroom flat built on top of an old, defunct one which retained the design. The flat was decorated in 1960s neon greens, oranges and blues, with Japanese-style sliding doors and rooms that could only fit a single bed and a wall of built-in drawers where I threw in everything I owned – bras and candles and notebooks and headphones, all sharing space. These tiny spaces help you understand your body better and I always felt bigger in them, filling a room just by being in it. I was an Alice in Wonderland swelling until her arms and legs stuck out of the house, taking over, punching through the restrictive space.

In the kitchen was a black breakfast bar and in the living room a leather sofa, full bachelor pad chic, so for comfort I often retreated into my bedroom to waste hours playing Candy Crush while my housemate settled into Splashy Fish in hers. We had a homophobic landlord who would turn up unannounced at any moment, and who threatened to keep our deposit because we absent-mindedly left half a tub of Bailey's Häagen-Dazs in the freezer after the deep clean. In a fit of rage he spat, 'I thought lesbians were supposed to be clean!' before slamming our front door.

# Surrey House – How we're taught we're all the same

By the time I got to university in 2006, the New Labour project was in full swing and my pursuit of higher education made me a willing participant in it. New Labour's 'national crusade'[*] of social mobility, the idea that you could raise your social class through education, swept me along on a buoyant, naïve cloud of promise.

Tony Blair's cry of 'Education! Education! Education!' which posited that you could learn your way out of inequality, entered my home through rousing televised speeches that were parroted by my mum. She took it on as a maniacal chant and a devotional prayer. Eventually, it stuck, encouraging me to pursue that most elusive of things, the thing that took my nanaji to Beresford Road – a Better Life.

The politics of New Labour, though less socially conservative, continued the emphasis Thatcher placed on individual

---

[*] As Gordon Brown put it in 2008 ... and many more times after that.

success and enterprise. Thatcherism profoundly shaped and enforced ideas of neoliberalism, which were continued by John Major, who, among other things, took aim at 'feckless' single mothers like mine in his 1993 'Back to Basics' speech (which was widely interpreted as enforcing traditional family values).* In 1997, after eighteen years of Tory governance, Blair proudly proclaimed that 'the new Britain is a meritocracy where we break down the barriers of class, religion, race and culture'. (Incidentally, he used the word 'meritocracy' more than any other PM in history.) And in 1999, he famously set a target to send 50 per cent of young people in Britain to university. This fantastical Britain where everyone was equal and 'things could only get better'† was the one I grew up in, ready to make my way without any minor irritations like race, gender or poverty slowing me down.

The fact that I loved learning was a coup for my mum, who was outside the matrix of school and largely left it up to me to organise my academic life. When I was at Hayes Manor, an older Polish English teacher with a brunette bob and lots of patience, Miss Polatajko, singled me out as a 'gifted' child and gave me some extra reading in lunch breaks. The list included Blyton, Shakespeare and Emily Brontë, and my favourite of them all, *Anne of Green Gables*, who had spent her life moving between homes and orphanages. I admired Anne's precociousness and wondered if 'Miss' had seen the same in me, too. This might have been true but more probable was

---

* It made way for Tory MPs to go on attack mode, like John Redwood in 1993 condemning 'young women [who] have babies with no apparent intention of even trying marriage or a stable relationship with the father of the child'.

† As D:Ream sang in Labour's campaign track.

that she was trying to prepare me for a very specific kind of cultural initiation, encouraging an early reverence for writers that were new to me but who other people took very seriously. She saw these as books that would help prepare me for a time when I might need to reference them, books that would propel me up the rungs of the social ladder.

Going to university for me was, on the one hand, an escape, and on the other, it was inevitable – I was always going to go, even if it wasn't clear from the government data. In Year 11, I was given a burgundy faux-leather-bound 'Record of Achievement' by my school and asked to write all my dreams for the future in it, what I hoped to achieve, to share my ambitions. Many of my classmates wrote that they wanted to be explorers, criminologists or *Big Brother* contestants. My goal was simple: 'Go to university'. That was as far as my imagination could extend, and for most of my school life this was my only aspiration.

After doing my A levels and spending a highly stressful period scrambling around to fill out forms, photocopying benefits letters at the college library and sweating over maintenance grants, I finally got in. My mum felt the sting of a certain kind of loss – for working-class people in particular, once your child goes to university they never really come to back to you in the same way – but mostly she felt an immense sense of pride. I was ready to start a new life as the first person in my whole family to go to university, where all I had to do to succeed in my English degree was sit and read books. Goldsmiths, where even the name sounded precious; Dick Whittington's choice.

## CHEAP PLYWOOD DESKS

The London I returned to could not have been more different to the London of my formative teenage years. I lived in Surrey House halls in New Cross in my first year, historically provided to students from the county of Surrey since 1907. It was sold as a '19th Century mansion with a new modern annexe' (built in 1982) which housed eight people per floor over six floors, forty-eight people in total. It was much smaller than the adjacent mansion building, which had twenty-two people sharing two bathrooms per floor (the annexe had en suites) and because I missed the deadline I was allocated accommodation rather than choosing it. I, thankfully, was in the annexe.

Living in halls also placed me in what it turns out is a particularly British tradition of living away from home to study. This dates back as far as the Middle Ages, when Britain's first universities were made up of bands of travelling scholars who the historian William Whyte describes as having 'mobility . . . in their blood'.[1] In the 1900s, country-to-city migrations propelled by the Industrial Revolution also made the idea of moving away to study more appealing. People across class divides were leaving home for the hope of betterment, and for something else too: to find an intellectual gathering of peers. This is an idea that has continued. Living in shared halls of residence is still the most popular choice of accommodation for university applicants in the UK.

This isn't a universal phenomenon, although we've come to think of it that way. In Scotland, students tend to stay at home, as they do in Ireland, where nearly half of undergraduates live with their parents. In Australia, students are more likely to live in the family home than anywhere else. Across Europe as a whole, on average, 36 per cent of students live in their parental home and only 18 per cent reside in student accommodation. Even in America, with its long tradition of residential universities and its growing industry of student accommodation providers, nearly 40 per cent of students live at home and 77 per cent attend college in their home state.[2]

My halls consisted of the usual trappings of single occupancy university accommodation: uniform lemon-yellow and lime-green curtains organised into a pattern of tessellated squares, a tight single bed, a 6-foot corkboard and a shelf, where I put the most valuable things I owned at the time: second-hand critical theory books and Rimmel lip liners. I remember the clinical, asylum-like smell of bleach and new carpet which hit me in the face as soon as I walked into the empty room. My door, like all the ones in the building, was a shiny faux-pine fire door, and when it closed, the heaviness of it concealed light and sound, as if I had disappeared.

To make the room feel less like a sanatorium I spent hours looking at that corkboard like it was engaging me in an identity test that I had to pass. I ended up going full embarrassing angst-ridden teen, with Don't Panic! posters, pictures of my siblings, quotes from Sylvia Plath and . . . a few rogue stickers of Vladimir Lenin. I bought CDs, preciously wrapping them in socks for safe transit, by Placebo (*Without You I'm Nothing*), Erykah Badu (*Baduizm*), Kanye West (*The College Dropout*), Dizzee Rascal (*Boy in da Corner*), Alanis Morissette (*Jagged Little Pill*) and Peaches (*The Teaches of Peaches*), and an unofficial mixtape of the grime artists of Channel U where the cover art was a blur of artists photocopied in black and white. I played these in religious rotation and cut out the covers into a collage – this disparate group of people making friends on my wall to encourage me to do the same.

I had never owned a laptop before and so I bought one for £300 from Ken,* a middle-aged, shiny-headed dealer on my mum's estate who you could find in possession of anything from illegal turtles to bouncy castles. The brandless laptop he sold me, the only non-Mac on my floor, had no built-in Wi-Fi and a Russian start-up screen, and in the night it would intermittently turn itself on with an industrial whirr.

I spent the majority of my time hunched over a cheap plywood desk fixed to the wall, with a wheatish-coloured shiny vinyl top. It was the kind of standard issue stock that the thousands of people who have ever bought furniture from IKEA, lived in student halls or experienced the institutional trappings of council building waiting rooms will recognise, from the warped bubbles that form on these desks at any contact with water, to the jagged chipboard that scratches your thighs underneath. When I sat at my noisy keyboard I would watch the glue on the plywood laminate come unstuck, exposing the layers of fake wood, and fight the urge to peel the layers apart.

Going to university is a process of uprooting yourself, or for many, it begins the process of moving from place to place. There is something inherently transient about furniture like this, which continued to crop up in the rooms I rented for years after I graduated. (It isn't a big stretch to link the mass

---

* Three years ago he successfully sold 'rubble from Bethlehem' to residents of my mum's estate for £20 a pop.

proliferation of cheap furniture with the general state of housing acquisition for students, much of which is private sector and low quality.) These rooms, which for many are their first experience of a home away from home, set up a generation of revolving tenants (though many students don't think of themselves that way) to be housed in rooms filled with items which are not built to last. When I was alone in those first weeks of halls, I was comforted by the idea that we were all sitting at our desks, with their uniform design, having the exact same experience.

Despite the range of British housing stock and their diverse histories, these details can feel ubiquitous. My friend Charlotte's university accommodation, Albert Stern House (formerly the Sephardi Beth Holim Hospital) in east London, was part of Queen Mary University and was erected as an elderly people's home. It overlooked a graveyard, and she describes wistfully looking out of the window over to the cemetery as she wrote essays. I ask her about the furniture of the room, presumably also steeped in the history of a specific place and time, caught between life and death. 'Oh,' she tells me with a shrug, 'it was that same cheap stuff from IKEA.'

## Working-class cosplay

The uniformity of halls could trick you into thinking that you were all on a level playing field. It is possible that the smugness I initially felt – that other students had paid extortionate private school fees, came from stable wealth and still ended up in the same kind of room as me – was premature. In hindsight, Goldsmiths, at that time, felt like a mad, lawless place where I became numb to people's displays of excess. These were often shrugged off as 'creative expression' or eccentricities, like the time someone came to the local pub on Halloween dressed as an aborted foetus, or the student who made violent porn zines as art, or even the band in the halls across from me who made songs with titles like 'Poo in My Mouth'.*

There was little time to dwell on this because owing to the fees, I felt pressure to enjoy Goldsmiths – and sometimes I really did – but it was hard to ignore how dizzy it was on its own cultural cachet. The university had enjoyed notoriety during the Britpop era of the mid-1990s as the home of Blur founding members Graham Coxon and Alex James (I was on Team Oasis, so really, who cared?) and the mass of Young British Artists who had graduated from the art department. Upon reflection, it made sense that so many of the students were obsessed with Blur because they were not just a pastiche to them – most of the people in my halls had grown up in very big houses in the country and were enjoying working-class identity as another thing to try on.

I was also at this time at the mercy of nu rave, a music genre that quickly made its way through the country, bringing an epidemic of 'The' bands into my halls: The Klaxons, The Wombats, The Futureheads. The music was jarring, a clanging distortion of noise that wasn't as free and as exciting to me as metal, but somehow clean and curbed, play-acting at real resistance.

I spent a lot of my time in university (when I wasn't

---

* Inexplicably, this band later featured in the pages of the *Observer Music Monthly*.

harbouring feelings of unrequited love towards the dirty-fingernailed Soviet Workers Party bros who collected Soviet-era propaganda posters and invited me over to – silently – watch *La Haine*, or fighting for my life when someone absent-mindedly put a plastic kettle on the metal hob and nearly killed us with the toxic fumes) watching grime videos on YouTube and Channel U, a music culture connected to UK garage, jungle and reggae. Black music at that time felt like resistance against a culture of excess and a singular white male point of view that dominated the mainstream. The era, which is now referred to as a period of 'indie sleaze', idealised foppish celebrities like Pete Doherty and Russell Brand,* and it wasn't unusual to see upper-middle-class bohemians in lectures dressed like Victorian rakes and quoting Oscar Wilde.

I was attracted to the DIY nature of grime, which wasn't necessarily about building a better life, but about celebration. It opened up the internet for me too and I obsessively followed blogs, made my own, shared others, gorged on glittery Myspace stickers and perused grime forums. I went to gigs on my own and made lifelong friends on dancefloors. Alongside reading Dante and Virginia Woolf I listened to Rinse FM and watched F64 freestyles on SBTV and felt grateful that those artists were sharing a little bit of their home with me.

It was also at Goldsmiths that I became exposed to

---

* I wasn't immune to all of this. I also was pushed into submission by queuing for apple-red Kate Moss skinny jeans as part of her Topshop collaboration, and had a picture of M.I.A. and her Roland MC-505 on my wall, torn out of the cult mag of the time called *Super Super*.

eye-watering wealth for the first time. But in those early weeks, you could deceive yourself into feeling like you were all the same, dealing with universal truths that are supposed to bind you – living away from home, recipe swapping, panicking about deadlines, buying a fitted bedsheet. That came undone pretty quickly. (For context, Princess Beatrice, currently ninth in line to the throne, was there at the same time I was. I once showed her how to use the vending machine in the library as an act of public service.) I felt my own lack of money acutely. At the same time, I knew I was privileged to learn just for the sake of it. I was not on a vocational course to get a job like a lot of my friends from Hayes Manor were. By the end of my degree it became a grim joke at Goldsmiths that, as arts and humanities students heading into a recession, we'd better start trading on good luck.

I often wonder what the experience is like for middle-class students who were untouched by this idea of social mobility growing up, who were always going to go to university, who thought about class as a horizontal line. I know now that class is both in flux and is complicated and sprawling, but when I was in university I was convinced it was fixed – that if I didn't complete my degree, my structural positioning would stick. I bought into the myth of hard work, grit and determination that set people against each other, which has always perpetuated working-class demonisation. I was one of the 'good ones' who had 'made it', as New Labour increasingly split working-class people this way, and Tony Blair would probably have gleefully put me on a prospectus somewhere. When I was nineteen, I thought of class as cultural, that it was about distinguishing between cheeses, reading Chaucer, feeling at home at the theatre. In some ways, all those felt achievable – more so than buying property, and perhaps a generation of people who'd heard about meritocracy from politicians liked to believe the same thing.

As much as we might like to think of class as high art, taste and education, it is organised as it has always been – by wealth and property. So class should be understood not just as about culture – although that plays a significant part, of course – but as a material and capital condition, or, how wealth enables you to have very different life experiences, outcomes and, sometimes, the power to oppress. After all, cultural capital will hardly afford you a stable home. My situation enabled me to have a life that can be reduced to a New Labour 'success story' but I find it hard to see myself as a beacon of hope and light – my housing situation has been precarious ever since I graduated and it still is.

While I ran around in skinny jeans and Perspex jewellery,* political power was being passed from Tony Blair to Gordon Brown. I was the first generation to pay the 'topped-up' annual university fee of £3,000, up from £1,050 the year before. I received a full maintenance grant, a partial scholar-ship and a student loan, expanded my overdraft limit to pay for rent during university, and thought very little of it. It was an abstract amount, a means to an end. Mine was deemed to be one of the poorest households in the country, in need of full financial help, and more than a decade after graduating, I am still in debt. The Conservative–Lib Dem coalition would go on, in 2010, to bump up tuition fees threefold. Today, the

---

* ☹

average student's debt on graduation day in England is more than £45,000 in maintenance and tuition loans.

The central challenge to affordability is that rents in student accommodation over time have risen by *more* than inflation, while the maximum student loan for living costs have risen *only* by inflation.[3] This knowledge is particularly galling when you consider that student accommodation in the UK is worth around £53 billion a year, as students' rent levels increase exponentially. Student rent currently accounts for 73 per cent of student loans, up from 58 per cent only six years ago. To get a sense of just how much money that is, consider that the current rent in Surrey House's annexe is upwards of £200 per week,[4] which means that one year of rent and tuition fees cost £18,600, and that's not including the rising cost of living. For working-class students, the parameters have shifted so severely that the idea of 'travelling scholars' moving for no other reason than the pleasure of intellectual and cultural expansion feels unfathomable.

With the fee bump in mind, in my first year I worked as a waitress for a catering company which moved venues every week, and learned just how many times a body can run up and down stairs in an hour. It was an easy gig to get. The other waitresses were also young and expendable, just required to be invisible statues that filled glasses and so no-one bothered to learn your name. I was paid around £30 a night to serve wealthy people canapés at Lottery winner events, dinner to bankers at the Natural History Museum (dinosaurs eating around dinosaurs, ha ha), wine to art dealers in secret passages in London Bridge. The latter event was the first time somebody had ever clicked their fingers at me (but not the last). As

I was embarking on a journey of self-betterment through this so-called social mobility, it began to occur to me that these people really didn't care that I knew about Roland Barthes and the *fin de siècle*. I was just another invisible uniformed waitress, sweating and rushing upstairs before fragile swirls of chocolate on wobbly domes of panna cotta melted. I would return from various strange corners of the city, in the dark, key card in hand, to the halls where very few other people worked, flop on my bed and gaze at those yellow and green curtains before falling asleep, the exact same view as everyone else in the building.

One time, I applied to be a 'student supporter' for two well-paid days' work when prospective students came to the open day. I was part of a group who wore electric blue branded T-shirts we could 'make our own' so I spent some time pulling the neck down around my bum to stretch it out, and folded the sleeves and attached hair clips to them – I look like I go here, I thought. I enjoyed it a lot, playing the part of the university's PR team, and I thought about how the money I was being paid would be spent – back into the university, ultimately, for books and food and rent. The visitors asked me what I didn't like about Goldsmiths, and when I told them it was the class and wealth disparity, I noticed that this response was met with excitement – who is really rich? Is there anyone famous here? Many prospective students weren't put off by any of the things I was – they were the selling point. After that, I spent the second day in a café, catching up on my reading. No-one realised I was gone.

## DESIGNING FOR LONELINESS

Student halls try to solve the problem of how to bring people together by their design, with varying degrees of success. Design is important in deciding who meets who, or at least how often, and under what, to borrow a poetic phrase from a halls design manifesto, 'circumstances of casualness'.[5] Research from social psychologists like Leon Festinger and colleagues shows how places designed to encourage people to bump into each other allow for the beginnings of relationships.[6] These design considerations are particularly important in student halls to stave off loneliness, something that almost one in four students experience, according to the Higher Education Policy Institute.

According to one UK-based study,[7] levels of psychological distress increase on entering university and do not return to pre-registration levels throughout the degree course. During lockdown, when students spent more of their time indoors than ever before, more than half of all students in England said their mental health had worsened since the beginning of term.[8] In 2021, research published in *BMC Public Health* found that much of this can be directly linked to the design and quality of accommodation.[9] How might we design these buildings so they serve students better?

Loneliness should be taken seriously. In the eighteenth and nineteenth centuries in America, following a period of mass migration thanks to industrialisation, the country was awash with homesickness, so much so that medical practitioners at the time recognised it as a dangerous and primary form of mental illness. It is interesting to consider how we might incorporate social design if we still took homesickness this seriously, because even with the advent of technology, it persists.

At Goldsmiths, I didn't recognise what I felt as homesickness, but I did mostly live on a pretty depressing diet of Quorn burgers in pitta, tins of sweetcorn and sleeves of Maryland chocolate chip cookies. Sometimes, when I was lonely I would avoid speaking to people in the kitchen and eat bowls of Fruit 'n Fibre in my room, melting chocolate over it with a lighter. Looking back, maybe I did find halls a little difficult.

## SOCIAL MOBILITY IS A MYTH

University housing can be improved with thoughtful design and a model that builds care and student well-being into the accommodation. But what about the gulf between class, income and life experiences? Uniform design is purposeful, creating the illusion that students are 'all in it together'. In fact: the design of your rooms might all be the same, but you are not.

There are countless ways that the myth of meritocracy unravels; we are not equal because these structures just aren't designed for many working-class people of colour to thrive on an equal footing. Only 660 Gypsy or Traveller students were registered in higher education in 2020/21, according to the Office for Students.[10] Only 6 per cent of care leavers ever reach university.[11] Half of England's universities have less than 5 per cent poor white students.[12] Ethnic minority graduates in Britain are between 5 per cent and 15 per cent less likely to be employed than their white British peers six months after graduation – and many can expect to earn less for years afterwards.[13] In January 2017, for the third year in a row, Higher Education Statistics Agency figures recorded no Black academics in the elite staff category of managers, directors and senior officials.[14] In 2018, one in five trans students were encouraged by university staff to hide or disguise that they are trans.[15]

Students absorb these ideas of who has power and agency and they can go on to be spread around the world. Just imagine the students who benefit from this corrosive structural racism who go on to become landlords, estate agents, developers and beyond and how that might perpetuate the cycle.

Despite selling social mobility as emancipatory, the New Labour project was unsuccessful in rebuilding a social safety net for everyone, as sociologist Jo Littler observes in *Against Meritocracy: Culture, Powers and Myths of Mobility*. Littler's book was published in 2017, and in a crisis that is growing every day, I speak to her about where we find ourselves now. 'The fact that over the past few decades we've had an increase in inequality is the single most telling issue and rebuttal to the idea of meritocracy,' she explains over Zoom. I ask her whether she thinks the bigger signifier of class today is a degree or owning a house. After much sighing she comes to the inevitable conclusion that it's the latter, thanks to 'the shift between a younger generation of people who have more likelihood of getting a degree than a home'. Her conclusion is that for large swathes of current graduates 'a degree can feel like … an expensive life raft'.

## Up the students!

This idea of university as a life raft is a potent one. But rather than submitting to the inevitability of graduating straight into a housing crisis, pushback can – and should – start in halls. This might be where the real education starts.

Student housing provision has changed,* and no longer sits solely within the control of universities. In fact, almost half of residences are owned by private providers, working independently or alongside university partners. But this does not often mean better-quality housing. TikTok's spoof 'Things that just make sense' viral videos parody high-style interior design accounts and make this point well, documenting the shitty light fixtures, leaky taps and broken plaster so common in the landscape of new-builds and forlorn, decrepit, old student accommodation. Rent strikes during and after the pandemic prove that students are not powerless to demand better conditions. After all, when students don't see themselves as tenants, landlords are able to exploit them. In fact, the private company that owns Surrey House, Campus Living Villages (CLV), was criticised in 2021 by the then president of Goldsmiths students' union, Lauren Corelli, who claimed on Twitter that 'issues go back YEARS in Surrey House! Students have lived with RATS, mould, flats that are falling apart for YEARS while CLV turn a blind eye for profit', spurring on a Goldsmiths rent strike. The rise of this activism seems to suggest that, happily, things appear to be changing, as students increasingly

---

* Private sector involvement used to be confined to shared student housing in the community. Universities, for their part, owned and ran halls of residence.

see themselves as tenants who can resist extortionately high rental costs.

There are ways to protect students from the stormy seas of the outside rental market. Rent setting must be more transparent. Students living away from home for the first time should be involved in institutional rent setting, because the fight about the acquisition and future costs of halls is invariably a fight about class, and how to support low-income students. They deserve a say – after all, student spending does support more than £80 billion of UK economic output.[16] Perhaps the answer lies in fighting for means-testing rent setting; perhaps it is about exposing the details of private contracts; perhaps it is advocating for the reform or abolition of housing contracts. Maybe – most importantly – it is to continue to push back against the marketisation and privatisation of housing creeping into our academic institutions.

I have a lot of happy memories of university, even though nothing unravelled the myth of social mobility more effectively for me than Goldsmiths. My eyes were opened to these new worlds and I got an education that made me – slightly – less shocked when I encountered this particular brand of inequality in the workplace. I found glamour in late-night library sessions and mostly just rolled my eyes when posh people theorised in seminars about my lived experience. It was an imperfect cocoon in which to grow wings, but I don't know if I could have developed a wingspan anywhere else.

It took me years to realise how university had failed me, to finally rip that plywood laminate off that desk and see what it was really made of. While I loved Goldsmiths, it's now clear to me how the experience could have been improved: with an institutional reckoning in university spaces that explores (at the very least) decolonisation, and by supporting working-class students and their employment outcomes. Maybe more crucially, it would have been empowering to see myself as a tenant who had a stake in the community I had moved to, rather than passing through it in the way that many students can see themselves as transient in the towns that facilitate student life. Seeing myself as a tenant rather than a child of the university might have empowered me to have a voice about other things, too.

The end of my time in university saw the dying embers of New Labour's power in Britain. At my graduation, the dean delivered a speech acknowledging the recession that we were unceremoniously being launched into that tore the previous CV model to shreds, little flecks of paper like confetti around our feet as we danced in our caps and gowns. After they had lived independently for three years, most of my friends had to face the fact that renting in London post-recession, where jobs were thin on the ground and most training was unpaid or non-existent, was going to be a slog. Many of them were depressed at the thought of having to go back to their childhood homes, which they considered a kind of infantilisation, and one friend joked about the shame of having to go back to her home where she had a life-size poster of Thom Yorke beside her bed. I didn't have a room to go back to, only a bed to share with my mum. And so, on my waitress salary, despite the aimlessness, the lack of a guarantor, a global recession, a new coalition government and without any secure employment, I immediately became a renter.

# Amersham Grove – How we rent

The year after I graduated, I decided that rather than moving back home, I would house-share with two girls who were a saving grace for me in university. All three of us were ready to bob along on the tidal wave of recession anxiety together.

We went to so many flat viewings that it became clear that we would need to get used to rejections, finding places that we loved, organising who would have what room, only to be informed that we had been outbid. The house we finally ended up in came after weeks of searching when we were flattened by desperation. At the risk of sounding like a diva, matters were not helped by the fact that earlier that day an estate agent had taken us to a residence where the tenants were smoking billowing clouds of crack. As we walked through the flat where bodies were strewn out on mattresses, coming face to face with vomit encrusted on the sink, the agent sunnily informed us that he 'should've called first!' So when we saw Amersham Grove, we were tired and susceptible to the hard sell, believing him when he said there was stiff competition.

Out of sheer fatigue, we said yes to a three-bedroom terraced house tucked behind New Cross station, an area that we knew by now, and hoped for the best.

A recent listing from an estate agent describes this house as having a 'quaint façade archetypical of a Victorian terraced workers cottage'. *I* would describe it as a janky shithole. It was coated in muddy salmon pebbledash, and the walls were thin enough to hear coughing either side. There was no door in the living room. The frosted glass door in the bathroom meant that you could see the shadows of freshly showered naked bums as you ascended the stairs. The bathtub had a puzzling open hole underneath it. For some reason, water would often leak from the kitchen walls. Once, the kitchen flooded, and I had to scoop water up from the floor with nearby bowls and Tupperware and into the garden, splashing washing on the line. Our housemate, who had moved in sight unseen, was not impressed by the strength of our testimony that, owing to the size of the bedrooms, 'it was nice'.

I also realised for the first time that landlords can use the homes they let as storage facilities. This house was used to store countless standing bookshelves and three sofas squashed into the small living room, making it impossible to put anything else in there, including ourselves, without doing a sort of half roll-in. If you can have pathetic fallacy with a house, this was it – an emblem of the crumbling economy in the heart of a recession.

Three doors down from us was a house that had silver Christmas wrapping paper with little cartoon snowmen covering the windows. On occasion, the sweet, acrid, chemical smell of crack, like hot cleaning products and burnt sugar, would make its way through the street. To the right of us was a white professional couple who hosted 'cosmic disco' raves and woke us up by playing loud bass through the walls. I got really familiar with the cracks in the ceiling, staring up at them as a roster of some of the most terrible dance music ever concocted played next door. I would trace line illustrations in the cracked plaster to the music of Squarepusher, trying to get back to sleep, slowly losing my mind.

The sheer temporariness of this house was apparent from the off, so much so that I never unpacked the boxes of books from the front room, making it look like some kind of a disused warehouse. We didn't have the money or capacity to make the living room homely – we weren't running out to buy soft rugs and curl up in front of the TV, because on some level we always knew we were suspended, perpetually in transit.

In the downstairs bedroom an open fireplace had a slab of cardboard stuck with masking tape to the arch of its façade. At night, it would stretch and bend towards you and something behind it, which we named The Creature™, would scratch and flex the cardboard. We all lived in fear of what would happen here – would TC gnaw through the cardboard in the dead of the night, find its way onto a face and gnaw that too? My imagination, fuelled by general discomfort, amplified these nightmare images of what could be behind it – a rat mainlining steroids? A badger? An ex-boyfriend? Sometimes I would observe it during the day and run out screaming whenever it moved. The Creature was a living embodiment of what gnawed at me for months: the admin, the forms, the times I had to tell my housemates that I couldn't pay rent that month. Renting quickly lost its novelty and turned into an unbearable supernova of escalating costs and precarity, with me sucked into its black hole.

## GET UP OFF YOUR ASS, AND WORK

It was, in hindsight, not the best time to be starting the personal journey of private renting (although when is?), owing to the small issue of the global financial crash of 2008. Any semblance of hope I had of leaving university and going straight into an apprenticeship or training immediately dissipated into thin air. Abstract names like Lehman Brothers over *there* changed the job market over *here* and my degree was devalued overnight. The recession, put simply, was the result of an accumulation of a decade-long expansion in US housing market activity which peaked in 2006. The housing market was bloated, borrowing was overextended and when the financial markets began to tumble, the bricks came falling down. To quote Michael Burry in *The Big Short*, the 2015 film which charts the run-up to the crisis: 'The housing market is propped up on these bad loans . . . it's a time bomb.' The detritus of that explosion provided the landscape that we were renting in for the first time.

What followed was a devastating unemployment crisis. In the months after the recession the UK unemployment rate was 10 per cent, with almost 2.7 million people looking for work.[1] Youth unemployment was at a record high, with 18-to-24-year-olds accounting for almost 30 per cent of the rise in the unemployment rate. Average rents went up by 16 per cent between 2011 and 2018, while earnings rose by just 10 per cent. This period was the beginning of a national reimagining of work. Training opportunities shrivelled up through lack of funding and many millennials who graduated in the shadow of the recession still experience a training gap. News agencies reported all this with a predictable sense of bedlam. One story that sticks in my mind (that surely wasn't true?) was that graduates were sending out, on average, 100 CVs a month. Another told of a job seeker who wore a sandwich board on the Tube with his CV on it, encouraging people to take pictures for recruiters. Vox pops were done with people handing paper CVs to passers-by at Canary Wharf. More and more surreal and nonsensical stories abounded on how graduates were securing employment.

It was in this climate that I had my heart set on getting into a famously competitive industry. I tried anyway, and benefited from being on the cusp of journalism's move to the internet, writing – unpaid – in equal parts for print magazines, which offered bits and pieces of training, and online blogs, test sites, forums and publications that no-one really wanted to write for – sites that lived and died quickly, thousands of words lost into the space–time continuum of the digital ether, and happily so because they were, almost exclusively, all crap. As it turned out, I was crowbarring my way into an exclusive industry not designed for me and had I understood just how gatekept it really was, it might have been too much of a deterrent.[*] But I happily trundled on with my fifty jobs,

---

[*] Journalism is still laughably unequal. In 2022, the National Council for the Training of Journalists' 'Diversity in Journalism' report found that 80 per cent of journalists come from professional and upper-class backgrounds.

sending some money home, and bringing my own flask of tea to meetings with editors.

Having rent to pay made way for a chaotic and diverse array of jobs that I hoped would bring me closer to my chosen career. So, alongside signing up to every temp agency in the UK, I was also paid for the following: flyering on Brick Lane for a club night called Supa Dupa Fly in the freezing winter, taking pictures at grime and dubstep raves, writing reviews for the *NME* for £30 a pop, doing PR for a record label and writing bios for rappers, one of whom paid me in a brown paper bag full of cash on Deptford High Street. I sold Christmas cards at craft fairs, waitressed at a pizza restaurant and did the odd unpaid internship on my way to becoming a journalist.

Pursuing this dream took me to gigs, journalism courses, parties and events with a lot of free booze. I'd return home drunk to find a housemate in the same state after a shift waitressing at a theatre and crawling to the kitchen, her curls, Medusa-like, springing in all directions. Sometimes we would meet each other at crawl level, hysterical, banging about loudly, or I'd find her lying on the uncomfortable sofa in the living room. All of us were working multiple jobs – waitressing, front of house at theatres, bookshops, various versions of customer service hellscapes, unpaid internships. All this chaos, coupled with the energy of being in your early twenties and defiantly pushing back against the barrage of headlines telling us that there was no hope for anyone brazen enough to think they could acquire employment, made us feel that the ground was falling out from underneath us. But it also made for tight, lifelong friendships. We were hell-bent on finding joy amid the punishing cycle of knock-backs, and the friendship was the undercurrent keeping us all afloat. It's true that scattergun job applications, rereading tenancy agreements and stoically trundling to the estate agents are not often written into the tales of lasting love, but they were for us. For a while it felt like Alice, Fabi and I were part of a trifecta that saved me from completely bottoming out.

Having a degree and no money during my twenties was a completely different experience to the times I'd been hungry growing up. Often my lifestyle did not reflect just how little money I had. I wrote pieces that were either unpaid, or would be paid within 30 days. I had to foot the bill up until then. I was doing a lot of work experience at this time, where part of my job was interviewing celebrities from my bed, spending money I couldn't afford on phone bills, then spending hours doing the agonisingly slow work of transcription, letting the sound of Craig David's voice play out on half speed in the top room. I interviewed rappers at festivals I could never afford to go to if I was paying, flew on press trips, attended live gigs then returned to bed, delighted at the experience, glowing from the inside, luminous and warm – which was just as well because we couldn't afford to put the heating on.

## THE RENT IS TOO DAMN HIGH

Meanwhile, the insipid phrase 'Generation Rent' became a popular way to describe my peers who were facing historic challenges to getting on the home ownership ladder. The moniker caught the imagination of substantial parts of the media gleefully vilifying anyone who deigned to enjoy life's small pleasures, reducing a housing epidemic to an insatiable desire for (yawn) avocados on toast.

I have always known rent is expensive – too expensive – but never really knew what this meant in national data terms. In 2022, the UK is experiencing the longest pay squeeze on wages since the Napoleonic Wars, while rent has reached dizzying and record highs. Rents have doubled over the last decade, and Londoners on average spend two thirds of their income on it. This is by no means normal fare – across Europe, only Paris has higher rents (although the monthly minimum wage in France is the third highest in the world).[2] In Valencia, the average monthly rent for a one-bedroom apartment in the city is €944 (£819), compared to London's €1,940 (£1,683). Put your finger anywhere on a map of Europe and you'll find the same: €1,296 in Lisbon (£1,124), €1,502 in Berlin (£1,302) and Reykjavik, known for its high cost of living, notes an average monthly rent of €1,391 (£1,207).[3]

Amersham Grove was my first collision with estate agents. My mum, aunties and many of the people on my estate that I grew up with had never owned property. My early homes were either provided by the state or recommended to my mum by a friend. Meeting these first ports of call for the hell of private renting at age twenty-two really showed me what it means to be part of the expanded market reach of private housing. (I am not alone: nearly one in five households in England live in the private rented sector.[4]) Renting in London in my twenties in the midst of the recession taught me everything I know now, starting with the unrelenting march of leather-shoed estate agents.

Estate agents, in the modern context, work as intermediaries between tenants and homeowners or landlords. Before the twentieth century, working-class people rarely came into contact with agents because home ownership was for elites. Most of these early agencies (Chestertons, for example, is a family business dating back to 1805) also acted as auctioneers, chartered surveyors and valuers. Today, the UK estate agent industry is estimated to be worth approximately £9.1 billion.[5]

Estate agents are often the first face of a broken ecosystem that we see, and as a result, it is easy to attach loathing to them. In culture, little is done to improve their reputation. In the 2014 fly-on-the-office-wall six-parter from the BBC, *Under Offer: Estate Agents on the Job*, social pariah appears to be part of the job description. One agent, Darren Griffiths, speaking about revealing his occupation at dinner parties tells the camera, 'You get a better response if you say you're a mass murderer.' In 2021, Channel 4's BAFTA-winning comedy *Stath Lets Flats* follows the hapless Stath as he attempts to secure sales with bluster and incompetence.[*] *Stath Lets Flats* might be a comedy, but it's not far off the nation's view of estate agents. One 2018 study reported that 87 per cent of Brits have had a negative experience with an estate agent (91 per cent in the south of England, where the competition is presumably fiercer). In one episode of *Under Offer,* Griffiths gives some possible explanation for their unpopularity, citing the fact that they don't need any

---

[*] In the *Simpsons* episode 'Realty Bites', where Marge tries her hand at becoming an estate agent, her honesty hurts her sales, requiring her to get some advice from Lionel Hutz. 'Instead of small, it's cosy!' he tells her. They do a quick run through this new language. Marge: 'That's dilapidated.' Hutz: 'Rustic!' Marge: 'That house is . . . on fire.' Hutz: 'Motivated seller!'

qualifications for the role: 'That's probably why there's so many shady characters and why estate agents get such a bad name in this country because ... If you wanna be an estate agent, just open a shop.'

There may be a more innate explanation. Estate agents are hated because they are selling something more than a house. They're selling the promise of home, which cannot be easily reduced to a pile of bricks. There are, of course, logistical aspects to consider, like functioning windows and running water, but for people with the luxury to choose a home, what they're looking for is a feeling, a quality that connects us to the deepest part of ourselves, that doesn't welcome the hot breath of a suited stranger on our neck ready to take between 1 and 3.5 per cent commission. Estate agents, like all good salespeople, also legitimise the madness of house and rent prices, giving us the hard sell when they should be enrobing us in a foil blanket.

The details of the housing market are so notoriously complicated that information is also not weighted equally, which skews the dynamic of selling. While many other industries benefit from what is called 'information parity' (where customers generally know as much as, or more than, the salesperson thanks to competitive price checking and information readily available online), the housing market retains an 'information asymmetry' by design, where it is often impossible to know more than your estate agents after a few viewings of a house, or to price-compare a housing market that seems to have no earthly logic.

During the UK national lockdown in 2020, estate agents were one of the first industries to return to work. The first lockdown saw a seven-week shutdown between March and May, but they were deemed important enough to continue working, and during this period they were some of the only human contact that people got. The market had to continue, and so while the streets were empty, many estate agents were still driving around for viewings, framed as a beating heart of the economy.

The stereotype of an estate agent seems to exist in cultural stasis. It's certainly true that most of the ones I've dealt with could have come from any point in modern history, untouched by changes to society – still suit-clad, many still routinely making misogynistic comments about 'men of the house' or homophobic assumptions about girls living together, still clumsily stumbling over keys and hard-selling shitholes to you as if you'd never seen a bathroom in your life.

But let's not get personal. For all the perceived villainy of estate agents, the state is ultimately responsible for creating a private market which enables agencies to exploit tenants. It is interesting, then, that luxury estate agents, or 'estate brokers', have become aspirational. In the US, the stars of the popular scripted reality TV show *Selling Sunset* are blonde, coiffed and ultra-glam female agents of the Oppenheim Group who sell luxury properties on the sunset strip of West Hollywood. These shows, of which there are many (along with 'agent influencers' on Instagram), give the industry a slick sheen, selling power and status. Home ownership is high value, highly revered and always seen as the coveted end goal. In the UK, estate agencies framing the search for a house as a luxury experience often ape the design of metropolitan bars, offering glass bottles of water and modernist, curvy furniture.* The aspirational estate agency the Modern House presents itself as a lifestyle platform more concerned with design than the grisly business of letting fees. This lifestyle-ification of the process even filters down to merchandise. One estate agent, Portico, sells canvas tote bags with typographic designs that you might mistake as coming from a coffee or book shop, in case you want to proclaim your allegiance to your administrator.†

The private rental housing market is built on the lucrative idea of scarcity, which allows estate agents to make outlandish claims about how lucky you are to be in a room with them through storytelling sales techniques. While it's true that the rate of house building doesn't match our need, it is good business for estate agents to overblow this a little. This has long been used as a sales technique. In 1975 a famous 'scarcity principle' study by Stephen Worchel and colleagues illustrated the link between scarcity and desirability with cookies in a jar.[6] They put ten cookies in one jar and two of the same cookies in another jar and measured demand. The cookies that were in scarce supply were rated as most valuable, but crucially it was fluctuation that made them desirable – they moved from being abundant to in short supply and back again. The housing market has not only capitalised on this equation of scarcity with value but, crucially, mythologised

---

* Foxtons made headlines after its Brixton branch had its windows smashed and was sprayed with graffiti reading 'Yuppies Out'. The use of 'yuppies', a distinctly 80s slur to represent the 'young urban professionals' of the period, who under Thatcher bought property that amplified the gentrification of local communities, was striking, a lens onto how much London is still in bondage to policies of that period.

† The website encourages people to tweet or Instagram themselves carrying these tote bags, calling them, in all seriouslness, a 'London icon'.

it. It creates winners and losers of the housing crisis, braiding further competition into an already broken system. We are told to think of housing acquisition as rare, making winners of us when we achieve it, or more readily accepting if we don't – it is, after all, just how it is.

In a thriving market for estate agents, these tactics are encouraged and rewarded. The market is so competitive that it's quickly becoming the norm to speedily move into a house without seeing it, as my housemate Alice did. Eighty per cent of US millennials would buy a property without viewing it, according to a 2021 study by St Louis-based Clever Real Estate.[7] In 2021, in the Welsh town of Aberdare, thirteen houses were sold within three hours of being advertised after dozens of people slept outside the estate agent Bidmead Cook and Williams to bid for homes on a new estate.[8] In New Zealand, reported 'FOMO' – fear of missing out – was cited as a reason for house-buying spikes – a term that has become widely used to explain spikes across Europe and the US, too.

## Luxury, always luxury

For the majority of the population, home ownership is an unattainable luxury.

*The Times*' infamous property section frequently covers young influencers with keys in hand, ring-lit and filtered, looking out at their newly acquired homes. This trope is pervasive on Instagram, where an announcement culture of home ownership is rife. Young entrepreneurs present their homes, telling us that they acquired them through that glorious, delectable thing – Hard Work – and beam. In this context, where a neoliberal house-buying mania has a chokehold on wealthy western countries, a house is a thing for individual pursuit, which feels so very far away from the spirit of mortgage committees of the 1970s. It can be difficult to look at these glossy images wrapped in so much opulence and demand that housing is a right for everyone, because through this lens there are no rights, only rewards. The pandemic turned celebrity homes into content, with people marvelling at Zoom backdrops and gossiping about house prices, while *Architectural Digest* continues to take us into the fantasy of celebrity homes.

Meanwhile, in the buying market, house prices grow to outlandish, impossible heights. House prices rose by 197 per cent between 2000 and 2020.[9] The price of the average UK home has increased almost twice as much as the wages of the average UK worker over the past fifty years,[10] and for the first time since records began, the average first-time buyer is now older than thirty.[11] For most people, simply 'working hard' is not enough. (How does this work for those with chronic illnesses, for those who lose their job?) As Vicky Spratt suggests in her book *Tenants*, Britain is an 'inheritocracy' where solutions are often found in deposits, usually gifted by parents or family members. This is not on an individual level bad – but concealing these gifts validates the lie that we can have these rare things if we only hustle harder.

There are some government schemes designed to make it easier for people to buy homes, but even these are flawed, and changeable. Shared ownership is a scheme where you buy a share in a property (typically somewhere between 25 and 75 per cent), pay a mortgage on that share, and pay rent to a housing association for the remainder. By 'staircasing' (buying more equity over time), you can eventually become the sole owner of the property. But before then, you bear full responsibility for the costs without any of the legal benefits of ownership and can potentially lose all of your equity if you fall behind with your rent. Another option, Help to Buy, requires a 5 per cent deposit, and the government will lend you up to 20 per cent (40 per cent in London) interest-free for five years. But, as Johanna Noble explains in MoneySavingExpert, 'the loan is only for new-builds that are £400,000 or under in value – £600,000 in London – which can lead to unforeseen costs like ground rent, service charges, building safety and quality.' This is all without the obvious challenge that most people will only be able to borrow four to five times their annual income for a mortgage when, according to Simon Youel, the head of policy and advocacy at Positive Money, who spoke to *Vice* in 2021, London housing costs around twelve times the average income.

The truth is that every element of the housing market is gentrified. The housing-industrial complex has bent itself into shape to gentrify – or more accurately 'wealth-ify' – every element of buying a house. Despite the biggest housing crisis of a generation, the lure of house buying is still potent – still a signifier of cultural capital, a flag in the dirt declaring that you've made it. Not only because it can be cheaper than renting,* or may provide the security that

---

* According to the English Housing Survey 2020–21, on average, private renters spent 31 per cent of their income on rent. This figure was higher than for mortgagees (18 per cent).

renting doesn't as long as you can pay your mortgage and the market doesn't crash, but because it still represents a tantalising, glistening fantasy.

## PHOTOSHOP THE DREAM!

Not all prospective tenants are treated equally. Take the representations of properties online. Many prospective private tenants are catered to with slick, high-quality photographs on aggregate house-finding sites like Zoopla. There is a whole industry designed to prop this fantasy up. DCTR (as in 'doctoring', I assume) is a UK company which creates 'property imagery' for a certain clientele used to seeing properties in a certain way. With CGI and other forms of photo enhancement they create well-lit, filtered images of properties, which arguably make for lighter, brighter fictions. DCTR's founder, former estate agent John Durrant, explains his process of capturing a property to me over Zoom – where his background is a *Tron*-like graphic that looks like waves of fluorescent lasers, striking against his avuncular grey hair, white beard and polo shirt tucked into his jumper. 'I use a Canon camera, a wide-angle lens for interiors, longer lenses for exteriors, then use an HDR [high dynamic range] process that enables you to capture the full range of light, from the very light to very dark. You take several photographs at varying exposures and bend them together in a program called EnfuseGUI,' he explains with the air of someone with little interest in the artistic potential of these tools, and in fact says as much. 'I'm not interested in photography. All I'm interested in is making houses look amazing,' he tells me. 'They send the photographs to us and we professionally finish them in post[-production]. You can make a good 25, 30 per cent difference to the effectiveness of the photograph.'

I ask if, by doctoring photographs using photo-editing software, or even receiving pictures that have been caught with a fish-eye lens (to give the illusion of more space), he feels as if he is misrepresenting the quality of the properties.

He looks at me quizzically. 'The question really is, is there any danger that an estate agent might *undersell* a property? And take a picture that makes a £60,000 kitchen look like the lower deck of Noah's ark after a nasty storm?'*

Property marketing companies also enlist the services of models to make high-production videos. One of these particularly beautiful models, Michael, talks me through a shoot day for a recent video advertising an apartment block. 'We were asked to show local amenities,' he explains to me over the phone. 'They set up typical scenarios so in the bathroom I was pretending to shave, brush my teeth, or to just walk through the rooms, pretend to prepare a meal in the kitchen, and watch TV. They're selling you an aspirational lifestyle – like, if you lived in this house this is what it could look like and this is the kind of people that could live in these houses.' He reveals something peculiar about the casting call: 'One of the questions was whether I was a homeowner, which I am,' he notes offhandedly. This detail rings in my head for some time after – maybe it's not just the people who are being sold to, but every person recruited as part of the game who must believe in it. These are all part of a system – images like

---

* The sigh I sighed must have been heard around the world.

Durrant's hook you in, and once you're through the door, the estate agent can begin a sales pitch.

If you are bidding on social housing in the UK the experience could not be more different. A lot of councils organise their housing stock using bidding systems for people on a social housing waiting list, which are known as 'choice-based lettings',* but they don't exactly help you make that choice. On Home Connections, an allocations site for social housing for Lambeth, the photos of available homes are tiny blurred squares – most properties only have one picture showing the outside of an estate or a terraced house. Sometimes, there isn't even a picture, just an address to turn up to on moving day. (These ones show as a white box with a red border and text inside reading 'No Image Found'.) The implication is clear – you get what you're given and you'll be grateful for it. Even the copy on the website reads as if the style guide was written by Miss Trunchbull in her new role at the local council. Here's one:

> First floor flat with one double bedroom. This property is not served by a lift. There are at least 15 stairs to climb to get to the flat. Do not bid unless everybody in your household can manage stairs. We will not be able to nominate you if you are pregnant or there is a child in your household. The accepting applicant will be required to pay rent in advance when the sign up takes place. The amount required in advance will be the decision of the Housing Association.

---

* The logic is that this is a better system than being given housing sight unseen. I am unconvinced by this argument.

The tone is clear – shut up, and put up. Someone close to me recently used the Shropshire HomePoint application system to bid on a two-bedroom new-build property in Shrewsbury and was given a list of baffling requirements. Hearing her talk about it was depressing to say the least: 'They told me I was only allowed to bid once a week on a Monday, and if you don't answer your phone within three rings the housing association will automatically move onto the next person,' she says. You're treated with such hostility that you might find yourself longing for a bit of slimy estate agent sycophancy. It's worth mentioning that the last point about the three rings isn't lawful – so it may not be formal policy, just the bad practice of the local team, one with potentially devastating consequences, that is almost impossible to prove.

## ADMIN IS DESIGNED TO KEEP SOME PEOPLE OUT

Once you've found a place to live, there is another arbitrary, unglamorous mountain to climb: admin. I had to quickly learn a host of new words: break clauses, cleaning fees, credit checks. At Amersham Grove I was pummelled with emails about tenancy fees and had to beg, steal and borrow a 'guarantor', someone in my life who earned £30,000 a year,* and who was close enough to insure me should I miss a rent payment. (My cash-in-hand and low-paid jobs meant that I was not an ideal bet from a landlord's perspective.) The only person I knew at the time who earned over £30,000 and was

---

* That was the requirement at the time. Usually guarantors are expected to be making at least three times the annual rent price of the property in order to be accepted by the letting agent or private landlord.

willing was my editor at the *Guardian*, who I suspect went above and beyond his job description when he agreed to help me, although luckily, in the end a friend's parent stepped in.

After years of moving, being evicted and being ignored by housing associations, I had simply accepted that I had no rights against the omnipotent administrative powers that be. I had submitted to the way of things like an inert bloated slug watching the salt slowly being poured over my body.

It is easy to become overwhelmed like this because the housing-industrial complex is administerial, arduous and exclusive. Tenants awaiting a visa cannot rent property under the Right to Reside policy, which destabilises huge portions of the population. This creates a black market for lettings by unscrupulous landlords who know that the client's lack of a right to rent means that they will not run the risk of enforcing any of their legal rights. Then there are those on zero-hours contracts, care leavers, members of the GRT (Gypsy, Roma, Traveller) community, people who are estranged from their families. Trans tenants are at the behest of the Gender Recognition Act of 2004, which governs the process by which some trans people are able to change their legal gender and obtain a birth certificate. Many landlords ask for ID that may require a gender recognition certificate. This is a lengthy, arduous process. Click on a government website to apply for a gender recognition certificate in 2022 and it will ask if you're eighteen or over if you've been diagnosed with gender dysphoria, and various other invasive questions that include asking 'whether you intend to live in your acquired gender for the rest of your life'. That these questions are required as part of an official administrative process to rent a room may be a contribution, among others, to a situation where one in four trans people in the UK have experienced homelessness at some point in their lives. None of this is a level playing field.

Renting requires a classist admin fluency. The admin I already knew, of managing housing associations, budgeting benefits and writing complaint letters, was useless when I became a private renter. To be a really financially sound adult, it seemed that I needed to know about guarantors and credit scores and felt patronised when I didn't. (As someone who remains too cautious to even get a Tesco Clubcard, I was pretty incredulous when one estate agent recommended that I get a credit card to improve my credit score. I thought that was in bad taste considering that reliance on credit was part of the reason that the global economy was in this mess.)

During this time, despite the government advice to 'catch it, bin it, kill it', I caught swine flu, a result of generally not looking after myself through skipping meals and flyering in icy conditions in thin Primark jackets at night. I spent a week in bed in my room, shivering and hallucinating, circling galaxies, imagining the signs of local estate agent Peter James in neon Technicolor like a *Fantasia* montage, where my months of rent anxiety bubbled to the surface. I saw my fantasy houses appear in vending machines that unfurled and hit the base as I entered pound coins and retrieved them with a claw, dreamed that I bought every house on the Monopoly board, and once, that I died in my sleep – erasing my credit history, leaving guarantor checks and deposit fees behind me.

## Taking power back

Many landlords are simply not equipped to deal with the job, thanks to the fact that there is no formal training for the position. Many may not even have money to pay for smashed windows or a broken boiler and so the whole cycle becomes highly stressed. A stressed landlord with little money to pay for a new boiler, a stressed tenant, all leading back to a stressed state.

We need to radically reimagine the parameters of what it means to be a benevolent landlord. The bar is so low that we often accept way more than we should, and get less than we deserve. Sharing knowledge about this process has to become the work of the individual and communities, as well as institutions. What would it mean to have a lesson in school about guarantors, or to hand out dummy tenancy agreements? To have Instagram pages dedicated to information sharing? To facilitate pop-up workshops? For now, I make it my business to tell any youngsters about the dreary and unglamorous side of admin. (I have never pretended to be fun.)

The one benevolent landlord I had understood that rents did not have to be set above the market rate, that it was possible to provide housing that paid a mortgage without using the tenant as a slot machine that required shaking down every month. Profiteering ramps up in times of crisis. We tend to burrow down and save every penny, extracting as much as we can from what assets we have. This is not the behaviour of a healthy society. Difficult times pose a challenge on how to work together, whether to discuss rent waiving (something seen successfully during the pandemic), or resist evictions. (This is, if we are thinking of less radical solutions in the short term – the long-term goal, I hope, is to abolish the current system of landlords altogether.) In my locality, grassroots organisations like the London Renters Union, for instance, front campaigns titled 'Can't Pay! Won't Pay!' They help people negotiate rent strikes and reductions, under the recognition that Black and Brown tenants are disproportionately under threat of rent debt and homelessness. Landlords and estate agents are all arms of the same body. The thing is, we have arms too, to punch out, grab information and try to begin pushing the ooze from on top of us.

## CLEAN-UP WOMAN

I was still obsessed with the black abyss that lay behind that fireplace, but after some months I had learned to manage – or at least live with – it. We stacked bricks in front of The Creature, doubled up on cardboard fortifications, and I learned to walk by without screaming. Amersham Grove was, all in all, the kind of place which is only funny in retrospect, an anecdote told with a grimace at dinner parties (which I did), because to find it really funny would be to suggest that there is enough distance between then and now. In truth, an Amersham Grove might easily be in my future. My next house, even.

Before we moved out it became clear that cleaning affected our deposit, and so we were sent into a spiral about what abstract cleaning standard we were expected to deliver. We had all heard tales of landlords keeping deposits because of a sock left under a sofa, and one of my friends told me she was deducted £200 for not cleaning the fridge properly (she missed out a shelf). So we went for a maniacal approach to scrubbing, propelled by fear. The threat of losing money I desperately needed had a direct effect on the intensity with which I cleaned that stupid fucking house. We became hopped up on a kind of mass hysteria and found ourselves cleaning places no-one in their right mind would check – corners of the inside of cupboards, the top of the fridge until it shone, steam-cleaning sofas and carpet. I found myself on my hands and knees scrubbing the floors, with the spectre of a nameless, faceless landlord standing over me. My housemate took it upon herself to take hundreds of pictures of each room on a digital camera to prove there was no damage that we had added, except maybe the crime of just existing, and so please, could we not be charged for this? She sent around 50 gigabytes of jpegs to the estate agents in question, which, to our amazement, worked.

I learned about how to navigate the system at my first proper rental. It was grinding, but not enough to dampen my enthusiasm for a novel stage of my life. I was still excited to look for another place, pleased to be part of a system that allowed me to do this over and over, and maybe get a better one next time. I was already in submission to the fact that I would never own a house, so I figured that I had better get really good at playing this game. I thought my experience would make renting better, easier, fairer the second time around. I was wrong.

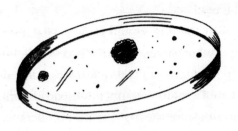

## Pepys Road – How we protect
## our health

Pepys Road was the first of many rentals in London where I had mould, which presented as a lightning bolt that had struck and cracked the wall in my bedroom, splintering into electric tendrils.

I moved to this first-floor flat in New Cross in 2010 with my same housemates and an added boyfriend. It was one of the thousands of Victorian conversions across London, on a long, leafy road favoured by students which was named after the celebrated diarist Samuel Pepys, another Londoner who lived through his own plague epidemic in the 1600s. Though historical accounts assure me that Pepys was not among the group of high-risk people who had to endure cramped housing or 'mixed with the poor'.\* The road did not mirror the man, then, but did represent some of the stories that make up

---

\* In fact, biographer Claire Tomalin wrote in *Samuel Pepys: The Unequalled Self* (2002) that 1665, when the plague was wreaking havoc in London, was 'one of the happiest years of his life', where he quadrupled his fortune.

this city – of a decrepit, failing present built on the sovereign myths of the past.

After the issues of Amersham Grove, a flat felt more manageable than a whole house. The bar was in hell, but I was still excited to live somewhere where features – like doors – just worked. I shared a room with my boyfriend but only his name was on the tenancy for the first few months because I couldn't get a guarantor organised in time. Sometimes, we'd have spot checks from a landlord who didn't know we were sharing a room, and I'd run around madly while the girls kept the landlord busy at the door, kicking my shoes under the bed, removing any trace of female presence in the bedroom (how easy it is to erase yourself). By the time I was able to add my name, the mould had got totally out of control and I was more than ready to start really powering up my complaint mode.

Alongside the mould that grew up the wall, another haunting image of that period was seeing the sky turn grey and pour with rain as I watched, live on TV, the town car drive the new prime minister, David Cameron, into Buckingham Palace in 2010. The powerful rhetoric of New Labour's neoliberal meritocracy – that your success is hinged to you, that only you decide your quality of life – intensified under Cameron's political project. He dreamed of turning Britain into an 'Aspiration Nation' (a phrase first used at the 2012 Conservative Party conference, but which underpinned his whole time in power), celebrating those who '*wanted* to be better off' (subtext: whatever you want, get it yourself). The main thing I aspired towards in 2010 was a room to live in that wouldn't make me sick.

If you live in the UK, you will probably encounter mould

at some point in your life. It's a pervasive and severe symptom of British housing thanks to the age and condition of our housing stock. The World Health Organization (WHO) estimates that between 10 and 50 per cent of European indoor environments where people live, work and play are damp.[1] In 2020, official figures reported that an average of 3 per cent of households in England had damp in at least one room of their home[2] – that's around 850,000 homes. There are two main types of damp which cause mould – rising, where groundwater seeps into the bricks of a building, and penetrating, caused by leaky roofs, or faulty guttering. This house had both. Over time, the mould in my room was spreading, rising like an infernal smoke.

Mould is very bad for us.* It can produce allergens that cause skin rashes and asthma attacks, infections and depression, where mycotoxins can cause lesions in the frontal cortex and result in dopamine dysfunction. It can be really serious – fungi like *Aspergillus fumigatus* can cause lung infections such as farmer's lung, and *Stachybotrys chartarum* (black mould) can cause organ failure. When mould toxins accumulate in the body it can lead to brain fog because mould spores act as irritants, which can trigger the body to mount an immune response. This can lead to inflammation throughout the body, and chronic inflammation in the brain might result in long-lasting cognitive impairment – or even kill us. It's also hardly a fringe matter. While it affects us all,

---

* As far back as biblical times toxic mould would grow on stones inside or outside houses and was rightly feared. Once discovered in or outside a house, the stones on which it grew would be taken and thrown outside the cities it was found in. Its discovery led to house demolitions and contamination fears and was, basically, taken much more seriously than landlords do now.

it's estimated that 5 per cent of the UK population are *particularly* sensitive to fungal spores – over 3 million people.[3] In 2022, the death of two-year-old Awaab Ishak, which was a direct result of exposure to mould, made national headlines and reinforced how dangerous a public health issue this can be when left unchecked. Landlords are dealing with matters of public health way above their station. Regardless of the condition of the house, more often than not, the rent gets paid, which means that landlords are rarely motivated to fix the issue.

In an effort to learn more about mould, I travel to Cranfield University one January morning in 2022 to speak to Naresh Magan, professor of applied mycology. We meet over chamomile tea in the atrium of the campus, a slick glass building – where mould could surely never settle – as students mill around us. Prof. Magan is immediately likeable – an expert in the field for thirty-five years, he left apartheid South Africa to study in the UK, finding passion in fungi. Dressed in navy cords and jumper with a soft sweep of white hair not quite reaching the top of his head and neat, silver glasses, the first thing he does, with a twinkle in his eyes, is to finesse my hackneyed, inaccurate language. 'The fungus is not a plant,'* he emphasises. 'And it's not an animal. It's in between. It is its own thing. It is made up of different kinds of proteins and carbohydrates and so on. And then there is the nucleus, and it may be multicellular.'

He explained that fungi are able, from a single spore, to colonise large surface areas, using enzymes to degrade

---

* Interestingly, fungus needs oxygen, and will produce carbon dioxide. Fungi, they're just like us!

materials and absorb any nutrients present. They can grow on something as seemingly un-nutritious as a brick. He also explained that lungs happen to be a perfect site of reproduction for mould spores; at 37 degrees Celsius, they act as a warm, moist Petri dish. But not all spores are dangerous to our health. As Prof. Magan notes, 'we are all breathing in a thick microbial soup', and 'airborne inoculum' – the name for spores clustered together – is everywhere, moved by hoovers, coughs or even by someone entering a room.

He makes a connection between this knowledge and housing solutions. After a natural disaster like Hurricane Katrina for example, mycologists were called to measure for damp in the houses that were saturated with water. And there is already some – albeit limited – precedent for mycologists to consult on private building work. With this in mind, I raise Prof. Magan's blood pressure by telling him some of the solutions I've heard from landlords. He frowns. 'Ventilation is always useful. But if you have a damp wall and the water's coming from outside, because you've got a leaky pipe or gutter, that's not going to help much. In reality, there is very little you can do aside from rebuilding.' It sounds hopeless, but there are other ways to advocate for our own lungs made fragile by the mould-infested rooms so many of us find ourselves in.

## Are you there, Landlord? It's me, Kieran

When I complained to my landlord about the mould – equipped with much less information than I have now – I was advised to get something called a 'damp trap' to solve my problem. Dutifully, I trundled along to Khan's on

Peckham High Street, a local superstore stocked full of most things a person needs to survive this life, and left with a plastic damp trap for a quid. These boxes are full of silica and various other toxic substances (including anhydrous calcium chloride, a corrosive, blinding chemical which the trap warns against skin contact with) which are supposed to absorb moisture in the air. I put the little chemical-filled plastic boxes in the corners of my bedroom and when that failed, my landlord advised that I simply bleach the wall. I stoically did what I was told, ruining dishcloths and tea towels, soaking them in boiling water and bleach, cleaning the smudge and destroying the colonies of life from the wall that had migrated to my chest, only to find them reappearing a few weeks later. My asthmatic housemate at the time was told to paint over hers – something, by the way, which doesn't really work on bad cases because fungi are designed to thrive on porous surfaces and a single cell can reproduce a millionfold. A can of run-of-the-mill Dulux is just not designed to counteract this kind of biological warfare long term. The surface simply chips, peels and bubbles as evidence of an ecosystem gaining ground, getting ready to win the war.

I became obsessed with the creeping black patch rising up the wall, which seemed to grow bigger the more I tried to extinguish it. When I rolled over at night my arm would brush against the cold, wet mould and I'd flinch. I thought about the mould colonising the complex latticework of fibres and tubes in my lungs, cilia-clogged pockets, and beat myself up, wishing I'd never had so many cigarettes in club smoking areas. I imagined tiny little weapon-wielding spore-men occupying my chest. I gazed at the stain on hungover mornings, making shapes in the growth patterns like cloud formations in the sky. I saw ugly, Rorschach-like images of minotaurs that kept coming back every time I wiped it with a damp cloth. I wrote long email complaints to my landlord, frustrated and annoyed. He suggested that I stop drying clothes in the house.

I also became addicted to Reddit threads and community message boards on Mumsnet – the dark sides of the domestic internet – and was sent links to industrial-grade mould killer that you could buy on the black market. I imagine now, with more knowledge, all the morphological features of the different spores I inhaled – microscopic matter with thick-walled spheres, long, thin, spiked surfaces, tiny clusters of oval-like seeds.

I started feeling the impact of my chest tightening, which at first I put down to paranoia, but it then became a frequent heaviness. My then boyfriend would make jokes about me as *The Secret Garden*'s sickly protagonist Colin, who is afraid to go outside because of the 'spores'.* After a while, the smell became more noticeable – an earthy bouquet of dirt with just a few notes of putrid decay. I was self-conscious about it, dousing myself in Body Shop vanilla perfume so I perpetually smelled like a big marshmallow. As a music fan, I even had to cut that down, not wanting to sing and dance in my room in case I inhaled too deeply. I stopped inviting friends over out of embarrassment and burned incense in

---

* In the 1993 film adaptation, Colin has a meltdown at what he calls 'the little things in the wind that get stuck to your lungs!!' and the freakout he has is guttural, wailing and thumping the floor.

my room to give it a new scent identity. I got a warning from the landlord about this after he came over to do a spot check – as if I were a professional arsonist whose plan to burn down my own home had been foiled just in time. I used the opportunity to ask him about the mould again, and he said he'd get to it – in the meantime, maybe I should open a window? When the mould inevitably occupied my body, attacked my lungs and made its way through my bloodstream, giving me various chest infections, I thought about that fucking window comment, and each breath I took made me crumple my body in defeat.

Constant moving hinders being able to easily advocate for your health. As a workaround for this, I managed to retain the same GP for longer than I should have by not telling them that I had moved. When asked for my address at the front desk, I memorised old postcodes. Luckily, postcodes are designed to be memorable – according to a Royal Mail survey, 92 per cent of people can recall their home postcode, thanks to the teams of cognitive psychologists who came up with them in the 1950s. They are a product of various research findings: that short-term memory has a capacity of between five and seven pieces of information, and mixed numbers and letters are easier to remember. This helped, because though I felt guilty for scamming our sacred NHS, it did really help my chest that I was able to spend that winter talking to a GP that had known me for years.

I longed for a fit-for-purpose centralised database to log complaints against landlords. There was one, for a time, but it was, to use a term from a housing lawyer friend, 'useless'. As it happens, rogue landlords can easily move from borough to borough enacting their worst practices. It is a perverse system where tenants are required to jump through countless referencing hoops but landlords aren't required to provide testimony from former tenants. Landlords rely on tenants to pay their mortgages to keep them afloat, a fact never far from my mind when I was struggling to breathe. I like to imagine how these reviews would read – long pieces of irate literature, built to go viral.

But this is not a matter of dragging and cancelling individual landlords on Twitter (though that might be a start) because the stakes are bigger than the theatre of online rage. The consequences of untreated mould can be fatal, and they are not felt equally. Poorer families are more likely to suffer from poor indoor air quality.[4] Of these, Black and Brown households are more likely to have damp problems than White British households.[5] Disabled people are often left in conditions that can accelerate disabilities. Health is tied up with how we live, our personal sense of agency and the extent to which we are able to advocate for it.

During the first year of the Covid-19 pandemic, the images of airborne spores flying around in red and blue were plastered all over the media. News reports spent months telling us that our lungs were precious, but also fragile and exposed. The death count in BAME communities was disproportionately high. In May 2020, Public Health England recorded earth-shattering data that, as a woman of colour, rocked me and my community: BAME patients who had contracted Covid-19 had a 10–50 per cent higher risk of death than white patients, and within that group, Black patients were at highest risk.[6] This is directly related to unequal housing and access to healthcare (as well as employment and pre-existing co-morbidities). The virus has further exposed just how desperate the housing crisis is, and that our health is impacted by our living conditions, doubly so for people of colour. Part of the national conversation should have been about putting pressure on landlords, giving them the opportunity to think about what to do about the damp and mouldy conditions of their housing stock. It was not. Rogue landlords bank on our frustration and lack of agency to accept these potentially fatal terms.

Then there is the racial health gap. This phrase refers to evidence that white patients receive better treatment from healthcare providers than racially marginalised communities owing to individual and systemic racial bias, where subconscious racism can affect how we diagnose, treat and care for non-white patients. This racial health gap spans across everything from the assumption that Black people have a higher pain tolerance, to poor education on how certain illnesses exhibit on darker skin, to disproportionately high rates of death in childbirth. This is coupled with the fact there are specific medical areas in which people of colour require specific attention – asking questions about how migration affects bodies, or the ability to break down vitamin D and lactose, for instance.

With this in mind, it's curious that there is no accessible research that looks into potential racialised elements of mould-related illnesses – asking the question whether BAME people with co-morbidities are affected differently. Prof. Magan offhandedly suggests that widespread skin spore allergy testing might be a place to begin. The more I reflect on this the more I realise that this could be truly revolutionary work.

## LET THEM EAT CHEESE

Artists around the world have begun to explore mould in new ways in their work. After all, mould is fascinating, and fungi themselves are having what trend writers might call a 'moment'. In music, North Carolina-based artist MycoLyco and Vancouver's Tarun Nayar have become stars of #mushtok – the mycology-centric corner of TikTok – by attaching modular synths to mushrooms and letting the music do its thing. It sounds a bit like pitchy ambient electro: imagine the product of a few weeks in a studio with Brian Eno and Kraftwerk. Activist collectives like @fungi.futures put on events and workshops to investigate the 'potential to map radical alternative futures'. On Netflix, the acclaimed documentary *Fantastic Fungi* explores the majesty of mushrooms, while exhibitions like 'Mushrooms: The Art, Design and Future of Fungi', which I visited at Somerset House in 2020, zoned in on their medicinal uses and cultural impact, and the future possibilities of eco-design. In 2021, *Vogue* ran the headline 'You aren't tripping: fungi are taking over fashion'.[7]

The distinctly unfashionable spatter of mottled mould, like a black fissure being released as a spray across the corner of my Pepys Road bedroom wall, was devoid of glamour. I chat about this with Avril Corroon, a visual artist based in south London who grew up around the damp conditions of Westmeath and Dublin. Her work sets out to explore the 'potential for damp as a material' for art. We talk in her Deptford studio where there are clusters of mould cultures which she has collected from her bedroom and fermented to make a cheese culture. Her plan, she says, her curly hair bouncing in mischief, is to make cheese that looks artisanal, wrapped beautifully, with the fantastical intention of feeding it to her landlord.

The work (which is imagined, to be clear – she doesn't *actually* plan on poisoning her landlord) reappropriates the fetishised mould in expensive cheese. It looks convincing too, up to the veins that perfectly emulate those in Stilton. (Imagine the scene! The landlord slowly unwrapping the package to consume their own mould!) Her point is that everything packaged as a luxury item is based on the exploitation of others – and that includes housing.

Dark twisted fantasies aside, Corroon's latest project, 'Got Damp', explores how to present mould as a material condition, born out of negligence, in a way that confronts the public with the reality of people's lives. After doing numerous call-outs for damp houses (including flashing red capitals on Instagram posts asking 'Got Damp?'*), she interviewed people and took samples from their homes to exhibit. 'Mould is still something that we fear because it reminds us of our own decay,' she explains. 'Its proximity is dangerous.' She sighs. 'If you can propel yourself 200 years into the future people will be like, "I can't believe they lived

---

* A phrase that harks back to 1971, when residents of Thamesmead organised to highlight the issue of water seepage in their newly built homes. A visiting MP, with delegates from the Greater London Council, was greeted by a poster so powerful it led to remedial repairs. In the windows of residents were three accusatory words: 'I'VE GOT DAMP'.

in damp", like we are about people putting lead make-up on their face.'

I ask her what it means to take this material out of working-class homes and into more middle-class gallery spaces to be presented – and even admired. After all, for any work on this subject to be meaningful, it should always circle back to empowering the tenants or else, what's the point? 'I hope that it is an accusation,' she emphasises. 'It is political and confrontational by nature.' I troll her by saying that her work might be ripe for gentrification – I wouldn't be surprised to hear local art students imploring her to make opulent mould necklaces out of resin. She grins, leaning into her Irish lilt, 'Well, they can fuck off.'

Before I leave, Corroon teaches me how to make DIY spore traps to catch mould spores in the air. The process includes filling Petri dishes with a mix of agar and barley malt (the malt is a nutrient source to encourage growth, while the agar, a seaweed extract, is used to solidify the medium). She leaves them open for four hours or so, and then monitors which spores have been caught as they grow.

When I ask Prof. Magan his professional opinion on the efficacy of this, he baulks at the idea of uncontrolled conditions where unsterilised Petri dishes are used in dirty rooms. This is unsurprising, seeing as we have this conversation in a sterile campus laboratory, both dressed in lab coats and goggles. He makes some initial exclamations about the precise measurements being off, and how an aerosol collection device would do a much better job. But before I leave the lab, to save me from my own unscientific mind, he gives me a parting gift – two perfectly sterile dishes, one with a golden film labelled 'YES' (yeast extract, sucrose), and the other 'MEA' (malt extract, agar), and sends me on my way. After some back and forth he agrees that the DIY method will simulate a desired effect, though his emphasis on precision, I feel, must be passed on. (He advises that you spray dishes with alcohol first, making sure they are airtight, as if you're making jam.)

I do this later that evening, plotting Petri dishes around my house, and after a few days, they transform. One has white wads of cotton-like mould circles; in the other are colonies of green and orange specks with a deep grey outline which turns to black – the whole thing is fascinating and nauseating every time I allow myself to peer in. This kind of DIY work is empowering in its potential. It could be used by tenants' residents' associations (TRAs), as a way to document and prove the existence of dangerous spores like *Stachybotrys chartarum* to doubtful landlords.

## LIGHTS, CAMERA, ACTIONABLE ACTIVISM

Poor-quality living conditions, especially damp, are galvanising issues for communities exercising their political agency. Activism is its own sprawling, breathing life form – exposing cracks that have been hidden and demanding something better with persistence and quiet power.

Sometimes, solutions come in unpredictable forms. One of my favourites is a piece of equipment that is a key player in our history of mould activism: the Portapak. This heavy, unwieldy video recorder arrived in Britain in the late 1960s from Japan. From the mid-1970s through to the 1980s, tenants, film makers and artists used it to produce what came to be known as 'damp tapes' – videos that documented the level of damp (and other negligence) in homes. Much of the activism we benefit from today would not have been possible were it not for this camera, which by its very design forced collaboration (because, well, it was heavy).

The Portapak consisted of a playback deck that went over your shoulder, a separate camera and a microphone, and could require as many as three people to operate it. It also, crucially, had an instant playback feature. The closed loop of production afforded by the technology enabled marginalised communities to have agency over how the films were made and shown. These damp tapes were then shown on TV monitors at tenants' meetings, and to housing officers and local councils.

Ed Webb-Ingall is an artist and researcher whose book *The Story of Video Activism* explores in more detail the history and significance of the Portapak and community video activism. 'The story goes that the Sony Portapak, which was the one that most people used, was the equivalent of buying a small car, around £1,300,' he tells me over Zoom. 'They gave four to the Rolling Stones and one to each of the Beatles. Then John Lennon either lent or gave his Portapak to a guy called John "Hoppy" Hopkins, who lived in squats in north London and started using it to make videos.'

Many of these stories are hearsay, but it's true that Hopkins went on to form the Fantasy Factory, a facility that revolutionised low-tech video editing, bringing it within reach of community activists. And, so, Sony's original plan to gift technology to artists for behind-the-scenes musical footage became a crucial resource in the fight for safe housing as tenants saw the potential to embarrass local councils.

Webb-Ingall explains that the 'largely white, middle-class' squatters living around London in the 1970s documented their experiences with other tenants. They took the expensive equipment out of the hands of the elite and into mouldy kitchen corners. The groups that made these tapes include Swingbridge Media in Newcastle, who produced *Don't Talk Wet – Dry Up* (1983) with the North Kenton Residents Group; the Easthall Residents Association in Glasgow, who made *Dampbusters*; West London Media Workshop, in Notting Hill; and Albany Video, in south-east London.

The endgame of these damp tapes was not necessarily that a councillor would see the mould and come to fix it. Rather, it was to illustrate the collaborative nature of the work: showing that tenants could organise. The work was, in part, in the making. The very existence of the damp tapes showed councillors that building community was powerful and that the residents had a voice and the ability to use it.

Recording housing abuses is a tactic that tenants continue to employ. People brought cameras to housing meetings after the Grenfell disaster, recording responses of managers in real time. On TikTok, tenants post videos documenting their living conditions to thousands of followers. Activists like @KwajoHousing routinely upload videos of distressing mould-ridden housing conditions that go viral on Twitter, and in 2020, during the Covid-19 pandemic, Housing Action Southwark and Lambeth (HASL) invited their members living in overcrowded and temporary accommodation to use their smartphones to record the impact of government-sanctioned quarantine measures on their families. This method of recording to speak truth to power is not new – it is an element of our modern life that connects us to activists who have come before us.

Councils are still slow to act, and in some cases, sceptical about the severity of health dangers in homes across the country. Tenants today can push back on this inaction by gathering proof of cold spots, damp and mould in their homes. If, say, tenants' and residents' associations could crowdfund for, or be gifted, thermal-imaging cameras (TICs), they could share this equipment with local residents, and provide an opportunity for collective teaching, enabling more people to prove their poor living conditions to sceptical housing associations. As part of the writing of this book I spent some of my advance on a TIC for this exact purpose.

In theory, you could lodge a claim against your landlord for disrepair or unfitness for human habitation as a legal remedy to mould-related negligence. But this is very difficult in practice because there is, simply, a dearth of housing lawyers in this country. As of 2022, across England and Wales, 41 per cent – that's around 23 million people – do not have access to a local legal aid provider for housing advice.[8] Most disrepair claims now also fall outside the scope of legal aid, meaning that unless tenants can afford to pay a lawyer or can find one willing to work on a 'no win, no fee' basis, they will not be able to access representation.

Housing barrister Angharad Monk condenses the complexity of the system to me as concisely as she can. 'You can only get legal aid for disrepair claims if you can prove that there is a serious risk of harm to health and safety,' she explains. 'It can be argued that mould falls in this category but it often requires proof from a doctor's letter, so it is still very difficult. Mould is also very problematic in housing law as when it is caused by condensation resulting from design flaws (like poor ventilation) it is not considered to be "disrepair".' Until the Homes (Fitness for Human Habitation) Act was passed in 2018, mould caused by condensation was not actionable at all.

For Prof. Magan, local housing associations, TRAs and property developers would do well to build a relationship with mycologists – and an exciting future sees mycologists invited into discussions about social housing stock (what if this was standard across social housing?) and to feed into the unregulated market of the built environment. Though mycologists are occasionally employed as consultants on building projects, seeing this as par for the course would be transformative. I love to imagine this trifecta of art, science and community activism.

## DR MARTENS DON'T SOLVE, THEY STOMP'

We have a tendency to look back and to lament our youthful ignorance – if I had known what I know now, maybe I would have pushed harder to get that wall repointed. But really, would it have made a difference? My housemates and I tried our best and our complaints remained unanswered. I still have some of these sent emails, each one getting more desperate, riddled with spelling mistakes as my fingers shook with rage. I guess that only made me easier to ignore – not a serious candidate for response, and they became just another addition to the landfill of tenant complaint emails which clog the inboxes of landlords across the country.

I have one clear memory of stomping down the road in my Dr Martens one winter's afternoon to the estate agent in New Cross. I pleaded my case on deaf ears, which ended with me kicking over a bin and hollering at a perturbed lady behind a slow-moving Dell. This fit of mania got me banned from the offices. My housemates were annoyed that I ever thought my rage would have helped. I had made a bad situation worse, but what do you do when you have nothing but fury coursing through your veins and no power to effect change? When it comes to health, there is no respectable response.

During this time, my journalism was starting to take shape. I interviewed some of the most exciting artists of my career – Erykah Badu, Dr Dre, Mick Jagger – and went on thrilling press trips in five-star Marriotts in Miami after interviewing P. Diddy backstage – 5,000 miles(ish) of separation from my real world. When I returned from these trips, I would flop back onto my bed at home and dream of Miss Havisham's mould-ridden wedding cake. Though the mould was penetrating my dreams, in real life I could push it to the back of my mind. My career life was finally getting somewhere, and I felt the joy of building something, getting paid to write(!), spending hours in my room writing, occasionally huffing on bleach residue and feeling moments of pure joy whenever I got published.

Despite that, I didn't want to spend *all* my time at home sucking up spores so I went out a lot, saying yes to invitations I wouldn't have otherwise accepted. I went to the Turner Prize to see artists I wasn't excited by; I listened to 'soundscapes' at noise nights that sounded like thousands of nails hitting a concrete floor; I went to house parties hosted by people I didn't like, stayed on for afterparties and woke up on strange floors. I saw *Aida* at the National because I got a free ticket (I didn't like it) and attended two different amateur productions of *The Vagina Monologues* just because. The mould pushed my cultural palette forward, I guess.* I did also discover things I loved – exhibitions that moved me, cheap tickets to National Theatre shows that made me fall in love with theatre, the British Library sound archives, dhol players who made me feel close to my nanaji, and many, many friends and mentors (Emma, Rahul, Tim) who helped along the way. I am eternally in awe at how lucky I was to be held by all these things when I needed it.

My housemate's chest was suffering worse than mine, so we eventually made the decision to leave. After I packed, all that was left behind was a bed and the black stain on the wall, like the projected shadow of someone who had lived there. As I heaved boxes with a Polish mover he noticed it immediately, felt the moisture in the air. He lifted a box with a grimace, first to his knees, then again to his waist and gave me some advice: 'That looks like mould,' he whistled. 'The landlord should do something about that.'

---

* When I got a weekly clubs column in *Metro* I thought it had worked out perfectly because I could spend weekends out of my room.

# A note on some of the floors I've slept on

My earliest memories of sleeping on a floor, besides sleepovers with my cousins, are at my masiji Debbie's house. Between Meifod Cottage and the Swanage Waye house we had nowhere to live and so piled onto the living room floor of my aunty's house in Ealing. Her floor was covered with thin lino, a cheap alternative to wood. It was a slick, lacquered, nut-brown shade, easy to sweep and clean and fun to slide on in your socks. For a few months we made that floor home by layering cheap polyester quilts, jumpers, blankets and pillows on it in the evening, where my mum, my brother and I would sleep. The hard floor made itself known through the low-tog quilts. When you turned in the night your arm would slide across the floor, and if you slept on your side too long it felt like a gentle bruise on your hip when you woke up.

I loved it. If you ignored the faint odour of my aunty's Silk Cuts in the kitchen, it felt like a never-ending fantasy sleepover. I luxuriated in the space that stretched further than the confines of a single bed and felt like I could roll twenty times in either direction. I would starfish my body, imagining an *MTV Cribs*-size bed, and then in the morning, jump up to transform my bedroom back into the living room again. I didn't want to move from there.

Over the years, I became adept at quickly folding up mattresses and pillows and socks kicked off in the night, transforming living rooms back into communal space. Constant moving requires us to be invisibly in transit.

After a period of not being able to find work and a break-up, I moved into the spare room of my friend's younger brother. I was out at sea with no firm next place to live and I stayed in his house, inheriting my own stop-gap sibling from my friend. It was a proper boys' house – no houseplants and a strange, surreal poster above my bed. There was a bet between him and another housemate to buy the worst poster they could find – the sort of 'take me to your leader' calibre that you would find in the Perspex poster racks of a Virgin Megastore – and the one that ended up above my bed was a truly upsetting image of a monkey on the toilet with the word 'Shit'. During the stay, I was going on housemate auditions and at night I slept under that poster in a sort of hysteria-filled amusement, not feeling like I could take it down because this wasn't my house, and really, it summed up how I felt.

Another time, between moves, I briefly lived with a friend's older sister, and I got to know her as we shared a bed for a few weeks while my shit was in various places all over London – I'd kind of just let go of it out of sheer fatigue. It may be one of the reasons I do not like to let stuff go now. Sometimes I remember an item with a jolt, say a top that I love that I haven't seen since, and I wonder where it is before just releasing it into the world. It was probably in one of those boxes that never got collected. This was my first long stay in east London, in Hackney, where I didn't have my local community and so she shared hers with me. One day I came home to find that she had emptied a drawer, folded all my clothes and placed them gently inside. I often think about the loving folds, of how generous she was to share a small space – and a bed – with me.

Moving may not be your decision to make, especially if you are at the mercy of state negligence in the form of social housing, or private landlords, or a change in financial circumstance. I speak to counselling psychologist Dr Jaspreet Tehara on the impact this continual moving can have on our brains. 'If we don't have stability in our subsistence needs (food, shelter, warmth, clothing, hygiene) as a baseline, we can find it difficult to move on to other elements of life,' he tells me. 'It's harder to address more of the higher-order issues such as love and belonging, self-esteem and self-actualisation. So in living in places for short periods of time, we move from a position of thinking about living, to a position of focus[ing] toward existing.' In short, living in flux makes it harder for us to think about our own self-development. I often wonder what that means in a society where moving is an increasing part of the experience of modern life, and what it means that so many of us may not have the space to think about things as central as love and belonging.

With this in mind, I am grateful for people in my life who gave me brief respite from the adrenaline-fuelled, manic dance of moving, who let me catch my breath and stay still.

# Oswyth Road – How the internet has a say

There's a running joke that relationships are shaped by the housing crisis – that thousands of people in this country have propelled their unions forwards thanks to the promise of cheap shared rent. The joke isn't really a joke when you consider just how many people this is a real necessity for. A 2016 study by trade site Ziffit found that of over 2,000 people interviewed, almost a third admitted that financial security was a key reason they were with their current partner.[1]

My first real experience of love gave me an insight into what it means to share space as a couple. After scamming the landlord at Amersham Grove by sharing a room, my boyfriend and I moved to a tiny one-bedroom flat in New Cross Gate, a new-build that cost £700 a month and couldn't fit both of us in the kitchen at the same time. If we cooked, one of us would have to sit on the countertop. We danced around each other, restricted by meagre square footage, and argued quietly before storming off to different corners of the tiny bedroom. When we broke up, a year after we moved in, the heartache was acute but made worse by the fact that I couldn't afford to continue paying rent, so I had to find somewhere else to live.

The Splitting of Things™ led me to strange, previously concealed corners of the city. One of these was a storage facility called Big Yellow, branded in sunshine yellow for a distinctly un-sunshiny time of life, a business in part bankrolled by teary couples wandering up and down metal corridors like some kind of mad ministry for broken hearts. I paid £25.25 a week for a 20-square-foot room which housed all my most treasured things, and sometimes I would put myself inside there too, the small space reminding me of that kitchen, and cry.

My timing was off kilter with my friends' who were in tenancy contracts they couldn't get out of, and so after a break-up that snapped the muscles from my bones tendon by tendon, I was left flailing, broken and with nowhere to live. I whimpered on floors in Bristol with Kasha, in spare rooms in Wales with Tom, in my mum's bed, and in a box room in a friend's younger brother's flat in south London. I became a cliché: I reread *High Fidelity*. I listened to a lot of Fleetwood Mac. I dyed my hair. I smoked a lot of grotty weed. Then, finally, like many before me, I turned to the worst possible place for a vulnerable person in search of an ego boost: the internet.

It had become common around this time for someone in search of a spare room to participate in the unhinged, competitive process of housemate auditions. In 2014, I wrote about this trend for *Grazia*, which ran with the headline 'The housing Hunger Games' – an accurate portrayal of the fight-for-survival dystopian landscape of renting. As if we hadn't already half-killed ourselves trying to get a job in the recession, now finding a room was a battle to the death, too. In the year I was miserably scrolling through house-share sites, the Joseph Rowntree Foundation predicted that 1.5 million extra 18 to 30-year-olds would be priced out of buying their own homes within eight years.[2] This resulted in a flooded rental market, and sites such as SpareRoom boasted more than 3 million registered users in the UK. It is still the largest flat-share site in the country, with 2 million users a month. And the phenomenon is global – in the US there is Kangaroom, in Singapore Roomies, IndianRoomates in India, TokyoSharehouse in Japan.*

As you probably know, SpareRoom is a flatmate-finding service. It gathers all the prospective housemates in your area and lets you filter the search according to your preferences for anything from smokers, pet lovers, vegetarians, job titles to gender. Crucially, it asks you to upload a picture. After a while, trends begin to appear. (In 2014, Pantone declared 'Radiant Orchid', a muddy lilac blush, as the colour of the year and I'm not sure whether it was cause or effect, but you could see it popping up on walls, bedsheets and cushions in pictures.†)

The whole system is an imperfect solution to the fact that millennials (those born between 1981 and 2000) are

---

* I trawl through some of these and find universal constants: a pair of Malaysian Chinese sisters looking for a room near Tiong Bahru, a 'hygienic and sensible' single man looking for an apartment in west Singapore, an 11-room 'women's share house' in Shibuya for 44,000 yen (£266).

† In 2022, it is 'Very Peri', a kind of deep blue-toned violet, which apparently represents, among other things, 'possibility'.

victims of historically high rents and barriers to home ownership. Millennials are half as likely to own a home at the age of thirty as baby boomers (those born between 1946 and 1964) because of higher prices and low earnings growth. It is a symptom of the times – in the 1980s it would have taken a typical couple in their late twenties around three years to save for an average-sized deposit. Today, it would take nineteen. As rent prices increase – the median monthly rent in England between April 2021 and March 2022 was £730 (£1,430 in London), higher than at any other point in history, according to the Office for National Statistics (ONS) – more and more renters are turning to house-shares.[3] Renters are getting older, too. Those in their mid-thirties to mid-forties are three times more likely to rent than twenty years ago. This is directly linked to astronomical rent costs. SpareRoom's own data shows that there's been a 239 per cent increase in 55 to 64 year-olds looking for house-shares between 2011 and 2022.[4]

If you're interested in a listing on SpareRoom, you send a message and then meet up for an interview to view a room. I became part of a carousel of prospective tenants, sitting in strangers' kitchens, overhearing the person before me getting quizzed and cringing at their answers. Sometimes there were group interviews, all of us shuffling together like a sociopathic *Lord of the Flies* social experiment where the most brazen among us made loud jokes. Some people had the genius sales gene and chose to talk about things that were mainstream or acclaimed enough to elicit positive reaction: *The Wire*, *Friends*, how Gamu was robbed on *The X Factor*. Owing to my broken heart, it was too much of a strain to be fun. It was already a

Herculean effort to wander around strange rooms in the city looking for housemates.

This clambering towards respectability is alive in the buying market too, evidenced by the rise of 'buyer letters', which are personal letters sent from prospective buyers to sellers to give them an edge. These 'pick me' letters, often saccharine and fawning, are not unlike mass-produced wedding invites in style, with floral borders and calligraphy flourishes. There are even templates on Etsy with intimate cursive script that say things like 'We love your home' and, even more creepily, 'We know you've made many memories in your home ... we are just a young couple looking to find a family home to call *our* own'. Incidentally, after much searching, I have yet to find a buyer template with a picture of a non-white couple.*

At one of these particularly hellish property viewings, I was asked whether I liked Coldplay or Pedro Almodóvar films (cursed choices) to decipher whether I was a worthy candidate (*what* do these choices say about a person?). At another viewing at a housing co-op I was told that everyone did one big shop on a Sunday, everyone had to cook for the other five housemates at least once a week and there had to be a liberal approach to drug use – which I might have already worked out, considering the fluorescent green bong that greeted me when I walked in, the orange lava lamps illuminating the living room and the copies of *Fear and Loathing in Las Vegas* and *Mr Nice* on the shelf. Sure enough, after I looked at the (admittedly spacious) room, the guy showing me around had one last, hopeful question for me: 'So, do you take acid?'

---

\* I'm not advocating this kind of representation, merely observing.

Housemate auditions are problematic in many ways but are made truly sinister by the fact that tenants are given extended landlord powers to determine who lives in a house and who is rejected. This process, known as 'churning' (referring to a churn of tenants), benefits landlords who can then receive rent without having to go through the hassle of finding new tenants themselves. There are a number of ways this is organised: sometimes, housemates jointly pay a deposit, select a room and one – usually the most organised member – collects the rent and pays it over to the landlord. Sometimes, all tenants pay separate direct debits to landlords. Sometimes people sign tenancy agreements, sometimes they don't. Then, sooner or later, when one of the tenants wants to leave, they find a replacement, and all you can do is hope that the deposit handover goes smoothly.

Live-in landlords are another flawed and troubling feature that crops up in this process. They, more often than not, disrupt equal-power dynamics and indulge in power play (even if not consciously) because whatever happens, they will never be the one who has to move out. This is often justified by the promise of – hopefully – cheaper rent. We should not accept the terms that dictate that this is the only way to achieve that and instead, fight for cheaper, capped rent across the board.

The process of finding a new housemate can reveal an ugliness in otherwise reasonable people. In my experience, when tenants are granted the power to make these selections it can lead to uncomfortable and arbitrary policing. It also enables tenants to discriminate on the basis of race, class, sexuality, gender identity and age.

This process can be particularly egregious when the power

dynamics translate to men looking for female housemates. I have been on the receiving end of a few lascivious men asking what time I go to bed, or what I sleep in. In 2019, the Women's Budget Group reported that thanks to the gender pay gap, there was a gender housing gap too, and there was absolutely nowhere in the country that was affordable for a single woman on an average salary to buy or rent a home.* This puts many women at the mercy of house-shares and high-priced private renting, when they should have access to social housing. This is uniquely troubling; the number of women in England who are homeless and living in temporary accommodation has increased by 88 per cent in the last decade.

During this time, I was writing regularly for the music section of the *Guardian* and hosted a weekly music podcast for them, which unbeknown to me made me a candidate for bribery. One email I recently unearthed from this time reads:

> Hey Kieran!
>
> So ... There's one room left in what has been a very popular house so far. Although there are about a dozen people interested in the [£]520 room, I liked you and thought we'd get on. So here's the deal – you try and get [redacted] and I [*sic*] in the Guardian and the room's yours. Deal?

There was no deal. But I did eventually find a place. After months of housemate auditions, bobbing around on sofas and

---

* The same ONS data shows that across England, average rents take 43 per cent of women's median earnings and 28 per cent of men's.

in box rooms, I secured and moved to a four-person house-share in a dilapidated but very cheap (at £400 per month) house in Camberwell. I thought a lot about how refugees, or people without the ability to make the arbitrary cultural grade, would get past housemate auditions. I, it seemed, could pass thanks to the cultural capital afforded by the *Guardian* and Goldsmiths, a heady combination that sent me into a deep identity crisis and my first tentative taste of what I think is known as 'middle-class guilt'. The fatigue of moving had really got to me at this point because I would routinely take the wrong Tube back to my previous house, brain going through the motions, unable to distinguish between the spectres of an old life and my new one.

The house was a revolving cast of white women of my age. In my experience, living with white people, generally speaking, can come with its own tax – you can feel like you're not just representing yourself. With strangers, race is usually carefully danced around, and cultural inflections are open for fascinated dissection. Once, one of my housemates walked into my room and marvelled at my plastic tissue box, thinking it was a family heirloom jewellery box. I just let her believe I was part of some kind of royal Indian dynasty. In the first few weeks of moving in, another housemate called me 'coloured' in what she thought was a friendly, throwaway descriptor. One of the other housemates, Lerryn, who I had met just a few days earlier, to my surprise, jumped up, a blush rising up her face, and shut her down. We became friends immediately.

## A PLACE TO HEAL

An 1875 'Brief Account of the Parish of Camberwell'[5] suggests that the name may have originated as 'Cripple Well', and that the settlement developed as a hamlet where people from the City of London were expelled to when they had a contagious disease like leprosy. They came, allegedly, for treatment by the church and the clean, healing waters from the 'Camber Well'. It was, it seems, a place where people who were broken and rejected, whose support systems had turned their back on them, went to make their home on the margins. Whether or not this is true, it was the perfect backdrop for me, living disconnected in a community which for months didn't expand outside my house, in a single room, alone, waiting to be healed.

This house, then, felt like a win. (After countless interviews I'd failed to acquire at least six places, and like a bad date spent time spiralling about what it was about me that made them pass.) On a popular estate agent's site, a listing for the house next door bizarrely boasts that the property has 'an almost Dickensian view of London'. It would be more accurate to say that the interior was Dickensian, an old Victorian house prone to damp, cold, cracking plaster, a sunken roof and windows that rattled and shook in the night. It needed the kind of care that none of us were fully invested in giving it, and it was the first house I lived in that I felt completely unconnected to – I had moved in with strangers out of sheer misery and had no real attachment to the place. It had three bedrooms (four, including the living room) and two bathrooms, one so freezing that the draught would chill your bath water before you got in it.

It is relatively normal for renters not to have a living room. In 2019, 20 per cent of people aged 20–30 (often described as Generation Rent) in London didn't have a living room at all.[6] In the same year, 90 per cent of the properties on house-sharing websites advertising rooms for rent in London had no separate living room. An increasing number of landlords are letting out living spaces as extra bedrooms for increased profit, squeezing money from any space they can. And in a desperate and competitive market, they can get away with it. This has become normalised in rental accommodation. In 2018, Patrik Schumacher, who took over as head of Zaha Hadid Architects, argued that millennials didn't need living rooms, as news stories abounded on how 'hotel-room-sized' studio flats were ideal for young people who led busy lives.

To put it lightly, none of this is ideal. The National Sleep Foundation has consistently advised against working in your bedroom. The cognitive association between bed and work leads to poor sleep, which in turn harms your mental health. I knew this, but I still spent hours propped up against the head-board like most of my friends; my spine slowly curving as I bent over my laptop, trying to make a writing career happen. I had a small tray which I would use as a makeshift desk on my lap, and I put chocolate Hobnobs in the cup holder for a treat. As I lay in bed typing for hours, I was probably giving myself early onset scoliosis, and a specific, rent-crisis-related strain of RSI.

## URL v. IRL

We have to sell ourselves everywhere, all the time, under capitalism. This drive is fed by the internet and makes its way into our vulnerable moments. When searching for a place to call home, we often brand ourselves online as more interesting, more fun-loving, more sociable than we really are. This pressure has only swelled – it already seemed haywire in 2014 when I was searching for a room, when Instagram was only four years old, and I felt it even then. Since then, Instagram had grown from 10 million to 1 billion users.

It's not surprising that the internet has become embroiled in housemate natural selection. This process of uploading ourselves on sites like SpareRoom as part of a house-search illustrates just how much the internet has shaped us, becoming the lifeblood of our contemporary lives. Here, it acts as a useful filtering process, allowing us to cut through the sheer noise of housing demand. The way we are selected is invariably tied to how we perform online. Saleability has, depressingly, become an increasingly potent feature of the housing crisis.

Our IRL and URL lives cross over so much that we have gamified the banality of landlordism. In the game *Animal Crossing* your landlord appears as a digitised racoon. In *The Sims 2: Apartment Life* and *The Sims 4: City Living*, if a Sim has a good enough relationship with the landlord, there is a chance that their rent will be reduced. In the Metaverse, there are opportunities to buy residential land to build on. Landlord Real Estate Tycoon, which describes itself as an award-winning geo-localisation Monopoly-game, is basically Monopoly in app form, rewarding developers. (This has captured the imagination of the public: in 2021, Hasbro advertised a life-sized Monopoly game in Tottenham Court Road with the tagline 'Win the challenge. Buy the property. Own it all', as if we are not already living in a landlord's game hell.*)

Moving is so tedious that an increasing number of apps have gamified that, too. The Big Moving Adventure teaches kids about moving, while Unpacking is a surprisingly tender meditative puzzle game where we learn about our narrator by unpacking boxes and putting away their contents. Postdates (which is actually quite useful) is a third-party delivery service app for the retrieval of stuff after a break-up. Move House is a game that requires you to shift boxes from place to place and the user reviews pretty much sum up the real-life experience it imitates, with one reading: 'This looked like it was going to be a fun game. I was really looking forward to playing it when I downloaded it. It turned out to be a huge disappointment.'

The real world is often even less fun. The internet may pervade almost every element of our housing lives, but there is no logic to how deranged this relationship has become. In 2016, City Park residents in Salt Lake City were given a 'Facebook addendum', taped onto their door by their landlords. It claimed that each tenant needed to 'friend' the building's Facebook account within five days, or be faced with potential eviction. On TikTok and Instagram, houses often have their own renovation accounts. In the market-place, you can buy a house with bitcoin and in 2017, a house

---

* Ironically, the original Monopoly of 1904, titled The Landlord's Game, was intended by its creator Elizabeth Magie to be a warning about monopoly capitalism, a 'practical demonstration of the present system of land-grabbing with all its usual outcomes and consequences'.

in Essex made headlines after being the first property in the UK bought entirely with cryptocurrency. Home ownership has become so tied up with the idea of luxury that accounts on Instagram that routinely hold competitions to win houses online have started to pop up with worrying frequency. @ RaffleHouseUK (17,100 followers) offers the chance to 'WIN a Dream Home ... or tax-free cash!' @Omazeuk (33,500) invites you to 'WIN a Million Pound House', while crowd-funders use Twitter to help with housing deposits. In these cases it is the lucky ones that go viral, who might have a compelling enough story to achieve this goal – luck being part of the whole rigged game of home ownership.

Online, there is an unsaid requirement to perform an idealised version of our self who has good credit and a range of interests, is interesting and funny, and contributes a sense of 'worthiness'. In her essay collection *Trick Mirror,* journalist Jia Tolentino notes our 'optimised selves' as something she says is built into the design of the internet. She writes, 'As a medium, the internet is defined by a built-in performance incentive ... And, because the internet's central platforms are built around personal profiles, it can seem ... like the main purpose of this communication is to make yourself look good.' When it comes to housing, the stakes are higher than usual. This isn't about amassing an online following from Twitter hot takes, or the hope of a brand deal, but about the difference between having a place to call home or not.

Meanwhile, landlords, who already use their own bias to determine who lives in their houses, outsource this power to tenants, many of whom use social media as a way of find-ing people. The internet has propelled the already dizzying competition of the housing market by giving us opportunities to pick and choose from who an algorithm throws our way. Just as there's an online cyborgian 'look' – small nose, catlike eyes, contoured cheeks – there is an ideal housemate online, who would make us richer by association. You can see this being exploited when people upload themselves on Instagram or Facebook, doing open-source call-outs for rooms to rent, where the pictures of themselves are as mesmerising as the descriptions.

Many people don't even have the chance to be part of this game. These systems of selection ignore those with no internet (1.5 million people in the UK)[7], or those with no finessed and practised internet language, or those who are not filter-literate. How these people fare in the politics of online desirability is a consideration seldom made in the rush to amplify our online footprint.

Capitalism has normalised extraction. We extract value from our friends all the time, compartmentalising them into different categories depending on what they offer us. We might have a funny friend, a political friend, a party friend, and it can at times feel like we are collecting identities that reflect well on us, as if life was one big Instagram post. We live in a culture where marginalised communities are routinely expected to explain their identities to those outside of them. We have become used to asking ourselves the inevitable question: what do *I* get out of this?

Of course, it would be silly to suggest that we don't – or shouldn't – have preferences for the people we live with. An optimum housemate for me, for instance, might be someone who has a houseplant, reads bell hooks, enjoys Chicago house and would share a Domino's Two for Tuesday with me.* But this is a fantasy, not a prerequisite. Because no matter how big our list of preferences, should we be ascertaining 'value' in this way when the stakes are so high? Why should I benefit from someone else's need to be housed? These are questions with no clear answers, but what is clear is that making such huge assumptions about identity, respectability and value in a single meeting or arbitrary online description is bad for us – and bad for culture.

Data shows that over half of people google their dates before meeting them. There's no official research on how many prospective housemates are googled, but I'd wager that it is much, much higher. There are many reasons why you might do this. Loud racists online, for example, are best avoided, but the problem is that we're all acting on the internet so you need more than good luck if you're recruiting a housemate off the back of a good Twitter presence. This desire feeds a lie that abounds online: that we should be having optimal lives, perfect housemates and frictionless experiences all the time.

If you have any kind of social media presence it is almost assumed that you will be doxxed or at the very least surveilled – fair game for would-be dates, employers and housemates. A rogue opinion on the new Beyoncé album or political affiliation could make a pariah of you and mean the difference between a house being offered to you or not. These insidious ways of constructing respectability are potent, they feed into the entitlement that we all should be able to access

---

* One Tandoori Hot, one Veggie Volcano.

one another's private information. This is a world where our digital footprints have a direct line to our IRL selves.

## No curry smell! No Biryani Babes!

Self-branding and hyperactively selling yourself online can have 'rewards'. But there is a digital elephant in the chatroom – our online world is not a level playing field.

'Unconscious bias' or 'implicit bias' are terms to describe how prejudices can be drip-fed into our consciousness. In 2016, Dr Jennifer Eberhardt, a psychologist and author of *Biased: Uncovering the Hidden Prejudice That Shapes What We See, Think, and Do*, published a study alongside her colleagues showing that people who saw photos of Black families subconsciously associated them with bad neighbourhoods, no matter how middle class those families appeared. The last few years have seen plenty of projects and studies exploring solutions to the problem of unconscious bias, and the small but necessary steps we can take to unlearn our worst instincts. 'Prejudice habit breaking' encourages us to call out stereotypes, gather more individualised information about people, reflect on 'counter-stereotypical' examples, adopt the perspectives of others and increase interactions with different kinds of people.

This is potentially urgent work because there's no getting around the fact that all elements of the housing-industrial complex are racialised. In 2016, Fergus Wilson, one of the UK's biggest buy-to-let landlords, whose Kent property empire was then thought to number around 1,000 homes in Ashford and Maidstone, was made infamous after instructing estate agents not to rent to 'coloured' people 'because of the curry smell' which 'sticks to the carpet'.[8] (I think the 'coloured' here refers specifically to people who look like me.) Wilson also, incidentally, ordered agents at Evolution Properties not to rent to 'battered wives, single parents [and] low income and zero hours workers'. In 2017, the Equality and Human Rights Commission found this ban 'unlawful' and it was overturned,* but this is not to say that this kind of discrimination doesn't endure. When I called around local businesses in Ashford to ask locals what they thought of the ruling most were disgusted by Wilson's ban, but one lady told me, 'I thought he must have had a point.'

And this is not an issue limited to the UK. The welfare organisation Hong Kong Unison found that more than 90 per cent of those belonging to ethnic minority groups have been discriminated against when looking for housing. In 2016, French estate agent Laforêt advertised an apartment in Levallois-Perret, an expensive suburb of Paris, with a bold upper-case message which read: 'ATTENTION, IMPORTANT INFO FOR THE SELECTION OF A RENTER: French nationality, no blacks.' In 2021, David Merryman, the 56-year-old owner of dozens of rental properties in south-eastern Virginia worth over $5 million, told Black tenants that they should 'go back to Africa'. In 2022, Airbnb had to apologise after advertising a 'slave cabin' on their website, a former site of horror from the 1830s now offered as a place to stay and have breakfast. There are thousands of stories like these.

---

* Wilson called this ruling 'political correctness gone mad'.

It is the extreme examples that make headlines and the more nuanced instances of bias are harder to identify and prosecute. Unconscious bias is a particular problem in a highly competitive rental world. One study in 2016 conducted by professors at Harvard Business School revealed that 'requests [on Airbnb] from guests with distinctively African-American names are roughly 16 per cent less likely to be accepted relative to identical guests with distinctively White names'.[9] Anecdotal reports from the 2016 Twitter hashtag #AirbnbWhileBlack about Black people's struggle as both guests and hosts on the site went viral. Internationally, homes owned by people of colour are appraised for less than their value. In 2021, a Black couple in the US sued a company who valued their home $500,000 less than when a white friend posed as the owner (and added pictures of her white family and stripped the property of 'African art'). This idea, that white people are the most desirable tenants, persists.

The internet, the tech industry and the housing market are all broken when it comes to matters of race. One example of how that combination can come to a head is the relatively new – and unregulated – screening industry, which runs checks on prospective tenants. This industry has grown over the last two decades as the rental market and the real estate analytics market have boomed.[10] As news site The Markup explains, 'the companies produce cheap and fast – but not necessarily accurate – reports' but they are nonetheless used by an estimated nine out of ten landlords across the US.[11]

It can play out like this: in 2018, US citizen Marco Antonio Fernandez was asked to undergo a tenant screening for an apartment – a process involving credit, criminal record and eviction checks. The screening's algorithm-based software rejected him for an apartment after it found he had a drug conviction, confusing him with a Mexican alleged drug trafficker called Mario Alberto Fernández Santana.[12] Fernandez is one of many. There have been hundreds of federal lawsuits filed against screening companies over the past ten years. In the UK, the industry is growing rapidly. As it does, we need due diligence to prevent these new technologies enacting some of the worst (racist) practices of the current system.

This discrimination is woven into false narratives that demonise working-class people, especially those of colour. It was only in July 2020 that it was ruled unlawful to refuse tenure to a tenant in receipt of benefits. Before that, 'No DSS' (Department of Social Security) was a frequent and aggressive term used to deny housing to anyone on benefits, making housing in this country inaccessible for the vast majority of those most in need of it. The implication was that being on benefits rendered people untrustworthy, prone to leaving properties in feral states. Never mind that residents on benefits, like my mum, often make these houses more beautiful, and revel in the opportunity to take care of them. The representation of those who need help from the state continues to be so aggressive and effective that landlords who might never have come into contact with this demographic already believe that they don't want them, before they've even learned their names.

Some racism is protected by law. The UK's Right to Rent policy requires private landlords to check the immigration status of current and prospective tenants. In 2019, the High Court challenged this, proposing that this practice was racially discriminatory because it caused landlords to disfavour British citizens from minority ethnic backgrounds and foreign nationals who had a legal right to rent. But in 2020 the Home Office appealed against that ruling and won, claiming that though some landlords did discriminate, it was still 'justified' as a 'proportionate means of achieving its legitimate objective'.

## FRIENDSHIP

With this in mind, it's no wonder, perhaps, that I was excited to have managed this capricious system to be awarded the prize of my room in Camberwell. The excitement was short-lived.

This house in some ways resembled my experience of the internet: it was cool, detached, with little tribes forming, logging in and out at will. There was a novelty I enjoyed – new products in the bathroom, posters of bands I'd heard of but never *heard* (Bastille? news to me). I got to test new perfumes (great), got peer-pressured into sharing clothes (not great), saw various anonymous boys in the kitchen in the morning in their Calvin Klein boxers (sometimes great), and stumbled into dinner parties where I got a lot of free food by proxy (excellent).

The biggest source of my anxiety was a mouse infestation that added to my sense of disconnection: unloved rodents in an unloved house. I would wake up at night with a start, hyper-aware of any sound, a spider sense, homing in on the sound of a coat label quivering in the draught, a shadow on a wall, any imaginary rustle, mistrusting my senses as I felt a phantom running up my leg. My phobia of mice was exacerbated by the fact that I couldn't stop my housemates from eating Domino's in bed (as I'd spent many prior evenings doing myself). The landlord wouldn't pay for pest control, and it was too expensive (at £500) to pay for ourselves. So I trawled the local pound store for sticky pads, which were almost worse when they were effective. I would hear the blood-curdling squeaks of a trapped mouse and frantically shout for help. The mouse situation was exhausting, and out of my control. This was a house where I couldn't have the heating on when I wanted, felt the frustration of the cleaning rota, of the administrative tone of house meetings, and for me, heartbroken and single, of the need to assimilate if I wanted to make friends. My housemate Lerryn was experiencing the end of a relationship too, and we zoned in on one another like two planes circling aimlessly, looking for a place to land. She was working various café jobs, running around and coming back with pastries, ready to change clothes and beckon me out of the house. I was running around too, interviewing people, doing cover shifts at magazines, though I also had nothing to do for at least three days of the working week, which chimed perfectly with her café hours. And so, we spent time learning about each other's worlds, made fun of each other and met each other's families.

Over the year I listened to a lot of Chicago house. It took me out of my room and cemented my friendship with Lerryn, who was always up for joining me on a dancefloor. It's a genre that finds joy everywhere, birthed in tiny wood-panelled homes, town hall pubs and the corners of people's homes, where many of the pioneers were queer Black and Latinx dancers taking up space in a climate of hate. I channelled some of that Chicago ecstasy in south London, through listening to collectives like Teklife and RP Boo, lots of Frankie Knuckles and the vocal stylings of New Yorker Barbara Tucker. I went to clubs and wrote about finding my community on the dancefloor, at London club nights like Night Slugs, Livin' Proof, Visions and various others no longer with us (RIP). When I heard the mouse in my room scuttling about, I put on Boiler Room sets of MikeQ in New York and transported myself to another place, turned up my speakers and hoped the bass would scare it away. We spent a lot of weekends up against other bodies and throwing Dickens' *Bleak House* out of my mind.

The level of intimacy that develops in friendships brought together by crap housing situations is sometimes akin to romantic relationships. When I heard a squeak in my room in the middle of the night, I would pad across the hallway to get into bed with Lerryn. At the sound of the door opening, she would silently, sleepily, shuffle her bum forward to make room for me and I'd get in, falling asleep in silence. The comfort of these shared moments taught me a lot about how we find allies in housemates who get it, who get us. Sometimes, all the feelings of isolation, of support, of both dealing with a break-up and hurriedly having to move into a strange house, of coming from different worlds and meeting in the middle, are expressed in those moments of sleepy generosity and bum shuffles. Thank you, Lerryn, for making room for me.

## SPOILING MY BALLOT

The other problem with this system of auditions is that, like a job interview, once you're in, you feel a sense of responsibility to fulfil this covert contract that you may have agreed to. I had said that I cooked meals, baked cookies and went to the Camberwell College of Arts final degree show. I didn't do any of that. I lied in the interview, talking some nonsense about how Anish Kapoor was a genius and how much I loved sculpture, and was now under pressure to come up with the goods. And for some of the housemates, I suspected that I was falling short. Capitalism sees us all through what Marx calls our 'use value', referring to the features of a commodity that fulfil a human requirement, want or need, or which serve a useful purpose. My useful purpose was to operate a tagine and have an opinion on the Turner Prize. After I moved in, when I'd get high and come downstairs to the kitchen at 1 a.m. and shake my box of Fruit 'n Fibre to unearth pieces of dried coconut, waking up my housemate who slept in the living room, I had the distinct feeling that I wasn't adequately providing this use value.

My time at this house came depressingly full circle. After a year, one housemate moved out, toppling the power dynamic, and suddenly *I* was the overlord who had to host interviews for prospective tenants. I had moved from prole to ruling class, from serf to monarch in one fateful swoop and I tried to deflect power immediately, attempting to opt out of the whole system. This led to much messy conversation about having a say – I had the luxury of a vote but was purposely spoiling my ballot(!). I doubled down and ended up with a housemate I hated but had squandered my privilege to complain about it.

When I lived on the Green Man Lane Estate, we learned how to live together holistically. When I lived with Jafari, we learned how to protect each other, and when I lived alongside seven strangers in halls, it was an exercise in appreciating each other's differences. None of those people were cherry-picked for me. There is no perfect, curated housemate, and the search for one is usually fruitless, and misses the point of communal living. If we removed the selection process, would we all be easier to live with? I suspect yes, because it would force us to work out how to negotiate and compromise with one another, adopt conflict resolutions that work, learn from each other in ways that go beyond extraction, and become used to managing different kinds of people. These are all skills we should take beyond our front doors.

Eventually the owners of the house decided to sell and we all had to move out. Lerryn came with me, to start another adventure together. I had emerged from the heaviest debris of romantic wreckage thanks to friendship and laughs and many days spent in bed smoking and chatting like the grandparents from *Charlie and the Chocolate Factory*. I had gained something real from the mess of the internet hoop jumping and felt brand new. Then, as a new search began we turned to what we knew, a place that could help us realise our dream, and fired up the internet.

# A note on Stuff

We may like to believe that our lives could never be reduced to mere boxes of stuff. We like to believe that we, so special and important, require more drama to reflect the enormity of the event. But packing is a humbling process for my ego – it never takes as long as I think. The lives we lead can be picked up and put somewhere else over the course of a weekend.

I have moved so many times in my life that I should have the choreography down. But I've never quite perfected the sequence of packing, then neatly unpacking a new life. There have been many occasions where I could have finessed this dance, but instead got so fatigued I just scooped up my belongings in various Sainsbury's carrier bags and threw them into a car. When I moved from Amersham Grove I was so tired I tried to throw my table out of the window rather than carrying it down the stairs. My housemate Fabi told me she was sitting in the living room and saw pencil shavings and bits of Blu-Tack fall from above like debris from a nuclear storm and figured I had lost it. When she came upstairs she found me heaving the legs at an angle ready to launch the table into the street.

Despite the act of moving being touted as one of the most stressful things we can do in our lives, I find the packing up is the easier part – it is more difficult for me to imagine how to make something 'my own' without just filling it with a load of stuff, as if the stuff is an extension of me. I want to just enter a space, fill it with my impeccable energy and let the work of home be done, my *vibe* doing the labour for me. Occasionally I end up going full Marie Kondo – whose book *The Life-Changing Magic of Tidying Up* has sold more than ten million copies – and gleefully throw out bags of possessions; other times I cling sentimentally to old trainer boxes that once housed Jordan Vs, now filled with old gig tickets.

When I can't buy furniture to make a house feel like home, I use workarounds – adding flourishes to existing, often neutral, furniture using blankets or carefully putting up pictures with Command strips. Once, out of sheer desperation for a shelf, my housemate, not wanting to email the landlord and begin what could be months of back and forth about purchasing shelves, got high and posed a better solution. Rather than buying shelves we'd have to keep and carry to our next place, could we somehow staple cardboard boxes to the wall and use those instead? (Sigh.) Landlords want us to be traceless, to avoid picture frames on the wall, to preserve their commodity shells. At the same time, we are in an epidemic of overproduction.* Capitalism wants to

---

* As Marx noted back in 1848.

remove the traces of workers' hands and the conditions of labour from the things we own. This structural weight is bigger than us and our desire is, more often than not, by design. So, to submit or resist?

Moving encourages me to submit. In those moments something breaks inside me and I want *everything* because moving gives me permission to spend and reset – and suddenly, I feel entitled to nice things. I feel guilty for being a *champagne socialist*, glugging down a desire for mass-produced crap. In the middle of a climate crisis I still want cheaply made lamps and bookcases and candle holders. I want rugs and ceramics and jugs for imagined visitors and I want art posters to frame all the cover stories I've ever written and I want vases and . . . I want it all. I want to gorge on all the local wares, I want to buy my identity, gluttonously consume homewares, buy myself a life. I want to mimic the houses of the artists and writers and even politicians I've interviewed. For everything I want, I berate myself and keep walking past the shops, but it doesn't curb the desire.

I know that capitalism wants me to make a relationship with things instead of people. Larger systems than me encourage my desire for overpriced, pastel-coloured, body-positive candles, and to think that buying them is a radical feminist act. I know that the impulse towards consumption suffocates us, creating an insatiable market that corrupts our ideas of what it means to be a fully realised human. I rage about this in the day, but then at night in my dreams there I am, stroking my naked body against the buttery velvet of a jewel-tone blue sofa from Loaf that an algorithm somewhere has shown me every day that week, the one that's advertised on the side of the 21 bus. In this recurring dream, I run my fingers against the fabric telling myself a lie over and over again: I've made it.

We all feel buried and delighted by our stuff, and thinking about what to keep and what to release has become part and parcel of a very modern housing crisis. I reflect on hoarding after gorging on some episodes of a show with the same name. The show shames people with various traumas who build walls of stuff around them to protect them from the world, only for it to suffocate them. An estimated 2.5–6 per cent of the UK population (that's between approximately 1.5 and 4 million people)[1] are affected by hoarding in a way that becomes unmanageable, according to Hoarding Disorders UK, but the language and shame around this prohibits us from knowing the true figures. I suspect they are much higher. For those suffering with ADHD, where clutter can make symptoms feel worse, the advice to combat mess is to aim for 'baby steps' progress – that the act can be a mediation. In this context, clutter can appear as a series of mini failures or unmade decisions which creates acute stresses and overwhelms. 'Baby steps' progress is a useful way for us all – neurotypical and neurodivergent alike – to think about how we can manage this endless barrage of stuff weighing down on our ability to feel like we're managing well.

Watching *Hoarding* makes me wonder who can accumulate this way, filling rooms with stacks and piles, until I realise that now I am an accumulator, too. Some of the current items that I have carried around for ten years of moving in London consist of: a box of rusty Primark gold hoops (various sizes), a Geri Halliwell yoga DVD, some commemorative packets of Kate and William royal wedding condoms (?), tiny amounts of currencies from around the world and a box of phones including my old BlackBerry Messenger, Sony Ericsson and Nokia 3210. I cannot articulate why.

Of course, capitalism and accumulation go hand in hand, but when does hoarding become too nauseatingly grotesque? These shows want me to think it's when rats start running around in between bin bags but as we already know, this is because we have just normalised being exploited by those who hoard wealth at everyone else's expense.

William Morris's pursuit of the radical potential of beauty to transform human lives for the better continues to inspire ideas of home as a setting for art. His often-repeated quote 'Have nothing in your house that you do not know to be useful, or believe to be beautiful' tells me that the things I feel now have always been felt and considered, a comfort that connects me to homes past and present.

Why do we like the things we like? Is our taste our own or simply a product of a marketing industry bigger than us? I think that both are true – we are defined by advertising that encourages us to optimise our homes* but also focuses on the nostalgia of youth. We are pulled by the things that remind us of our early homes (in 2021, there was a 56 per cent increase in searches for lava lamps, the preserve of many 1990s households – and many 1960s/70s households before then, reinforcing the cyclical nature of these trends.[2] Our

---

\* The DIY and homeware sector thrived during the pandemic, as many people tried to buy new life experiences through colour and texture and sage green and painted arches and emerald bathroom tiles and pink velvet sofas and framed posters as an escape from the horror of outside. Online sales of DIY products grew by 50 per cent during the first lockdown, and the boost in the UK economy in late summer and early autumn 2020 was in large part thanks to a 9.9 per cent increase in DIY and homeware spending.

taste for this created by our own histories, which can feel like a brief respite from the rampant taste policing of capitalism.

In 2018, I investigated what happens to our digital assets after we die – our bitcoins, Apple libraries, Kindle books – and spoke to people who are writing digital control into their wills, appointing 'legacy contacts', or someone to take over their social media account when they die. This is meant to limit the conflict between family members who might have different ideas about their recently deceased loved one's online future. (My mum, I think, would want everything deleted, while my 25 year-old sister would probably want to scroll through my Twitter feed to connect with me in a uniquely Gen Z way.) I wonder where my stuff will go when I'm dead, and what I really have to give away, anyway. All my most precious things are precious only to me – a decades-old local newspaper where I got my first by-line, a clubs column in the daily *Metro* which got canned in The Cuts (like most of the clubs it described), international train tickets and love letters.

If I were to die now, the only substantial things I'd leave behind are a coffee table and a yellow vintage Versace jacket. Perhaps this is the enduring lure of IKEA furniture: the knowledge that it won't outlive you. A Billy bookcase doesn't remind me of my mortality, not like the oak dressers or wooden trunks that my mother-in-law bought in the 1980s when the world was different, built to last.

# Peckham Rye – How gentrification is a housing issue

In 2016, I finally landed in my 'dream' place,* renting a two-bedroom ground floor flat in a three-storey Georgian townhouse overlooking Peckham Rye. The view from the window in the living room (turned bedroom) was made famous in the 1760s thanks to William Blake's visions of angels that he claimed to see in one of its oak trees.

My flat, which I shared with Lerryn, overlooked the ghosts of Blake's poetry, as well as hairdressers, barbers and coffee shop pop-ups, with the latter becoming more and more of a fixture in the years that I lived there. I spent much of my time gazing at that patch of green from the huge sash window, sliding in my socks over shiny wooden floors, and stretching out in the wild garden at the back of the house, and I have never loved another place I've lived in as much. This flat had the kind of magic that facilitates other magical

---

* I may not dream of labour but I have let myself dream of home ownership, despite myself.

events: it was where I later fell in love, made zines, wrote essays for books and cover stories and began to engage in what continues to be some of the most fulfilling grassroots activism of my life. I listened to Sampha, a fellow south Londoner that made everything feel like astral projection. I let the music wash over me. I thought I had reached the end of my relentless carousel and found a place I could happily grow old in, my little joy pocket suddenly erasing what I had learned over twenty-eight years about how short-lived these moments can be.

Among this elation I experienced see-sawing bouts of deflation, knowing I lived in a house that I could never buy, and feeling the desire to get a foot on the housing ladder so I could give my mum a stake in it. Though the house had become a home much quicker than any other, I would still wake up and feel guilty about drinking oat milk lattes and complaining about editors not replying to my emails while my mum struggled to put money on her electricity meter. I felt more selfish somehow, in a place of luxury – when we were both struggling, strangely, it felt easier.

Some of my sweetest memories of this period take me back to the high street, where I spent a lot of my time. When I got addicted to chin chin, a local grocer would pre-emptively reach for the plastic water bottles filled with it when he saw me approaching. Another local at a nearby internet café regularly gave me discounts on print-outs as I sat in the hot room, waiting for Word documents to load. Sometimes, I took a walk to the local community radio station, Reprezent, and slumped on bean bags, listening in on shows and occasionally doing guest spots.

During this time, I had a brief relationship with a guy who worked in a nearby shop that sold hydroponic equipment and weed paraphernalia. He had an addiction to coconut snowballs and always wore gloves so as not to leave his finger-prints for 'government data' collection. Sometimes in bed he would keep me up spitting and raging at the new shops and restaurants that sold sweet chilli sauce for £1 (his own dad, a Turkish immigrant who owned a local café, gave it away for free), angry at the idea that white people pay more to be served by white people. He had lived in Peckham his whole life, and when he mentioned a proposed threat of demolition to his estate his rage landed. After all, I was also a transient local – part of a nomadic generation who had ended up in south London because of my university and stayed because it felt like home. His frustration put my feelings of early dis-placement into focus, uncovering what I'd buried about my younger years. At Green Man, I was too young to make the connection between my estate, the centre of my world, and a new café on the high street. Now, it's become a bad joke that coffee shops spell displacement.

## ASPECTS OF CHANGE

When I was growing up in Hayes I often heard stories of London cabbies refusing to go to Peckham and Brixton, a racialised fear promoted by substantial parts of the media after the Brixton riots in 1981. These refusals made life harder for locals who worked outside of the area and needed to return home, only to be told their neighbourhood was too dangerous.* Now, Peckham's SE15 is one of the most coveted postcodes in London.

Gentrification is a housing issue. It is also, undeniably, connected to public health, the local economy and education, but at its core it describes the battleground on which social cleansing and class warfare is fought. The first recorded use of the term is by the ever-prophetic Marxist sociologist Ruth Glass in her 1964 book *London: Aspects of Change*, where she both observed her reality and predicted our present. 'Once this process of "gentrification" starts in a district,' Glass wrote, 'it goes on until all or most of the original working-class occupiers are displaced, and the whole social character of the district is changed.' Glass was writing about her local area of Islington, but she could have been talking about any city in the country, and more than a few around the globe. Gentrification prices people out of their homes, aggravating and corroding historical communities, and particularly Black spaces, like acid.

Living in Peckham in 2015 was to live on a site of frenetically paced social and economic change. My presence didn't exactly pre-empt the shiny boot of gentrification that stomped across the high street, but I was there to witness the sheer speed at which wealthy property developers saw an opportunity to move in. To get a sense of how this shift

---

* There must be an international language of area desirability rates – In *Sex and the City* when Miranda deigns to leave Manhattan to view a house in (gasp!) Brooklyn, the taxi driver refuses to take her: 'I don't go to Brooklyn,' he smirks.

affected house prices, you might look at Talfourd Road, where a five-bedroom house in 2010 sold for £530,000. In 2019 the same property sold for £1,798, 000: an increase of 239 per cent.[1] (In Brixton, where I went on to rent, an influx of restaurants, farmers' markets, galleries, cafés and bars has led to a spike in rent and house prices, which have risen by 85 per cent in the past ten years.[2])

A year after I moved in, in 2017, a news story circulated widely about how renters across the UK were spending on average half of their income on rent. The story was big news, jump-starting the inevitable glut of thinkpieces from a slew of shocked, white, middle-class columnists who claimed this spelled an unsustainable rent crisis, as people on Twitter bemoaned the spending habits of young renters.[*] (This has only got worse – in 2022, at the time of writing, inflation has risen to terrifying levels, and 45 per cent of renters have experienced a price hike in the last year, with one in five saying that their rent hike had been in excess of £100.[3])

When this story came out, I was hanging onto my twenties, and was bemused by the reaction – who exactly was this news for? That my friends and I, few of whom had children or other dependants to care for, struggled to make rent was the defining truth of our financial lives. These, as the climate of clickbait news has encouraged, were deliberately provocative articles, but still said something startling about just how many people of a certain generation were genuinely shocked

---

[*] This has become a predictable part of the culture – Kirstie Allsopp tells us that if only we cancelled our Netflix subscriptions we might be able to afford a house. Currently, it would take around 2,274 years to buy an average priced house in the UK and 3,980 years in London.

about why everyone doesn't just *get* mortgages for financial security. Like, why don't you just *get* a job if you're struggling, or *get* a boyfriend if you're lonely? I was routinely spending £700 on rent (the average rent for a two-bedroom property in Peckham today is £2,357, so I would now be paying £1,268),[4] and making around £1,000 a month in freelance writing income, but I had a lot more money than when I was living on Kwik Save No Frills fish fingers on my aunt's floor. I was crushed by rent, but I had made a choice to live here and so I felt like I had forfeited my right to complain. I submitted to the idea that this kind of happiness just comes at a cost.

My very presence was part of the crop of gentrifiers able to pay above the average social rented costs. Writers, like artists and musicians, are part of what many consider a 'creative class' that can contribute to the gentrification process: making the place more 'cool' to upper-middle-class investors while also pricing out long-term locals, and then, inevitably, ending up being priced out themselves. Author and academic Joel Kotkin explores these 'geographies of hip coolness' in the context of cities in the US. He argues that it has actually *not* been profitable to cater to the creative classes, and 'affordability' has been driven up for those least able to manage it. (It poses the question: if the housing system is not even working for the upper middle classes, then who *is* it working for?) The south London that I had spent over a decade renting in was slowly changing all over, but Peckham High Street became particularly unrecognisable in two short years. The metamorphosis happened in real time. I was watching the water level slowly rise as armbands were sparingly given out to those who could afford them.

Property developers often defend demolitions and new-builds by claiming that they are 'regenerating' or improving these neighbourhoods. This language is used to justify the displacement of residents (known as 'decanting') living in estates, who are often not secured a right to return. This has political precedent. New Labour's 1999 'urban renaissance' project (code for gentrification) posited that working-class people could be 'resocialised' through contact with gentrifiers with more social capital. That the proximity to middle-class people would inspire working-class people to climb the ladder of social mobility themselves, as if inherited wealth was not a crucial and significant barrier.

The political right clings to a belief in trickle-down economics, arguing that money pouring in from a wealthy few improves the economy for everyone. In reality, more often than not, money is siphoned and moves around in middle-class circles – a new coffee shop opens, which prices coffees and pastries at a mark-up that locals can't afford, which attracts wealthier customers, and the wealth flows between these communities. In fact, a 2021 Runnymede report titled *Pushed to the Margins* found that 'areas in London with high population churn subsequently have a loss in ethnic minority residents – meaning that ethnic minorities are the first to move out when an area becomes desirable'.[5] Any idea of 'regeneration' that renders locals homeless disintegrates under interrogation. While governments have sought the votes of buyers with the promise of affordable housing – introducing schemes such as Help to Buy and shared ownership – the quality and quantity of social housing has declined. This has paved the way for property developers to come in and fix the problem. The harm this does is generational – sowing lies and myths about what it means to be working class and to live on estates,* and why it is beneficial to have your home ripped from underneath you.

## THE ONLY LOCAL IN THE VILLAGE

Gentrification is a national concern and rural areas are not immune. In 2021, house prices in the countryside rose by 14 per cent,[6] twice as much as in cities. This rural gentrification is thanks to myriad factors: new buyers and renters who have responded to the pandemic by moving from city to country, the migration of older people into the countryside, affluent families buying second homes, and labour changes which have seen a shift from traditional agricultural jobs to services as cafés and restaurants cater for tourists.

This can change the make-up of local communities. A 2021 *Devon Live* report found that in a local survey of five Devon villages (Kingston, South Huish, Dalwood, Strete and Georgeham), between 66 and 95 per cent of properties are second homes, empty for most of the year.[7] Locals are being driven out of their towns and neighbourhoods. Later that year, the *Mirror* told the sensationally sorry tale of 88-year-old Norman Thomas, from Cwm-yr-Eglwys on the Pembrokeshire coast, who was the 'one local left' after most of the neighbouring houses had been bought as second

---

* In 2010 a BBC film crew was given permission to paint graffiti on the Heygate Estate while filming *Rules of Love* because the estate wasn't 'edgy' enough for them. I guess the BBC made Heygate *too* edgy because it was demolished in 2014.

homes.[8] The Normans of this world are increasing, but seldom heard from.

As the market expansion of expensive private housing continues unchecked, the casualties are vulnerable locals who have worked for a historical stake in the place – and often country – they call home. The only way to approach this death knell of community is with a complete rethinking of housing.

## WELCOME TO AIRSPACE

Gentrification brings with it a homogenised aesthetic. The writer Kyle Chayka in an essay for *The Verge* describes this aesthetic phenomenon in an apt and beautiful way, calling it 'AirSpace' – a frictionless experience of what he observes are hallmarks of comfort and quality. He uses examples you might recognise: 'reclaimed wood. Industrial lighting. Cortados'. He also describes the ultimate effect of this design aesthetic: 'The coffee roaster Four Barrel in San Francisco looks like the Australian Toby's Estate in Brooklyn looks like The Coffee Collective in Copenhagen looks like Bear Pond Espresso in Tokyo. You can get a dry cortado with perfect latte art at any of them, then Instagram it on a marble countertop and further spread the aesthetic to your followers.' You might recognise it in the glut of black shop interiors with tiny white writing. You may not even know what the hallmarks are, but you select cafés and restaurants based on a quality that you recognise as high-standard.

This all contributes to the hackneyed image of the gentrifier as a moustachioed hipster, who you might find, say, cycling around Williamsburg on a penny-farthing. For a few months in 2015, I lived in Crown Heights in Brooklyn for work and it was there that I first really *got* the aesthetic of gentrification. I don't know if Brooklyn was an innovator in gentrifying the neighbourhood, though it is worth mentioning because it is often cited as the ground zero for some of the calling cards of gentrification: SoulCycle, barre workouts, 'pop-up' Indian street food served by white people in Carhartt beanies. It's not easy to explain why these offerings were popular in the first place, but it is easy to explain why they spread: taste is globalised now thanks to easy travel, and the market serves a predominantly white upper middle class who have money to spend on leisure and trend 'experiences', including paying for overpriced bowls of cereal and riding vehicles from the 1870s. It is by now common to the point of parody to see coffee shops in monochrome, a wall painted in 'millennial pink', twee avocado illustrations on restaurant menus and minimalist furniture in a craft beer shop. These sights crop up in the US and the UK, and increasingly in Continental cities like Berlin, Lisbon and Paris, and beyond.

One example that comes to mind from 2014, in a now-viral moment, is often recalled when we talk about this subject. The owners of the newly opened Cereal Killer Café were asked by Channel 4's Symeon Brown whether it was reasonable to charge £3.20 for a bowl of cereal in one of the poorest boroughs in London (Tower Hamlets, where some 49 per cent of children live below the poverty line). They tentatively responded that it was 'cheap for the area', before swiftly cutting the camera. Were the owners in this instance providing a neat analogy for financially steamrolling a deprived area with no awareness of local sensitivities? Undoubtedly. But the Cereal Killer Café's owners were a symptom of something larger, more sinister than overpriced Lucky Charms.

Of course, neither they nor the Flat Whiters are responsible for the housing crisis. Fewer coffee shops do not stop our cities from increasingly becoming capital assets for property developers. To direct too much vitriol at individuals (and to police how people spend their money to treat themselves in very bleak times) is to let government off the hook. The government has exacerbated housing inequality, which has impacted local business, public health and even food poverty. When arguments about silly rich southerners spending money on brunch feature on right-wing talking-head shows, these are diversions, and the government is happy to let us fight among ourselves. It is important to realise that these things are all connected.

## FIRE, FIRE, GENTRIFIER!

So our ire may not always be best targeted *solely* on individuals, but that's not to say that all resistance, or reclamation, is fruitless. In June 2020, when community organisers Bring Brooklyn Black protested in the streets of Brooklyn following the death of George Floyd chanting 'Fire, fire, gentrifier!' and 'Black people used to live here!' to brunch-consuming onlookers, it was hard not to smile. Gentrification is a noun, but it is also a doing word – it does something to us, against us, and we can do something back to it, too.

Those activists were right to make a connection to race when you consider that Black, Asian and minority ethnic communities are more likely to experience housing stress than their white counterparts.[9] Homelessness has risen from 18 per cent to 36 per cent in BAME communities in the UK in the last two decades, and in 2020, the government's annual statutory homeless report revealed that Black people are three times more likely to be homeless than people from all other ethnicities combined.[10] But any idea of regeneration must also be critical of class politics – middle-class communities of colour can also contribute to displacement. In 2020, the London School of Economics released research showing that the private rented sector has seen communities displaced by 'ethnic middle-class owner-occupiers'. Dr Antoine Paccoud, lead author of the paper, commented: 'In the case of buy-to-let gentrification, the inequality is between the multiple property owners who own the rented dwellings and those who are not able to keep up in economic terms with the upscaling of their areas as middle-class renters, be they White British or not.'[11] Buying a home provides security for marginalised communities in a country where there are few other viable alternatives for feeling secure. But we should interrogate how any move towards ownership impacts our own communities, because if we don't, it is unclear who else will.

Saying that, this is not the threat that it might have been reported as – according to Runnymede, just 35 per cent of Black and ethnic minority people own their own homes in London, compared to 62 per cent of white British people.[12]

## HAVE FAITH IN YOUR OWN BAD TASTE

There is a connection to be made between the aesthetics of gentrification and interior design trends. Advancing technology has given visual currency new weight. Instagram and *Architectural Digest* don't just glamorise the idea of home ownership, they also glamorise a specific way of presenting your home once you acquire it – and this often has its roots in elite ideas of what constitutes 'good' taste. An influencer could move for free using a removals brand and furnish their house with free sponsored brand content from a homeware company, all while selling us the dream of a stylish interior they themselves didn't buy. This is how social media blurs the lines between models and real life, between personal choice and advertising.

An industry of 'dressers' or 'property stagers', for instance, can design your home to make it more sellable – adorning rooms with tasteful art posters and Herman Miller chairs. According to Rightmove, a staged home sells for an average of 8 per cent more than a non-staged home.[13] Alongside the casually racist references to 'plantation shutters', the websites of some of these offerings show a Rolodex of gallery walls, light, wooden floors, exposed brick and many, many monsteras. This connects taste to a financial incentive that appeals to buyers with money and an ability to update as fashions change.

This is not to undermine the cultural importance of interior trends, which can reflect our moment back at us. During the height of the pandemic, many people who were trapped inside painted arches on walls like portals to elsewhere, the equivalent of the painted vistas and windowscapes sometimes commissioned in prisons. Wooden dado rails became fashionable, allowing people to alter the proportions of a room with visual tricks that transformed their familiar views, giving the illusion of more space. A grey epidemic has taken over living rooms across the nation. One Farrow and Ball shade, officially known as Elephant's Breath (paint colour no. 229), was named 'Colour of the Decade' in 2022, typifying a frictionless retreat from our decade of unease and disorder. The neutral tone which has appeared on sofas, rugs, lampshades and walls provides a monotony and refuge from the unprecedented chaos of our social and political realities.

In 2022, Kim Kardashian introduced us to her minimalist, clinical home courtesy of *Vogue*. In a now viral video she showed us the smooth cement, brutalist edges and neutral tones of her interiors of the $65 million mansion which became aspirational even as they were lambasted. People bought 'invisible' sinks and storage solutions to recreate the serenity of that existence and rub away the tedium of messy life.* The message appeared to be a masterclass in self-control, only keeping what 'sparks joy' in curated homes, without letting anything unseemly spill out. There is already pushback to this. Towards the end of 2022, following the cost-of-living crisis and impending economic downturn, we saw a rejection of *that* grey and instead a swing towards the bright colours and mixed patterns of maximalist aesthetics. This is

---

* Working-class taste has long been criticised as being 'trashy' – anti-minimalist, cramped – where middle-class homes with the same chaos are 'maximalist'. Like denying food to stay skinny, there is something inherently uncomfortable to me about rich people and minimalist decor – taking up space to fill it with nothing.

in part thanks to more people entertaining in their homes and wanting them to feel like a full, exciting experience to rival restaurants. It may also be a reclamation of our new chaotic realities. Beyoncé's newly released album *Renaissance* was hailed by the *Guardian* as 'a maximalist tour de force', while TikTok saw maximalist fashion influencers amass millions of followers, and in August 2022, *Esquire* even ran a piece about the contemporary relevance of the 'maximalist novel'.

Of course, homes reflect personal style too – few people change the entirety of their home's look as dictated by *Elle Decoration* – but it is interesting to note that taste is, increasingly, formed in places like Instagram, where 91 per cent of influencers are white,[14] and is dictated by whoever controls consumption, and enforced by anyone who has proximity to consumer capital.

Some of the reason for this may lie in who exactly makes these decisions. In 2020, the Diversity in Interior Design Survey, the UK's first-ever such survey, found that 46 per cent of Black, Asian and minority ethnic interior designers were the only person of colour in their workplace, while only 15 per cent of respondents considered themselves as coming from a disadvantaged socio-economic background[15] – in an office of thirty people, that's less than five. So, white, middle-class, 'taste makers' decide what is desirable, their peers confirm, and we are left with self-fulfilling prophecies.

Working-class people are often encouraged to achieve that aspirational thing – a home that represents an upper-middle-class fantasy, which is synonymous with good taste. 'Trashy' or kitsch aesthetics, like, say, a leopard-print sofa, or my mum's cushion with my pixelated face on it, are usually desired ironically, if at all. Classism is inherently tied up with this, and when maverick aesthetes like the director John Waters tell us to 'believe in your own bad taste', it can feel like a radical rejection. Ione Gamble, author and editor of *Polyester* zine, formed from that Waters quote, breaks this down well: 'The upper classes in this country rule everything,' she says. 'There's this dominant belief that working-class people can't make good decisions because they're not making the right aesthetic decisions – if you can't even decorate your home or dress yourself in a tasteful way, then why should you be trusted to make decisions about your own life, or about how our country is run?' She is right to make this political connection. 'Good taste' is not just an abstract term, it is yoked in ideas of class, and sometimes power, where people of different social classes and structural positioning are catered to differently.

## DEMOLITION

In 2014, a couple of years before I moved to Peckham, I lived in a tiny box room with some friends off Walworth Road in south London where you could hear the crash of demolition at any point of the day. The victim of the wrecking ball, at that time, was the mighty Heygate Estate. The view from my room shifted every day as homes fell away and were replaced with cranes. At night, I would dream about them, as Transformers in the darkness, gleefully smashing through brick; Optimus Prime controlled remotely by a property developer. I heard the crack and groan of copper railing coming down, balconies resisting the onslaught, and dreamed of bits of scaffolding falling around me. After it was all over, only one in five tenants (216 out of 1,034) remained in the borough after the 'regeneration' (which also removed 283 of the 406 mature trees).[16] Rebranded as Elephant Park, the area currently stands as a shiny, soulless pocket of the city.

So what is the real value of a brick? Who keeps the remnants of these demolished sites? What is the value of a pound of rock from the estate where your kids were born, raised, and fell in love? In 1982, the feminist design co-operative Matrix, made up of majority white feminist architects, collaborated with Bangladeshi members of the local community in Whitechapel to build the Jagonari women's educational centre – named after the Nazrul Islam poem 'J'ago Nari Jago Banhishikha', meaning 'Women Awake', or 'Rise Up'. It provided services based on the needs of local women in the area, including childcare, training, offender programmes and support for victims of domestic violence. To build relationships with the local women, the architects felt it was important to share their language and understanding of the construction, so that everyone involved could join in and have a stake in the building. One of the ways that they did this was by going on group 'brick picnics' (bricknics?) where the women ate together and did rubbings of bricks with paper and crayon as they wandered around the city, picking their favourite types. The architects listened, incorporating the women's suggestions into the design of the building, which as a result was uniquely loved by its service users. Imagine if we included residents in the decision making at these early stages of building homes.

What can we do when homes are routinely neglected,

demolished or sold to the highest bidder while the property developers devastate communities? In addition to applying government pressure, if we have agency to make these choices, we must think deeply about where we choose to live. Educating would-be buyers and renters about the histories of these social housing burial grounds is crucial. The geography of UK housing would look very different if we started saying no to property built on the archives of some of the poorest immigrant communities in the country. After all, driving out some of our poorest communities who are not granted a right of return *should* feel nauseating, and we should respond accordingly. What if those who could afford to, who knew that homes for sale had been made possible by the decimation of communities, simply refused them? We should urge each other to learn more about these histories. We determine the market, and we do have a say.

Demolition is aggressive by its very nature. It smashes our security, evicts us, takes away our resources and fractures communities. It attacks our sense of safety through state negligence and the flippant greed of free-market capitalism. The psychological toll of demolition is not something that has been researched extensively, but we do know that proximity to it incurs anxiety, depression and paranoia,[17] and that any sustained noise is considered pollution, or at the very least, 'anti-social'. The environmental philosopher Glenn Albrecht coined the beautiful term *solastalgia* in his 2005 journal article of the same name, to describe the feeling of distress associated with environmental change close to your home, and I think putting new language to what will be an increasing feature of urban life is useful and comforting. The concept can be found in clinical psychology and health policy relating to climate change disruption and has been used by researchers in the US looking into the effects of wildfires in California on people's sense of home.

Many of us who have lived in precarious housing, or watched the estates we grew up in crumble around us, feel this sense of loss acutely. We develop reverence for bricks, for seemingly lifeless blocks of dried clay that hold up the places that we call home. We tend to assume that the places familiar to us will exist for ever. But if you have felt first hand the unchecked mania of property developers that devastate areas with reckless abandon, you know that this is not true. When we can't return to our homes, all we have is nostalgia. We have become so used to the dizzying pace of displacement and changing cities that we can think very little of it – we see housing cost hikes, and feel like all we can do is deeply, *deeply*, sigh.

One of my favourite words used to describe this loss is the Welsh '*hiraeth*'. It describes a deep longing for a home, a feeling, a place or person that is beyond this plane of existence. Many of us are in a state of grief about what we lose through displacement. In 2015, psychologist Margaret Stroebe and colleagues considered the possibility of homesickness as a 'mini-grief'.[18] This idea of the emotional fraying of a connection to a home requires us to bury something and move on – I myself have buried many in my life.

After all these mini-griefs, I have rebuilt again. I have bargained with my mum, a landlord, an estate agent; I've felt fury, and guilt that I didn't appreciate home enough when I had the chance. I've moved towards acceptance and hope – for another place that I could find joy in. Now I think what we really grieve for are the alternative futures for ourselves that we were not able to live.

## BODIES

We mould our bodies to the places we live. We are creatures of adaptation and during the pandemic-enforced lockdown, many of us developed a specific kind of muscle memory that rooted us to our homes. During the immediate aftermath of the first lockdown, when students were slowly going back to school, I helped to run some workshops with primary school children on how to document their pandemic through dance, song and story. During the preparation of this over Zoom, a teacher made a throwaway comment that has stayed with me: that one of her Reception pupils, on returning to school, had forgotten how to use the stairs after spending the majority of lockdown in his ground-floor flat.

We have forensic knowledge of the beats of our home, its sounds and creaks, the way they speak to us, the forgotten corners. We can run through the narrow corridors of our house and avoid sharp edges which would impale a newbie. Many people in the city right now are learning to live in one room, to find their quiet in tight spaces, and just as old sofas retain the imprints of our bodies, so too do the houses we occupy.

My father-in-law once told me about attending house parties in Brixton in the 1970s where the walls would get a smear from rub-a-dub dancing – bodies squashed and gyrating in slow, steady circular motions against the walls to lovers rock:

Janet Kay and Dennis Brown. After it was over, the residue of parties and dances and thrill was left behind, maybe from the indigo dye in a pair of jeans, or the scrape of a belt. This might be why the spirit of that music persists in Brixton, still singing in the walls. Houses are transformed by the people inside them.

My body had become part of my house in Peckham Rye, muscles lengthened by the lack of tension. But, it was also shaped by the world outside. A house can trick us into thinking that our domestic domain is all that matters, all that exists, that we can shut out the whole world and all that remains is us. But a house is just a *piece* of the world that we are part of. We affect the physics of a place, the frequency of the streets – we change and are changed by them and often need to pay into them in meaningful ways to allow other bodies to lengthen, too.

When I fell in love while I lived here, it was, as some people will recognise, a kind of brief, kaleidoscopic mania. The intensity of the love felt so teenage, so earth-shattering, that when I physically felt my ribcage shift to make way for my heart expanding I felt like it couldn't possibly be real. It was a core-shaking kind of feeling, where your body vibrates on its own frequency and all you can do is join it. It's too neat to say that a life of short-lived homes had resulted in many short-lived relationships but it is also true that love and lifestyles do often follow one another. I wasn't really settled in my life in the way of secure housing – I'm still not – but after that initial jolt of love *something* settled inside me. It was the kind of love that made it possible for me to dream of a stability that I had never had in my housing life. When I was with him, I saw how he changed the physics of a room, how the walls and the chairs and the tables in it were just there to bounce the love around, like a laser. He had lived in the same house for ten years (which was unfathomable to me) and would drive through the borders of Brixton to Peckham to visit me, sometimes taking the route that passed the registry office we would later get married in. On my wedding day, live dhol players beat the drums and as I held his hand my nanaji was with me, reminding me that there is joy in always building to something more.

It confirmed that home is where you make it – in yourself, in other people, and if you're very lucky, in a romantic partner. Being with someone that felt like home did not afford me housing stability – there is very little that can – but it afforded me the space to imagine better for myself. And it made me appreciate it too. I know home, by any translation, is not easy to come by.

Case in point: after two sacred years, I was, inevitably, priced out of this flat. My rent rose astronomically, and I had to move away from the house I thought I would spend many more summers in. Fantasies and fiction can be baked into where we live, into beguiling and carefully curated ideas of ourselves which rarely take into account the less inspiring reality of soaring living costs and insecure incomes. I was shaken from this heady enchantment of middle-class make-believe, and crushed to leave it. I wished I could cling onto it for just a moment longer, gazing at light-filled sash windows and illuminated oak floorboards, longing for just one more day in that heady daydream.

Love is unstable, unpredictable, and it requires work. It

alone can't give us the complete feeling of safety or diminish our sense of precarity, but it is a good place to start. We must fill our homes with love, flood them, buckle the walls under the weight of it, for ourselves, for the things we love, for what they give us, and for what we give them. I bring those houses with me. I remember that we are not in isolation to the places we live. I know that negligence happens, so we must reject negligence wherever we can in our own lives; that displacement reigns, but we should not displace; that bricks tumble and we must pick them up and build something again. As my life continues to take me from one place to the next, I am written into the histories of all the houses I've lived in, many of which, like this flat, have given me the space to dream. I have not stopped dreaming.

# Conclusion
## All the houses we live in –
## How to fight

If a lifetime of moving has taught me anything, it is how to fight. All those experiences arguing with housing officers, huffing mould fumes and forcing smiles at housemate auditions have been training: mostly, on how to get knocked down and get back up.

Housing is a human right. We are often told that to acquire a home is simply too difficult, and we are told that this is out of our control. We must reject these terms. It's important to remember that you do not have secure housing because you 'deserve' or have 'earned' it. It is a great privilege to be housing secure and with this security, we must demand the same for others.

Negligence, after all, can't be reduced to dodgy buildings – it is in the insidious cycle of the media, in political rhetoric, in the slow speed of responses from governments, councils, developers and landlords. It is festering on the tongues of those who determine who is and who isn't respectable. It is everywhere, and locating it is our work.

It is our responsibility to continue to organise even as buildings fall around us. To archive histories, to tell our own stories, to provide legal help, care and support, to make noise, and to build strong communities elsewhere. It can be easy to create distance where it does not exist, telling ourselves that we are worlds away from an estate 5 metres from our house, or from an immigrant family next door separated by an 8-centimetre-thick wall.

## POLICY SOLUTIONS AND BEYOND

The housing market has allowed for very little imagination about how it can be improved. There are some obvious solutions that we should demand from government now: rent controls in the private sector, securing a 'right to return' for all residents living in estates undergoing regeneration schemes, enforcing the (bare minimum, in my opinion) 35 per cent genuinely affordable housing target set for developments, making sure annual housing MOTs by landlords are written into law, abolishing rent debt and evictions, ensuring that all developers commit to building good-quality social housing in higher numbers, taxing second homes, capping the national rate by which rent is allowed to increase. And this is before we even scratch the surface of eradicating the racism that abounds in all these structures.

We should insist on writing house and tenancy administration into the curriculum, so all of us can have a base knowledge of this system and how to navigate it. We should make it our business to be proactive – creating workshops, joining tenants' unions, rejecting austerity measures, sharing information, teaching the young people in our lives about tenancy agreements.* We must look, too, at global solutions. In 1974, Jamaican prime minister Michael Manley set up a National Housing Trust, which collected a tax from workers. Low-income families were able to withdraw money from the trust at low interest rates to purchase a house or land to build their own. On retirement, you got back the contributions you'd made. It was not a perfect system, but the imaginative approach to democratic housing remains inspiring to me. In Oakland, California, Moms 4 Housing, a collective of home-less and marginally housed mothers, organise together to take over empty homes (there are four times as many empty homes in Oakland as there are homeless people). In Toronto, it is standard for decision makers to consult with the community on new developments, perhaps best seen in the approach to redevelop the Lawrence Heights green space. In Scotland, in May 1915, a joint meeting of Glasgow Labour Housing Committee and the Women's Housing Association called the first rent strike, creating a blueprint which continues to improve housing conditions for working-class people.

## The revolutionary potential of rethinking ownership

As we face what seems like unending austerity and recession, we must also look for answers beyond political party lines for

---

* While we're at it, we should tax the 1 per cent, abolish bankers' bonuses, invest in the NHS and state education, and then sit back and see just how this impacts housing.

281

how we dig ourselves out of this quagmire. The state might provide social housing but it does not grant liberation from inequality, or even safety. Policy may be a starting point for change, but it is *a* place rather than *the* place to focus our attentions. We have to reject the dominant narrative of competition, of being grateful for what we're given, and instead, focus on community. 'Care' in these terms looks like anything from sharing food, translating letters, helping with the school run, offering to make doctors' calls, helping to clean, to literally just knocking on your neighbour's door to check in. These are problems that people face across the political spectrum.

The reality is that the current system of home ownership is a game of luck in a rigged system. Most working-class people I know who have bought a house have done so through exceptional circumstances. Sometimes it was thanks to unexpected bonuses at a record label when an artist went astronomical, sometimes the result of a council house sold at a profit by chance. Perhaps you come into an unexpected inheritance, perhaps your partner has an inheritance that helps lift you, too; perhaps you have secure employment, or you win a house on Instagram, or you are one of the lucky ones who actually benefits from a government scheme. None of these is necessarily a Bad Thing – this is not an exercise in guilt, but it is an opportunity for us to think about how dishonest the whole system is, how it is built on thin wisps of cloud that could blow away at any moment.

Capitalism pits us against each other in continual competition. We should learn from our marginalised communities, particularly our queer siblings, on how to redesign alternatives so that home ownership is not the only goal. We should also challenge these ideas of the individual pursuit of narrow success as the status quo. Buying a house will not grant you security from the state. We must challenge the state's immigration policy, and any idea that liberation can be bought with a down payment. We may not see this kind of change in my lifetime, but it is worth fighting for now. The project of building a better world, after all, is not just about reimagining housing, it is about bearing witness to the structures around us that create harm and dismantling them.

There is a spectrum of proposed solutions to the housing crisis, from working with government to radical abolitionist ideas. These solutions are open to trial and error, and discussion with our peers. Lola Olufemi is a Black feminist writer from north London whose books *Feminism Interrupted* and *Experiments in Imagining Otherwise* urge us to consider how we can ask for more and to imagine what that can be. 'I think there are so few, such limited routes of thinking about justice, and how we actually might live communally,' they tell me. 'We're encouraged to place all of our hopes and dreams and ideas of stability into home ownership. Politics doesn't end there, around housing. It can't end there if we're trying to build a world that is entirely transformed. This means assessing, even as a dispossessed person, how your dreams of stability are tied up into an idea that is false.'

They continue: 'When I say I want the existence of private property to end, I don't say that I want this in a fictional future, I mean I actually think that this is possible, and that we could live in different ways.'

After we speak I write a list of questions on a pink Postit

above my desk: *What if home didn't need to be earned? What if we allowed ourselves to think radically? What if we used squatting as a springboard to consider how we occupy public space? If we have to think about ownership, how do we make it work for us?*

## EDUCATE, AGITATE, ORGANISE

The housing crisis does not affect everyone equally. To move forward at all, we must confront the prejudices in the housing system. We must begin with the fact that racism, transphobia, ableism and classism are built into the fabric of housing in the UK. Working-class people of colour are often seen as expendable and short term. In 2020, the Runnymede Trust reported that all Black and minority ethnic groups in Britain 'are more likely to be in the lowest paid work ... to be living in poverty [and to be paying] higher housing costs in England's large cities (especially London)'.[1] Immigrant homes are often first on the chopping block when it comes to displacement. But what we lose when we lose immigrant homes is monumental.

It is important to recognise that many people are dealing with overlapping prejudices. In the movement for Black lives we must also advocate for the rights of trans people, in the pursuit of what disabled activists call 'cripping the movement' we must fight for those who are working class. It is far more useful to understand the society we live in if we work together to enact change, all while learning from our different challenges. When we inevitably lose some of our battles, we must shout louder about them, amplifying our resistance. When the fabric of activism becomes frayed over time, we must double-, triple-stitch it more colourfully, more robustly, than before.

Homelessness is, of course, the undercurrent of all this, the snake circling at our heels threatening to bite us at any moment. Homelessness is closer to our lives than we would like to think, with many people just one pay cheque away from losing their homes. That doesn't stop the state from demonising and actively targeting homeless people through a lack of supplemental housing or care, and hostile architecture like spiked benches and sonic deterrents.* But the streets are ours too. As well as offering immediate practical solutions like good-quality emergency accommodation, we need new and creative possibilities. This should come, in part, from designers, artists, writers and tenants with the same thought in mind: we can do better.

For so long, marginalised communities have existed in supposed disconnection from 'universal' concerns. They have existed as an aside – an 'also' category. When we talk about feminism, for instance, we might tack on at the end '. . . and of course this is worse for X communities', with little interrogation of how these issues are connected. But it is on these margins that creative activism lives. What if we put marginalised communities in the centre of our designs? The history of property ownership is based on exclusion, and yet reimagining has always happened. In 1964, Black feminist writer June Jordan joined forces with the architect Buckminster Fuller on the 'Skyrise for Harlem': a plan for public housing for 250,000 of the neighbourhood's residents, most of them

---

* Luxury residents and even supermarkets play noise music to deter people from sleeping rough. In 2019 in West Palm Beach, Florida, 'Baby Shark' was played for this purpose outside luxury apartments.

Black, that made urban dwelling sacrosanct. Her plans for this 'collaborative architectural redesign' included light-filled towers, balconies, concert halls, theatres and athletics fields. In the 1980s, the London-based feminist architects' practice Matrix challenged the patriarchal design of the built environment, running workshops for women on reading house blueprints and fixing appliances. The core idea of the original Bauhaus,* a German design collective through the 1920s, was based on an approach where art existed to serve a social role. Today, there are thousands of minds inspired by this work through collectives like Decosm, Decolonise Architecture and the DisOrdinary Architecture Project, which works with disabled activists. We must commit to intersectional design.

Our homes too are under threat from the climate emergency. We will need to commit to Green New Deals and urgently retrofit homes to Green Homes standards. We must try and understand the connections between the climate crisis and housing challenges. We will need to find and construct new pathways in a new world – something immigrants are well versed at doing and making. Immigration brings with it sophisticated ideas of building, and creative imagination, and making something from nothing. We know that trans people, sex workers and care leavers, people who are or have been homeless, make a lot of very little. These are the skills we will need in a future world.

---

* German for 'building house'.

## ALL THE HOUSES I'VE EVER LIVED IN

There were times when writing this book that I became incandescent with rage, and adrenaline would make my fingers shake, typing my words quicker than I could think them. I would listen to stories of eviction and bite the right side of my bottom lip so hard it swelled, feel the blood pumping through, and taste its sweet, iron-y tang.

My partner would have to rub the bottom of my back in social situations. I developed a whooshing of pulsing blood in my left ear, and for months I could only hear a throbbing which my doctor called tinnitus but I knew was actually unfiltered frustration. In the course of the writing, I have gently allowed myself to listen, to deploy the cool waters of patience before fury. I have learned how to move forward in my anger, using this energy to get me up and out when I haven't always felt like it.

Those were also the moments I told myself to focus on the friendships, design details and hysterical laughter that four walls can afford us. I know that sanctuary can be fought for, lost, and fought for all over again. There are the things we bring with us, the tissue boxes and curtains and embossed wallpaper. And though it feels perverse, we can even find joy in a housing market that enriches the lives of so many as it dispossesses thousands of others.

It can be difficult not to feel like you are on a conveyor belt of temporary living, in constant suspension, as the market dictates that we dart from place to place. This way of living will be part of Gen Z's future, and Gen Alpha's after that. A system that is infected with unconscious bias is obviously not fit for purpose for a future world and it might take a lifetime to overhaul. That is OK – activism is, after all, about advocating for fights you don't always win right away – but if we should shout ourselves hoarse about anything, it should be about ensuring home for everyone.

Moving has been a huge part of my life but it no longer feels so much like a crashing, uncontrollable tide. Now, it is open water to swim through, thanks to new tools I have to resist, more structural agency, allowing me to throw down sandbags before the water drowns me. I have found sanctuary in friendships and the beauty of other people's creative imagination – window designs, damp tapes and bailiff resistance; the kindness of the people who have nurtured me; the beds and floors that have shaped my back.

There are always ways to push back. When the prices rise and the buildings fall and the heartbreak sets in, when I think of what has already been lost, I remind myself that there is always hope. When it comes to finding home for ourselves and each other, what else can we do but repeat the mantra of history? It tells us that there is only one thing to hope for: that we will fight, and we will win.

# Epilogue

I grapple with, as much as I delight in, the idea of home ownership. How do we find peace in a system that so surgically – and frequently – disenfranchises us? Owning a home is rife with countless problems, and yet, it can still ground us in a chaotic, destabilising world. During the writing of this book, I used the advance to put a deposit down on a flat with my partner, benefiting in large part from his generational wealth. How do I square my politics of equal wealth distribution with that?

Sometimes, it still feels like my life of moving always has – precarious, expensive, difficult. At other times, it feels like staying still. I have something no-one in my immediate family has, a place of my own that might provide solace not just for me but for a community that I can share with. What new responsibility does home ownership give me? There are no easy answers to these questions but ownership is not the fairy tale ending where we acquire castles and raise the drawbridge.

Though my sense of temporality has not changed, I feel the joy of finding solace and beauty in a house that makes me feel held, delighting – and I mean *delighting* – in domestic details like painting walls and grouting tiles. It is grounding to know that I am not in isolation to the street, city, country or world that I live in. In all my moments that I am settled (though this also hangs in the balance of the success of my relationship and faith in my current employment) I begin to really understand what it means to feel this way and why we should all feel it. It has ignited more fire: space here freed up to fight *there*.

I do not believe in a 'for ever home'. I do not believe in an inheritocracy. I do not believe the housing system works for anyone, even those who feel housing-secure. I know the market, my scenario and my political life are in flux all the time, and that it is by exceptional circumstance that I am granted the privilege of what thousands of people are not, where even then, precarity is never extinguished. This is not success, or evidence of housing acquisition working as it should.

My life is still full of possibility, of change – it must be. If I have children, I will tell them that building home is radical work, and feeling safe, secure and supported by a community is essential. It is vital. I will hold them close and tell them that we can always make home together. That if there is even one thing we can do, however small, to distribute our privileges, we should do it.

Home is a gift and I revel in it every day. After so many years of feeling choked, I have somewhere that I want to plant a root system so deep it carves its way into the earth, tangled and strong – finding water in the dirt, growing deeper and deeper until no trampling can kill it. Maybe we are all looking to grow roots that are immovable. If so, I hope we will all be allowed fertile enough ground to try.

# Acknowledgements

I would not have been able to write a word of this book were it not for the mighty activists who have fought so that we might live with dignity and respect. Thank you to all of those who understand and recognise that home is a human right that should be accessible to everyone, and who have fought and continue to fight for it. This book is for anyone who believes that a better world is possible.

Thanks to the diligence and sharpness of my editor Assallah Tahir, who approached edits with thoughtfulness and me with patience and kindness. I feel so lucky to have had you with me. Thanks to Holly Ovenden for my beautiful cover and wonderful illustrations, and to Rhiannon Carroll, Amy Fulwood and the wider Simon & Schuster family for believing in this book. To my agent Carrie Plitt, who was an early champion of me, and made a dream come true.

Thank you to Goldsmiths Special Collections & Archives and the helpful staff that filled the gaps, and to the George

Padmore Institute for taking me back to the best parts of the 1970s. Thank you from the bottom of my heart to the staff of the King's College Hospital women's surgical unit, who intervened during this process and gave me the strength to continue.

For all the people who have encouraged this book to get across the line, from voice notes to excitement when I needed it: Farrah, Kasha, Amad and Sian Rowe and Tom and Lemara; and my peers that inspire me: Lola Olufemi, Ione Gamble, Bridget Minamore, Reni Eddo-Lodge, Sita Balani, Symeon Brown and anyone else who is brave enough to write in these precarious times.

Thank you to Nikesh Shukla, for generosity and encouragement. To Amandeep Singh, thank you for your constant kindness and support. Thank you to those early readers who were crucial to building my confidence. Ruth Saxelby – from the *FADER* years to now, you inspire me. Thanks to Angharad Monk, for your mighty legal brain, and Billie Muraben, for your impressive design insight.

My friends have been a source of jokes and fun and respite during the whole project, much of which was written during very solitary lockdown moments. Thank you to Emma Warren – it has been a thrilling pleasure to be going through this process at the same time as you. Thank you for always getting it.

To every iteration of the group chat – Clara, Sindhuja, Bolu, thank you for your jokes and unwavering confidence in me. Kirby and Bridget especially, thank you for the humbling, for making me double-check my dates ten times, for stickers and cusses and voice notes and love.

To all my housemates past and present, you are in these pages. Alice and Fabi, Lerryn and Alice W, for laughs and love and friendship which got me through the hell (and highs) of my twenties. Chris, thanks for your generosity of spirit, brains and many phone calls in a world where people rarely call(!).

To my in-laws Sian and Linc, thank you for sharing your wisdom, for reminding me that the work is never done, but it is always worth fighting for.

To my mum, who has always made home for me, for us, I love you. You have taught me so much about how we find joy, thank you for all those decorated bedrooms. To my brother Callum, and Chloe and Theo and Teddy, I am always grateful for your support and smiles and encouragement. To my dad, who I remain in awe of, who taught me to look at buildings and really *see* them.

To my sister Naomi, this book is for you. I hope it fills some of the gaps in your own personal history – no home was ever really complete until you came along. Your patience and kindness are always an inspiration. Thank you for being a reminder that there is room for joy and activism. I love you so much, you make me laugh every day and you are what makes me optimistic for the work ahead.

To Rob, thank you for making home with me. There is no-one that I would rather write next to, and I wonder how this book would have got over the line without having your voice as a supporter on the sidelines. Thank you for showing me the real, core-shaking power of love and how we can employ it to build, and hope for, a better world.

Thanks to the awe-inspiring organisations that understand

that we can only rise by building up together: London Renters Union, INQUEST, CARAG, HASL, Sisters Uncut, Migrants Organise and many, many more.

# ENDNOTES

## BERESFORD ROAD – HOW A HISTORY OF ACTIVISM GOT US HERE

1. 'Virtual CSSA: Of Matchbooks and Gold Jewellery', University College London, 29 April 2021, https://www.ucl.ac.uk/institute-of-advanced-studies/events/2021/apr/virtual-cssa-matchbooks-and-gold-jewellery (accessed 2 September 2022).
2. *Race Today.* July–August, 1976, Volume 8, from the archive of the George Padmore Institute
3. Ibid.

## GREEN MAN LANE ESTATE – HOW WE LIVE WITH SOCIAL HOUSING NEGLIGENCE

1. Jessica Elgot, 'Council homes sold off almost three times as fast as new ones are built', *Guardian*, 28 June 2017, https://www.theguardian.com/society/2017/jun/28/council-homes-sold-off-almost-three-times-as-fast-as-new-ones-are-built (accessed 9 September 2022).
2. Reshima Sharma, 'Briefing: The Social Housing Deficit', Shelter, October 2021, https://england.shelter.org.uk/professional_resources/policy_and_research/policy_library/briefing_the_social_housing_deficit (accessed 5 September 2022).

3. Ibid.
4. Mark Townsend, 'Grenfell families want inquiry to look at role of "race and class" in tragedy', *Observer*, 26 July 2020, https://www.theguardian.com/uk-news/2020/jul/26/grenfell-families-want-inquiry-to-look-at-role-of-race-and-class-in-tragedy (accessed 5 September 2022).
5. 'Green Man Lane', Ealing Council, https://www.ealing.gov.uk/info/201104/housing_regeneration/373/green_man_lane (accessed 14 September 2022).
6. 'Green Man Lane, Ealing', Rydon, https://www.rydon.co.uk/green-man-lane (accessed 14 September 2022).

## YEADING LANE – HOW WE FEEL 'SAFE' AT HOME

1. Shanti Das, '"Pay up, or it trebles": bailiffs accused of strong-arm tactics in UK', *Observer*, 10 April 2022, https://www.theguardian.com/money/2022/apr/10/uk-councils-turn-to-bailiffs-to-collect-tolls (accessed 5 September 2022).
2. Ibid.
3. Ibid.
4. 'Doorbell Camera Market Size, Share & Trends Analysis Report by Product (Wired, Wireless), by Distribution Channel (Online, Offline), by Region, and Segment Forecasts, 2019–2025', Grand View Research, https://www.grandviewresearch.com/industry-analysis/doorbell-camera-market (accessed 5 September 2022).
5. Rani Molla, 'Amazon Ring sales nearly tripled in December despite hacks', *Vox*, 21 January 2020, https://www.vox.com/recode/2020/1/21/21070402/amazon-ring-sales-jumpshot-data (accessed 14 September 2022).
6. Megan Wollerton, 'Neighborhood security cameras sacrifice privacy to solve crimes', *CNET*, 27 March 2018, https://www.cnet.com/home/smart-home/neighborhood-security-cameras-sacrifice-privacy-to-solve-crimes/ (accessed 14 September 2022).

7. Duncan Hodges, 'Mapping smart home vulnerabilities to cyber-enabled crime', Centre for Research and Evidence on Security Threats, 17 February 2021, https://crestresearch.ac.uk/comment/mapping-smart-home-vulnerabilities-to-cyber-enabled-crime (accessed 5 September 2022).

8. Chris Gilliard and David Golumbia, 'Luxury Surveillance', *Real Life*, 6 July 2021, https://reallifemag.com/luxury-surveillance (accessed 5 September 2022).

9. Warren Lewis, 'Millions of Brits fear their neighbours' exterior décor is driving down the value of their property', *Property Reporter*, 13 December 2017, https://www.propertyreporter.co.uk/property/illions-of-brits-fear-their-neighbours-exterior-decor-is-driving-down-the-value-of-their-property.html (accessed 5 September 2022).

10. Patrisse Cullors, *An Abolitionist's Handbook: 12 Steps to Changing Yourself and the World* (New York: St Martin's Press, 2021) page 12.

## MEIFOD COTTAGE – HOW WE BREATHE IN GREEN SPACE

1. Rob Evans, 'Half of England is owned by less than 1% of the population', *Guardian*, 17 April 2019, https://www.theguardian.com/money/2019/apr/17/who-owns-england-thousand-secret-landowners-author (accessed 5 September 2022).

2. 'English Housing Survey 2018–19: Second Homes', https://assets.publishing.service.gov.uk/government/uploads/system/uploads/attachment_data/file/898190/2020_EHS_second_homes_factsheet.pdf (accessed 14 September 2022).

3. James Tapper and Suzanne Bearne, 'Staycation boom forces tenants out of seaside resort homes', *Observer*, 30 May 2021, https://www.theguardian.com/business/2021/may/30/staycation-boom-forces-tenants-out-of-seaside-resort-homes (accessed 14 September 2022).

4. Liam Geraghty, 'Almost 230,000 households are experiencing homelessness this Christmas', *Big Issue*, 23 December 2001, https://

www.bigissue.com/news/housing/almost-230000-households-are-experiencing-the-worst-forms-of-homelessness-this-christmas (accessed 5 September 2022).

5. James Fox, *The World According to Colour: A Cultural History* (London: Allen Lane, 2021) page 198.

6. Francisca Rockey, 'The death of Ella Adoo-Kissi-Debrah: Why are black people more likely to be exposed to toxic air?', *Euronews*, 4 January 2021, https://www.euronews.com/green/2021/01/04/the-death-of-ella-adoo-kissi-debrah-why-are-black-people-more-likely-to-be-exposed-to-toxi (accessed 14 September 2022); Adam Vaughan, 'London's black communities disproportionately exposed to air pollution – study', *Guardian*, 10 October 2016, https://www.theguardian.com/environment/2016/oct/10/londons-black-communities-disproportionately-exposed-to-air-pollution-study (accessed 6 September 2022).

7. Faima Bakar, '"I can't breathe": how racism impacts air quality and endangers life', *Metro*, 25 March 2021, https://metro.co.uk/2021/03/25/how-racism-shows-up-in-the-air-in-parks-on-roads-and-housing-14093213/ (accessed 14 September 2022).

8. Jonathan Lambert, 'Study finds racial gap between who causes air pollution and who breathes it', NPR, 11 March 2019, https://www.npr.org/sections/health-shots/2019/03/11/702348935/study-finds-racial-gap-between-who-causes-air-pollution-and-who-breathes-it (accessed 6 September 2022).

9. George Weigel, 'More herbs, more indoors: millennials shape gardening trends for 2017', *PennLive*, 29 December 2016, https://www.pennlive.com/gardening/2016/12/garden_trends_of_2017.html (accessed 6 September 2022).

10. 'Houseplant Statistics in 2022 (incl. Covid & Millennials), Garden Pals, 9 May 2022, https://gardenpals.com/houseplant-statistics/ (accessed 6 November 22).

11. Dan Hancox and Dr Kasia Tee, 'Houseplants or Revolution?', *Cursed Objects* podcast, 6 April 2021.

12. Frances E. Kuo and William C. Sullivan, 'Environment and

Crime in the Inner City: Does Vegetation Reduce Crime?', *Environment and Behavior* 33:3 (2001): 343–67.

13. 'Statistical Digest of Rural England: Population', Department for Environment, Food and Rural Affairs, 28 October 2021, https://assets.publishing.service.gov.uk/government/uploads/system/uploads/attachment_data/file/1028819/Rural_population__Oct_2021.pdf (accessed 6 September 2022).

14. See Alessio Russo and Giuseppe T. Cirella, 'Modern Compact Cities: How Much Greenery Do We Need?', *International Journal of Environmental Research and Public Health* 15 (2018): 2180.

## W. R. DAVIES – HOW TO LIVE IN PLACES NOT MEANT TO BE LIVED IN

1. Carol Ann Quarini, 'The Domestic Veil: Exploring the Net Curtain through the Uncanny and the Gothic', PhD thesis, University of Brighton, 2015, available at https://cris.brighton.ac.uk/ws/portal-files/portal/4756821/Carol+Quarini+PhD+thesis+CD+version.pdf (accessed 6 September 2022).

2. Tom de Castella, 'Why can't the UK build 240,000 homes a year?', BBC News, 13 January 2015, https://www.bbc.co.uk/news/magazine-30776306 (accessed 6 September 2022).

3. 'New housing design in England overwhelmingly "mediocre" or "poor"', UCL News, 21 January 2020, https://www.ucl.ac.uk/news/2020/jan/new-housing-design-england-overwhelmingly-mediocre-or-poor (accessed 7 September 2022).

4. Kevin Gulliver, *Forty Years of Struggle: A Window on Race and Housing, Disadvantage and Exclusion*, Human City Institute, https://humancityinstitute.files.wordpress.com/2017/01/forty-years-of-struggle.pdf (accessed 14 September 2022).

5. '"Nightmare" rental shortage for disabled people, EHRC finds', BBC News, 11 May 2018, https://www.bbc.co.uk/news/business-44061522 (accessed 7 September 2022).

6. 'BRE report finds poor housing is costing NHS £1.4bn a year', BRE, 9 November 2021, https://bregroup.com/press-releases/bre-report-finds-poor-housing-is-costing-nhs-1-4bn-a-year (accessed 7 September 2022).

A NOTE ON KINDNESS

1. 'Fostering in England 2020 to 2021: Main Findings', Ofsted, 11 November 2021, https://www.gov.uk/government/statistics/fostering-in-england-1-april-2020-to-31-march-2021/fostering-in-england-2020-to-2021-main-findings (accessed 7 September 2022).

MILL LANE – HOW WE MAKE A CASE FOR WELFARE

1. 'Universal Credit Statistics, 29 April 2013 to 8 July 2021', Department for Work and Pensions, 17 August 2021, https://www.gov.uk/government/statistics/universal-credit-statistics-29-april-2013-to-8-july-2021/ (accessed 7 September 2022).
2. Shané Schutte, 'UK offers some of the least generous benefits in Europe', Real Business, 18 February 2016, https://realbusiness.co.uk/uk-offers-some-of-the-least-generous-benefits-in-europe (accessed 7 September 2022).
3. Becky Hall, 'Is the UK the best welfare country in the world?', CashFloat blog, 2 August 2022, https://www.cashfloat.co.uk/blog/money-borrowing/best-welfare-country (accessed 7 September 2022).

## Surrey House – How we're taught we're all the same

1. William Whyte, 'Somewhere to Live: Why British Students Study Away from Home – and Why It Matters', Higher Education Policy Institute, November 2019, p. 13, https://www.hepi.ac.uk/wp-content/uploads/2019/11/HEPI_Somewhere-to-live_Report-121-FINAL.pdf (accessed 7 September 2022).
2. Ibid., pp. 9–10.
3. Sarah Jones and Martin Blakey, 'Student Accommodation: The Facts', Higher Education Policy Institute, August 2020, p. 26, https://www.hepi.ac.uk/wp-content/uploads/2020/08/HEPI-Student-Accommodation-Report-FINAL.pdf (accessed 8 September 2022).
4. 'Surrey House', Goldsmiths University of London, https://www.gold.ac.uk/accommodation/halls/surrey-house (accessed 8 September 2022).
5. Martin Heilweil, 'The Influence of Dormitory Architecture on Resident Behavior', *Environment and Behavior*, December 1973, pp. 377–412.
6. Leon Festinger, Stanley Schachter and Kurt Back, *Social Pressures in Informal Groups: A Study of Human Factors in Housing* (Ann Arbor: Research Center for Group Dynamics, Michigan University, 1950).
7. Joanne D. Worsley, Paula Harrison and Rhiannon Corcoran, 'The Role of Accommodation Environments in Student Mental Health and Wellbeing', *BMC Public Health* 21 (2021): 573, https://doi.org/10.1186/s12889-021-10602-5 (accessed 8 September 2022).
8. Sally Weale, 'More than half of students polled report mental health slump', *Guardian*, 9 December 2020, https://www.theguardian.com/education/2020/dec/09/more-than-half-of-students-polled-report-mental-health-slump (accessed 8 September 2022).
9. Worsley et al., 'The Role of Accommodation Environments in Student Mental Health and Wellbeing'.

10. 'Gypsy, Roma and Traveller communities', Office for Students, 20 June 2022, https://www.officeforstudents.org.uk/advice-and-guidance/promoting-equal-opportunities/effective-practice/gypsy-roma-and-traveller-communities (accessed 8 September 2022).

11. 'Children looked after in England (including adoption and care leavers) year ending 31 March 2015', Department for Education, 1 October 2015, https://assets.publishing.service.gov.uk/government/uploads/system/uploads/attachment_data/file/464756/SFR34_2015_Text.pdf (accessed 8 September 2022).

12. Sean Coughlan, 'Half of universities have fewer than 5% poor white students', BBC News, 14 February 2019, https://www.bbc.co.uk/news/education-47227157 (accessed 8 September 2022).

13. Wouter Zwysen and Simonetta Longhi, 'Labour Market Disadvantage of Ethnic Minority British Graduates: University Choice, Parental Background or Neighbourhood?', Institute for Social and Economic Research, January 2016, https://www.iser.essex.ac.uk/research/publications/working-papers/iser/2016-02.pdf (accessed 8 September 2022).

14. Richard Adams, 'British universities employ no black academics in top roles, figures show', *Guardian*, 19 January 2017, https://www.theguardian.com/education/2017/jan/19/british-universities-employ-no-black-academics-in-top-roles-figures-show (accessed 14 September 2022); 'Staff at higher education providers in the United Kingdom 2015/16', HESA, 19 January 2017, https://www.hesa.ac.uk/news/19-01-2017/sfr243-staff (accessed 8 September 2022).

15. Chaka L. Bachmann and Becca Gooch, 'LGBT in Britain: University Report', Stonewall, 2018, https://www.stonewall.org.uk/system/files/lgbt_in_britain_universities_report.pdf (accessed 8 September 2022).

16. 'NUS: Student contributions to the UK economy at national, regional and local levels', NEF Consulting, 2013, https://www.nefconsulting.com/our-work/clients/

nus-student-contributions-to-the-uk-economy-at-national-regional-and-local-levels/ (accessed 8 September 2022).

## AMERSHAM GROVE – HOW WE RENT

1. 'The 2008 recession 10 years on', Office for National Statistics, 30 April 2018, https://www.ons.gov.uk/economy/grossdomestic productgdp/articles/the2008recession10yearson/2018-04-30 (accessed 8 September 2022).
2. 'Expatistan's cost of living map of Europe', Expatistan, https://www.expatistan.com/cost-of-living/index/europe (accessed 8 September 2022).
3. 'Average monthly rental cost of a furnished one-bedroom apartment in select European cities as of 1st quarter 2021 and 1st quarter 2022', Statista, 11 April 2022, https://www.statista.com/statistics/503274/average-rental-cost-apartment-europe (accessed 8 September 2022).
4. 'English Housing Survey: Private Rented Sector, 2020–21', Department for Levelling Up, Housing & Communities, July 2022, https://assets.publishing.service.gov.uk/government/uploads/system/uploads/attachment_data/file/1088486/EHS_20-21_PRS_Report.pdf (accessed 8 September 2022).
5. Paul Whitney, 'Estate Agents Industry', Hallidays, 19 November 2021, https://www.hallidays.co.uk/views-and-insight/sector-report/estate-agents-industry (accessed 8 September 2022).
6. Stephen Worchel, Jerry Lee and Akanbi Adewole, 'Effects of Supply and Demand on Ratings of Object Value', *Journal of Personality and Social Psychology* 32:5 (1975): 906–14.
7. Darcel Rockett, 'Millennials want to buy homes so bad, 80% would purchase one without seeing it amid high-stakes COVID-19 market: survey', *Chicago Tribune*, 26 March 2021, https://www.chicagotribune.com/real-estate/ct-re-millennial-homebuying-trend-report-0317-20210326-lanzqfcelrhllblqk75nxlxnem-story.html (accessed 8 September 2022).

8. Lydia Stephens, 'People camped out over night at an estate agents just so they could be the first to put their names down for new housing estate', *WalesOnline*, 23 April 2021, https://www.walesonline.co.uk/lifestyle/welsh-homes/people-camped-out-over-night-20451131 (accessed 8 September 2022).

9. 'UK house prices up 197% since the Millennium, 43% in the last decade alone', Benham & Reeves, 21 February 2020, https://www.benhams.com/press-release/landlords-investors/london-leads-uk-house-price-increases-over-the-last-decade (accessed 8 September 2022).

10. James Sillars, 'House prices hit record high and barriers to ownership will become "more acute"', Sky News, 7 February 2022, https://news.sky.com/story/house-prices-hit-record-high-and-barriers-to-ownership-will-become-more-acute-12535323 (accessed 8 September 2022).

11. Richard Partington, 'Average UK first-time buyer is now older than 30, says Halifax', *Guardian*, 22 January 2022, https://www.theguardian.com/money/2022/jan/22/average-uk-first-time-buyer-is-now-older-than-30-says-halifax (accessed 8 September 2022).

## Pepys Road – How to protect our health

1. Dimosthenis A. Sarigiannis (ed.), 'Combined or Multiple Exposure to Health Stressors in Indoor Built Environments', World Health Organization, 2013, https://www.euro.who.int/__data/assets/pdf_file/0020/248600/Combined-or-multiple-exposure-to-health-stressors-in-indoor-built-environments.pdf (accessed 8 September 2022).

2. 'Housing with damp problems', Gov.uk, 8 October 2020, https://www.ethnicity-facts-figures.service.gov.uk/housing/housing-conditions/housing-with-damp-problems/latest (accessed 8 September 2022).

3. 'What are fungal spores?', University of Worcester, https://www.worcester.ac.uk/about/academic-schools/school-of-science-and-the-environment/science-and-the-environment-research/national-pollen-and-aerobiology-research-unit/What-are-fungal-spores.aspx (accessed 2 September 2022).

4. 'So what?', ARCC, 17 April 2015, https://www.arcc-network.org.uk/wp-content/so-what/So-what-UCL-indoor-air-quality.pdf (accessed 9 September 2022).

5. Caribbean 13 per cent, Bangladeshi 10 per cent, Black African 9 per cent and Pakistani 8 per cent; White British 3 per cent ('Housing with damp problems', Gov.uk).

6. 'Disparities in the Risk and Outcomes of Covid-19', Public Health England, August 2020, https://assets.publishing.service.gov.uk/government/uploads/system/uploads/attachment_data/file/908434/Disparities_in_the_risk_and_outcomes_of_COVID_August_2020_update.pdf (accessed 9 September 2022).

7. Emily Farra, 'You aren't tripping: fungi are taking over fashion', *Vogue*, 2 April 2021, https://www.vogue.com/article/fungi-mushrooms-fashion-inspiration-mycelium (accessed 9 September 2022).

8. 'Housing – legal aid deserts', Law Society, 7 June 2022, https://www.lawsociety.org.uk/campaigns/legal-aid-deserts/housing (accessed 9 September 2022).

## Oswyth Road – How the internet has a say

1. Deborah Cicurel, 'Should you move in with someone just to save on rent?', *Evening Standard*, 10 June 2016, https://www.standard.co.uk/lifestyle/should-you-move-in-with-someone-just-to-save-on-rent-a3268631.html (accessed 9 September 2022).

2. 'Generation rent: one million under-30s will be priced out of the housing market', *Telegraph*, 13 June 2012, https://www.telegraph.

co.uk/finance/property/news/9328406/Generation-rent-one-million-under-30s-will-be-priced-out-of-the-housing-market.html (accessed 9 September 2022).

3. 'Private rental market summary statistics in England: April 2020 to March 2021', Office for National Statistics, 16 June 2021, https://www.ons.gov.uk/peoplepopulationandcommunity/housing/bulletins/privaterentalmarketsummarystatisticsinengland/april-2020tomarch2021 (accessed 2 September 2022).

4. Becky Morton, 'Over-50s turn to house-shares to beat rising rents', BBC News, 21 August 2022, https://www.bbc.co.uk/news/business-62344571 (accessed 9 September 2022).

5. William Harnett Blanch, *Ye Parish of Camerwell: A Brief Account of the Parish of Camberwell, Its History and Antiquities* (London: E. W. Allen, 1875), p. 90.

6. Charlea Glanville, 'In defence of . . . living rooms', SpareRoom, 7 October 2019, https://blog.spareroom.co.uk/in-defence-of-living-rooms/ (accessed 12 September 2022).

7. Zoe Kleinman, 'Internet access: 1.5m UK homes still offline, Ofcom finds', BBC News, 28 April 2021, https://www.bbc.co.uk/news/technology-56906654 (accessed 12 September 2022).

8. May Bulman, 'Landlord who banned "coloured" people "because of curry smell" insists he's not racist and is happy to rent to "negroes"'. *Independent*, 30 March 2017, https://www.independent.co.uk/news/uk/home-news/landlord-who-banned-coloured-people-because-of-curry-smell-says-he-s-not-racist-a7657231.html (accessed 14 September 2022).

9. Benjamin Edelman, Michael Luca and Dan Svirsky, 'Racial Discrimination in the Sharing Economy: Evidence from a Field Experiment', *American Economic Journal: Applied Economics* 9:2 (2017): 1–22, available at https://www.benedelman.org/publications/airbnb-guest-discrimination-2016-09-16.pdf (accessed 12 September 2022).

10. Motoko Rich, 'SafeRent's math speeds up tenant evaluation process', *Wall Street Journal*, 2 August 2001, https://

www.wsj.com/articles/SB996702441926667410 (accessed 12 September 2022).

11. 'TransUnion independent landlord survey insights', TransUnion SmartMove, 7 August 2017, https://www.mysmartmove.com/SmartMove/blog/landlord-rental-market-survey-insights-infographic.page (accessed 12 September 2022).

12. Sanctions List Search, Office of Foreign Assets Control, https://sanctionssearch.ofac.treas.gov/Details.aspx?id=21070 (accessed 14 September 2022).

## A NOTE ON STUFF

1. 'Clutter image ratings', Hoarding Disorders UK, https://hoardingdisordersuk.org/research-and-resources/clutter-image-ratings/ (accessed 12 September 2022).

2. Fraser Simpson, 'The questionable retro lighting trend we never thought we'd see again is BACK ...', *Ideal Home*, 4 December 2020, https://www.idealhome.co.uk/news/lava-lamp-trend-262547 (accessed 12 September 2022).

## PECKHAM RYE – HOW GENTRIFICATION IS A HOUSING ISSUE

1. Rightmove, https://www.rightmove.co.uk/house-prices/details/england-79985507-9806305?s=68bf0e131eb6fa5772fec3c1c44ab1db-f9b3bd7fade67e493c6d4ead299838dc#/ (accessed 12 September 2022).

2. Prudence Ivey, 'Living and renting in Brixton: travel links, parking, schools, best streets – and the average cost of monthly rent', *Evening Standard*, 30 July 2019, https://www.standard.co.uk/homesandproperty/renting/living-and-renting-in-brixton-travel-links-parking-schools-best-streets-and-the-average-cost-of-monthly-rent-a132291.html (accessed 14 September 2022).

3.  '45% of private renters face rent hike', Generation Rent, 25 August 2022, https://www.generationrent.org/private_renters_face_45_rent_hike (accessed 12 September 2022).

4.  'Peckham Rent Summary', HOME. https://www.home.co.uk/for_rent/peckham/current_rents?location=peckham

5.  Adam Almeida, *Pushed to the Margins: A Quantitative Analysis of Gentrification in London in the 2010s*, Runnymede/Class, June 2021, https://assets.website-files.com/61488f992b58e687f1108c-7c/61d6fc536143d6219ea19fa4_Pushed-to-the-Margins-Gentrification-Report-min.pdf (accessed 12 September 2022).

6.  Robert Booth, 'Rural house prices in England and Wales rise twice as fast as in cities', *Guardian*, 20 June 2021, https://www.theguardian.com/society/2021/jun/20/rural-house-prices-in-england-and-wales-rise-twice-as-fast-as-in-cities (accessed 13 September 2022).

7.  'The Devon villages fighting against second homes and pricing out locals', *Devon Live*, 6 June 2021, https://www.devonlive.com/news/devon-news/devon-villages-fighting-against-second-5487760 (accessed 14 September 2022).

8.  Fiona Jackson, '"One local left" in village so stunning nearly all houses are millionaires' second homes', *Mirror*, 4 June 2021, https://www.mirror.co.uk/news/uk-news/one-local-left-village-stunning-24254136 (accessed 13 September 2022).

9.  Kevin Gulliver, *Forty Years of Struggle: A Window on Race and Housing, Disadvantage and Exclusion*, Human City Institute, https://humancityinstitute.files.wordpress.com/2017/01/forty-years-of-struggle.pdf (accessed 14 September 2022).

10. 'Statutory Homelessness Annual Report, 2019–20, England', Ministry of Housing, Communities and Local Government, 1 October 2020, https://assets.publishing.service.gov.uk/government/uploads/system/uploads/attachment_data/file/923123/Annual_Statutory_Homelessness_Release_2019-20.pdf (accessed 13 September 2022).

11. 'Gentrification in ethnically-mixed, disadvantaged urban areas

driven by middle-class ethnic minority renters', 22 May 2020, https://www.lse.ac.uk/News/Latest-news-from-LSE/2020/ e-May-20/Gentrification-in-ethnically-mixed-disadvantaged- urban-areas-driven-by-middle-class-ethnic-minority-renters (accessed 6 November 2022).

12. 'Race and class', Runnymede, https://www.runnymedetrust.org/ partnership-projects/race-and-class (accessed 13 September 2022).

13. 'What is home staging and will it help sell my house?', Rightmove, 2 October 2016, https://www.rightmove.co.uk/news/what-is- home-staging (accessed 13 September 2022).

14. Jacinda Santora, 'Key influencer marketing statistics you need to know for 2022', Influencer MarketingHub, 3 August 2022, https://influencermarketinghub.com/influencer-marketing- statistics (accessed 13 September 2022).

15. 'Diversity in Interior Design Survey', British Institute of Interior Design, https://biid.org.uk/sites/default/files/Final%20 British%20Institute%20of%20Interior%20Design%20diver- sity%20report_0.pdf (accessed 13 September 2022).

16. 'The Heygate diaspora', 35% Campaign, https://www.35percent. org/heygatepages/diaspora (accessed 13 September 2022).

17. Samir Qouta, Raija-Leena Punamäki and Eyad El Sarraj, 'House Demolition and Mental Health: Victims and Witnesses', *Journal of Social Distress and the Homeless* 7:4 (1998): 279–88.

18. Margaret Stroebe, Henk Schut and Maaike H. Nauta, 'Is Homesickness a "Mini-Grief"? Development of a Dual-Process Model', *Clinical Psychological Science* 4:2 (2016): 344–58.

## Conclusion

1. Omar Khan, *The Colour of Money: How Racial Inequalities Obstruct a Fair and Resilient Economy*, Runnymede, April 2020, p. 8, https://assets.website-files.com/61488f992b58e687f1108c7c/ 61bcc1c736554228b543c603_The%20Colour%20of%20

Money%20Report.pdf (accessed 13 September 2022).

# INDEX

# Index

# Index

# Index